Dispositions in Teacher Education

A volume in
Advances in Teacher Education

Series Editors:
James Raths, *University of Delaware*
Amy C. McAninch, *Rockhurst University*

Advances in Teacher Education

James Raths and Amy C. McAninch, Series Editors

What Counts as Knowledge in Teacher Education (2001)
edited by James Raths

Teacher Beliefs and Classroom Performance:
The Impact of Teacher Education (2003)
by James Raths and Amy C. McAninch

Dispositions in Teacher Education

edited by

Mary E. Diez
Alverno College

and

James Raths
University of Delaware

Information Age Publishing, Inc.
Charlotte, North Carolina • www.infoagepub.com

Library of Congress Cataloging-in-Publication Data

Dispositions in Teacher Education / edited by Mary E. Diez and James Raths.
    p. cm. -- (Advances in teacher education)
    Includes bibliographical references.
    ISBN-13: 978-1-59311-631-6 (pbk.)
    ISBN-13: 978-1-59311-632-3 (hardcover) 1. Teachers--United States--Attitudes. 2. Teachers--United States--Psychology. 3. Teachers--Training of--United States. I. Diez, Mary E. II. Raths, James D.
    LB1775.2.T423 2007
    371.1001'9--dc22

                                                                              2007020370

    ISBN 13: 978-1-59311-631-6 (pbk.)
            978-1-59311-632-3 (hardcover)
    ISBN 10: 1-59311-631-4 (pbk.)
            11-59311-632-2 (hardcover)

Printed in the United States of America

CONTENTS

PART III: PERSISTING ISSUES RAISED BY DISPOSITIONS

FOREWORD

Many people worked on this book to bring a nascent idea to fruition, but this is Larry Freeman's book. The authors were steadfast at crafting their chapters and responding to suggestions for improvement heard from members of the AERA (American Educational Research Association) audience to whom they presented and from coauthors, but Larry Freeman guided all their efforts in profound ways. The editors arranged the essays in the collection, suggested to authors how their chapters might be improved, but Larry's hand was everywhere. The editors and technicians at Information Age Publishing lent support to us and worked to put the materials we prepared into publishable shape, but make no mistake about it—this is Larry Freeman's book.

His deep thinking and his influence on the rest of us sing out of the pages he wrote in his two substantive chapters of this volume. We are so grateful for his leadership in this project.

Mary E. Diez
James Raths
Editors

PART I

THEORETICAL PERSPECTIVES

CHAPTER 1

AN OVERVIEW OF DISPOSITIONS IN TEACHER EDUCATION

Larry Freeman

INTRODUCTION

In the 1990s, without fanfare or much discussion, teacher educators began talking about the "dispositions" of teachers, administrators, and school service personnel. The traditional formulation of the domains of teacher education—knowledge, skills, and attitudes—was recast as knowledge, skills, and dispositions. The notion of attitudes had been deeply ingrained in talk about teacher education, as it has been, and continues to be, in talk about preparing professionals in any number of other professions. This recasting represented a major shift in thinking about teacher education and the attributes necessary for effective teaching and administering schools. In addition, this change was introduced and accepted rather rapidly given the usual pace of change in teacher education at the national level. Normally one would expect the teacher education profession to produce a parade of articles and conference presentations discussing and debating the concept of dispositions and then gradually to

Dispositions in Teacher Education, pp. 3–29
Copyright © 2007 by Information Age Publishing
All rights of reproduction in any form reserved.

integrate the notion into the everyday work of teacher education. That is not what happened. Without much documentable discussion at any level, the concept of dispositions became enshrined, within a decade, in the standards of the national teacher educational accrediting agency, the National Council for the Accreditation of Teacher Education (NCATE), and in the rules and regulations governing teacher certification in several states (see NCATE, 2002).

This change has resulted in countless meetings of departmental, divisional, and college faculties in teacher education institutions across the country as each faculty has attempted to delineate what it understands by the term "disposition." And the effort continues as evidenced by the existence of the Educator Disposition Symposium hosted annually for the last 3 years by Eastern Kentucky University and as evidenced by the number of papers now being presented at teacher education conferences. For instance, between the years 2003 and 2005, the number of presentations with the word disposition in the title grew from only a few to 43. Coming to terms with dispositions in programs preparing professional educators is an ongoing process.

PURPOSE OF THIS BOOK

The foregoing considerations suggest that significant questions need to be addressed in spite of the pressure to generate lists of dispositions—however relevant—and to assess—however crudely—whether candidates possess them. This book intends to address these questions and to offer potential pathways for ongoing thinking and development of the role of dispositions in teacher education. In this book the authors do not purport to settle these questions. For instance, there has been no attempt to arrive at a common definition of disposition or to stipulate such a definition. The several authors of the following chapters do not agree about the nature of dispositions and they do not agree on what constitutes a proper response to the other equally significant questions. Our intent is to explore these questions, to provide the reader with a variety of perspectives that will enrich the discourse about dispositions among teacher educators.

In the remainder of this chapter, my intent is to set the stage for the following explorations regarding dispositions in teacher education.

- promising theoretical perspectives that can generate useful ways of working with the concept of dispositions
- reflections on experience of practitioners' endeavors to implement programs that identify, cultivate, and assess dispositions

- issues concerning assessment and coaching that are raised by dispositions when considered a part of teacher education.

The rest of this chapter will address several questions that are fundamental to the exploration of the notion of disposition and its role in teacher education.

The first question is, why dispositions? The response to this question is divided in to three parts: (a) a brief history of the term, dispositions, and its use in the accreditation and regulation of teacher education; (b) alternatives to dispositions that might have been employed and their limitations; and (c) the attractiveness and dangers to teacher education in the use of the concept of dispositions.

The next section of this chapter addresses several questions that raise significant issues about dispositions:

1. What is a disposition?
2. How do we distinguish the dispositional from the nondispositional?
3. How are dispositions identified?
4. How do dispositions develop and change?
5. Are dispositions descriptive statements that characterize an individual's behavior or do dispositions cause behavior?

The responses to these questions will draw heavily on discussions of dispositions in other disciplines such as philosophy. These responses are intended to sketch some possible ways of thinking about dispositions that will enrich teacher educators' about dispositions.

WHY DISPOSITIONS?

A Brief History of Dispositions in Teacher Education

The traditional formulation of the domains of teacher education has been knowledge, skills, and attitudes. Attitudes as used in this phrase has been, in my experience—and I suspect in the experience of most teacher educators—a fuzzy and essentially useless concept. At one point in my career, I managed the teacher education program approval process at the Illinois state board of education. One of the tests that we used when reviewing programs was whether the program provided candidates with the knowledge, skills, and attitudes necessary to be an effective beginning teacher, administrator school service staff member. During the 9 years I held this position, we reviewed hundreds of preparation programs, and we cited a goodly number of programs for deficiencies regarding the knowledge and skills that they required of students. Not once did we cite a program for deficiencies in the area of attitudes. Institutions usually had little to say about the attitudes that they desired their graduates to exhibit. If they did, they were likely to be faith-based institutions and not the state-supported institutions that prepared the bulk of educational personnel. When institutions did describe the attitudes they desired in their graduates, my staff and I usually were hypervigilant about student rights and closely examined the assessment machinery used by the institution to insure that students would be fairly judged. This vigilance was based on knowledge and experience that working with attitudes is working with fuzzy, usually ill-defined, perhaps indefinable ideas and concepts.

Efforts to measure attitudes can be traced to as early as the 1920s when Thurstone (1928) published an article in which he held that an attitude denotes "the sum total of a man's inclinations and feelings, prejudice or bias, preconceived notions, ideas, fears, threats, and convictions about any specified topic" (p. 530). Faced with the question about how to measure attitudes, Thurstone turned to the notion of opinion which he termed "a verbal expression of attitude" (p. 530). He proposed getting at an individual's attitude by examining his opinion(s) on a specific issue. The problem that Thurstone did not address was the predictive relationship, if any, between attitudes and behavior.

While Thurstone relied on opinions to index attitudes, it appears that over time, there was a major initiative to connect attitudes and behavior. In 1992, Cook was proposing that attitudes can best be conceived as a tripartite entity composed of cognitive, affective, and behavioral components. That is, one's attitude toward a subject includes the person's perception or conceptualization of the subject, positive or negative feeling toward the subject, and the way the person intends to act toward the subject. The problem with the last component, of course, is that intention does not reliably serve as an index or predictor of subsequent behavior. It is commonplace that behavior often diverges from announced intention. Along with Katz and Raths (1985), we might observe that attitude is at best "a predisposition to action" or we might agree with Kenneth Burke (1945/1969) when he suggests that attitude is "incipient action" (p. 20) or when he suggests elsewhere that it is "a region of ambiguous possibilities" (Burke, 1945/1969, p. 242). What we know for sure is that attitude is not a reliable predictor of behavior. It is the gap between intention and actual behavior that renders attitudes unsuitable as a domain of teacher education, particularly when attention moves from what one intends to do to actual performance. Performance, not intention, has been emphasized in recent standard setting, accreditation, and administration of state level rules and regulations.

So far as I can determine from searching the teacher education literature, Donald Arnstine was the first to discuss the concept of dispositions in education extensively and to suggest the importance of dispositions in teaching (Arnstine, 1967). However, Arnstine's work had little impact on teacher education. It was left to Katz and Raths to introduce the notion of dispositions as a goal in teacher education in the middle 80s (Katz & Raths, 1985). In less than 7 years, the notion of dispositions was enshrined in the Interstate New Teacher Assessment and Support Consortium (INTASC) standards as an apparently well-developed concept (INTASC, 1992). In the space of no less than a decade, the old formulation of the domains of teacher education had been revised from "knowledge, skills, and attitudes" to "knowledge, skills, and dispositions." Further, there is little in the literature to suggest significant debates and discussions about this shift, which on the one hand appears rather innocuous and on the other, as we all know, has sometimes created consternation for teacher education administrators and faculty as they have attempted to understand and assess dispositions.

In their original paper that started or reinvigorated the discussion of the role of dispositions in teacher education, Katz and Raths (1985) do not explicitly argue for substituting dispositions for attitudes in the formulation, knowledge, skills, and attitudes. They do, however, discuss how they perceive the difference between attitudes and dispositions and observe that when attitudes is used in a conventional way, "the focus is upon pre-dispositions to act" and that "we employ the term disposition as a summary of actions observed." The authors conclude that

> among the reasons underlying our belief in the usefulness of their [dispositions'] inclusion [in teacher education], the most important is that they can orient our efforts toward designing and evaluating teacher education programs in terms of their enduring impact upon the candidates. (p. 307)

Katz and Raths suggest in this statement that adding dispositions to the domains of teacher education, if not substituting dispositions for attitudes, leads us to think more profoundly about how to educate teachers, to move away from checklists to observing more carefully, to move away from assuming that if a student displays the requisite knowledge, skills, and attitudes they will teach effectively to actually examining how a candidate teaches in a variety of situations.

A document that seems to have significantly shaped the profession's understanding of dispositions is *Minnesota's Vision for Teacher Education: Stronger Standards, New Partnerships*, produced by Minnesota's Task Force on Teacher Education in 1986.[1] This document introduces the concept of dispositions into policy considerations as follows: "Expected dispositions of beginning teachers must stem from the concept of an ideal teacher. The identified dispositions determine the range of skills needed by beginning teachers" (p. 34). The document continues: "Effective teachers are intentionally disposed to act in particular ways that best facilitate learning and can explain their patterns of behavior.... The frequency of particular actions within specified categories of circumstances determines the particular disposition (pp. 34-35). Here the Task Force follows the notion Katz and Raths developed as they relied on Buss and Craik (1983). They see dispositions as summary statements of the actions of an individual, an attribution used to characterize, but not explain, a pattern of behavior. The task force then proceeds to provide lists of dispositions under the headings, "Dispositions Toward Self," "Dispositions Toward the Learner," "Dispositions Towards Teaching," and "Dispositions Toward the Professions."

The influence of this document and the conversations surrounding it was heightened because Linda Darling-Hammond (1990) and her colleagues included Minnesota in a study they did for Rand. It may or may not be correct to do so, but it is tempting to see this Minnesota document exercising influence as Darling-Hammond chaired the group that produced the Interstate New Teacher Assessment and Support Consortium (INTASC) standards.[2] These standards, promulgated in 1992, enshrined dispositions in teacher education apparently with considerable permanence. INTASC's *Model Standards for Beginning Teacher Licensing and Development: A Resource for State Dialogue* (1992) included a list of dispositions related to each of 10 principles regarding the performance of teachers. This document, however, presented no discussion of how dispositions are conceived. As the decade progressed, NCATE (2002) worked on revising its standards and eventually promulgated standards known as Standards 2000 that incorporated the concept dispositions. Before and afterwards, the notion of dispositions was included in an increasing number of state rules and regulations governing the certification of teachers.[3] Eventually NCATE evolved a definition of dispositions that appears in a glossary the organization has prepared:

> The values, commitments, and professional ethics that influence behaviors toward students, families, colleagues, and communities and affect student learning, motivation, and development as well as the educator's own professional growth. Dispositions are guided by beliefs and attitudes related to values such as caring, fairness, honesty, responsibility, and social justice. For example, they might include a belief that all students can learn, a vision of high and challenging standards, or a commitment to a safe and supportive learning environment. (p. 52)

Nowhere in the documentation of its activities does NCATE provide discussion of any theoretical framework or sources for this conception of dispositions. On its face the definition appears to continue an allegiance to the notion of attitudes; the major advance is in the phrase "that influence behaviors." There is precious little in the definition to suggest that NCATE has moved to a performance based model of teacher education.

The authors of the 2000 NCATE standards and contemporaneous state certification rules and regulations apparently found the concept of attitude unable to do the job they had in mind. In spite of the NCATE definition, it appears they insisted on moving from quasi-predictors of performance such as attitude inventories to performance itself. During the 1990s—and perhaps earlier—the movement appears to have been one of moving from relying on proxies for performance to insisting that performance is what matters. Ironically, at about the same time that most states had adopted some arrangement for testing the knowledge of those who apply for certification as one means of assuring high quality teachers, influential teacher educators were taking the position that it takes more than knowledge to teach, that it takes more than skills acquired in methods courses, and it takes more than reciting the correct opinions about a variety of educational topics. What matters is performance. The full manifestation of this movement is evident in the NCATE 2000 standards. Standard 2 which focuses on assessment reveals this focus on candidate performance. The Standard requires that the "unit has an assessment system that collects and analyzes data on applicant qualifications, *candidate and graduate performance*, and unit operations to evaluate and improve the unit and its program" [emphasis added] (NCATE, 2002, p. 10). Further all the specialized professional groups—from early childhood and special education to educational administration—insist on performance assessment throughout the program, not only in student teaching or administration internships. Some of the guidelines, for example, those for educational administration, even provide examples of promising practices for candidate performance activities for those who are developing programs.

Alternatives to Dispositions

While it is evident that the concept of attitude, even if rehabilitated, would not do the job in an environment demanding performance assessment, it is unclear how or why the notion of dispositions came to prevail as the term of choice. Other available alternative concepts would seem to work as well or even better perhaps. A major criterion for choosing a replacement for attitude is that the concept must, it would seem, incorporate action, behavior and/or performance.

TEMPERAMENT

Given that many teacher educators have sought for years to model teacher education and certification on medicine and law, one would have thought that "temperament" as in "judicial temperament" might have been a good choice. The Chicago Bar Association, for instance, describes "judicial temperament" as follows:

> Among the qualities which comprise judicial temperament are patience, open-mindedness, courtesy, tact, firmness, understanding, compassion and humility. Because the judicial temperament requires an ability to deal with counsel, jurors, witnesses and parties calmly and courteously, and the willingness to hear and consider the views of all sides. It requires the ability to be even-tempered, yet firm; open-minded, yet willing and able to reach a decision; confident, yet not egocentric. Because of the range of topics and issues with which a judge may be required to deal, judicial temperament requires a willingness and ability to assimilate data outside the judge's own experience. It requires, moreover, an even disposition, buttressed by a keen sense of justice which creates an intellectual serenity in the approach to complex decisions, and forbearance under provocation. Judicial temperament also implies a mature sense of proportion; reverence for the law, but appreciation that the role of law is not static and unchanging; understanding of the judge's important role in the judicial process, yet recognition that the administration of justice and the rights of the parties transcend the judge's personal desires. Judicial temperament is typified by recognition that there must be compassion as the judge deals with matters put before him or her.
>
> Factors which indicate a lack of judicial temperament are also identifiable and understandable. Judicial temperament thus implies an absence of arrogance, impatience, pomposity, loquacity, irascibility, arbitrariness or tyranny. Judicial temperament is a quality which is not easily identifiable, but which does not wholly evade discovery. Its absence can usually be fairly ascertained. (Judicial Administration Division Lawyers' Conference, 1987)

A description of desirable teacher or educator temperament might be evolved similar to this definition of judicial temperament. But the use of the term temperament in teacher education, with its close affiliation with psychology, creates significant problems.

In pediatrics and developmental psychology, the term "temperament" has come to have a specialized meaning. Hedwig Teglasi defines it as follows: "Temperament is generally identified with a) the components of personality that are biological in origin ... b) traits that are relatively stable, cross situation ally consistent, and evident through the age span and diverse cultures ... and c) the style (how) rather than the content (what) or purpose (why) of behavior" (Teglasi, 1995). In this fairly specific usage, the term, temperament, emphasizes the aspects of human behavior over which humans have the least control and therefore the least likely to be influenced by education. Using temperament in this sense would have put teacher educators in the camp holding that good teachers are, for all practical purposes, born, not made.

TRAITS

If temperament will not do, why not traits? The concept traits is well established in the psychology of personality. Traits finds its use in distinguishing between individuals. We can say that Joe is who he is because of his "traits." That is Joe is distinguished from Jim because he appears more neurotic than the more stable Jim. Or Joan loves parties while Judy seeks solitude and some would say she borders on being a recluse. The notion of traits raises some significant problems because, unlike temperament, traits are sometimes used as a causal explanation as in Cate usually does not participate willingly in group activities because ... (here one would invoke a "trait"). Used this way, the notion of trait works much like temperament. Once a trait is established, it causes certain patterns of behavior. And, in fact, some would argue that various traits are linked to human biology, for example, extraversion is linked with the central nervous system reactivity and psychotism is linked to testosterone levels.

But adopting the notions of traits would not inevitably led to a causal or biological perspective. Some would argue that traits are no more than descriptive summaries of personal attributes. Traits, from this point of view, do not exist in the person but are attributions an observer makes based on the frequency of specific categories of observed behaviors. In this view, there is a virtually limitless supply of traits since traits are rooted in observation rather than in the nature of personalities. The reason for using traits as descriptive summaries is that they assist in distinguishing the typical behaviors of one person from those of another. Further, the nature of each trait can be stipulated since there is no assertion that a trait is embedded somewhere in nature.

Traits viewed as descriptive summaries of personal attributes have some obvious attractiveness for teacher educators. This view eliminates the bugaboo of biological determination. It avoids the question of whether traits are changeable. It simply asserts that given a category we can stipulate that certain, identifiable behaviors belong to this category.

This approach would seem to augur well for showing that when teachers display behaviors belonging to specified categories, they tend to positively or negatively affect learning.

Trait theory then seems to hold some promise for teacher educators. However, its use in psychology is, like many terms in psychology, complicated and loaded with baggage. Some use it as causal explanation and others as a descriptive summary. The biologically based notions of trait do not square with the experience of teacher educators. There is not a clear causal relationship between proposed biologically based traits and effectiveness as an educational professional. Experience will show that both introverted and extroverted individuals can function effectively as teachers and administrators. As we shall see later in a discussion of Katz and Raths contributions to the development of the notion of dispositions, the "descriptive summary" approach to traits or dispositions holds considerable promise.

HABITS

The construct, habits, would seem a promising replacement for the term attitude. John Dewey (1922), for instance, observes that "the dynamic force of Habit [sic] taken in connection with the continuity of habits with one another explains the unity of character and conduct, or speaking more concretely of motive and act, will and deed" (p. 43). In a subsequent discussion of the concept, will, he conjoins "habits" and "dispositions:"

> By will, common-sense understands something practical and moving. It understands the body of *habits, of active dispositions* which makes a man do what he does. Will is thus not something opposed to consequences or severed from them. It is a cause of consequences; it is causation in its personal aspect, the aspect immediately preceding action. It hardly seems conceivable to practical sense that by will is meant something which can be complete without reference to deeds prompted and results occasioned. [emphasis added] (p. 44)

Again, he seems to equate habits and dispositions when he says that "disposition is habitual, persistent" (p. 45).

However, Dewey (1922) clearly prefers the word habit to other candidates such as attitude or disposition:

> The word habit may seem twisted somewhat from its customary use when employed as we have been using it. But we need a word to express that kind of human activity which is influenced by prior activity and in that sense acquired; which contains within itself a certain ordering or systematization

of minor elements of action; which is projective, dynamic in quality, ready for overt manifestation; and which is operative in some subdued subordinate form even when not obviously dominating activity. Habit even in its ordinary usage comes nearer to denoting these facts than any other word. If the facts are recognized we may also use the words attitude and disposition. But unless we have first made clear to ourselves the facts which have been set forth under the name of habit, these words are more likely to be misleading than is the word habit. (pp. 40-41)

Dewey (1922) settles on the word "habit." He seems to have considerable company in this decision to use habit. Stephen Covey (1989) seems to be paraphrasing Dewey when he writes, "Our character, basically, is a composite of our habits" (p. 46). For Covey, a habit is "the intersection of *knowledge, skill,* and *desire* [emphasis in the original] (p. 47). And the term, "habits of mind," is now widely used; a Google search using "habits of mind" generates over 120,000 hits ranging from Web sites focusing on curriculum development and assessment to those presenting philosophies of education.

Others who have considered the choice between the terms, disposition and habit, have come to the opposite conclusion. Donald Arnstine (1967) explicitly distinguishes between habit and disposition. For Arnstine the difference between a habit and a disposition is that a habit is a behavior or pattern of behavior engaged in indiscriminately while a disposition is behavior that "varies to suit different circumstances." When a person acts dispositionally rather than habitually, "the *quality* of his acts may be repeatable, but the acts *themselves* are not" (pp. 28-29). Arnstine then goes on to argue that habits, unlike dispositions, are the consequence of conditioning.

In their frequently cited article, "Dispositions as Goals for Teacher Education," Katz and Raths (1985) prefer the term disposition to habit "because teaching is a profession, that is, an occupation that brings rationality to bear on performance." They use the term habit to refer to "acts that are neither intentional nor consequent to reflection" and the term disposition to refer to "a pattern of acts that are intentional on the part of the teacher in a particular context and at particular times." They go on to allow, however, "we see dispositions as 'habits of mind'—not as mindless habits" (p. 303.)

Others who have wrestled with the choice between habit and disposition have come to a conclusion similar to Katz and Raths. For instance, Ron Richhart (2002) who writes about the dispositions associated with critical thinking or intellectual character settles on disposition after giving habit its due:

Like Dewey, I wish to invoke by the chosen term the volitional, acquired, and overarching nature of patterns of behavior. I feel the term *disposition* does this better than *habit* because we tend to understand a disposition as a tendency toward a general type of action. When we talk about someone having a friendly disposition, we understand that to mean that the person tends to approach situations in a certain way and to display a general set of actions we associate with friendliness. No one action is specified, but rather a whole range of related actions and responses may be evident. Dispositional behavior isn't automatic, though it does provide a gentle nudging that helps to bring out the behavior.

   In contrast, the term *habit* often denotes a mindless and automatic response that is not readily controllable. Unlike *disposition*, *habit* tends to describe specific actions or behaviors, quite often those with a negative bent, and is thus less broad and descriptive of general behavioral trends. (p. 20)

If the concern were about performance absent intention, then the notion of habit would seem a likely choice. Habits are all about behavior and require little theoretical speculation about causality, intention or thought patterns. Further, the notion of habits can be narrowed to specific realms of human behavior as in "health habits" or "habits of mind." One can easily imagine a category of habits known as "educator habits" or "pedagogical habits." The attractiveness of this notion is that habits does not carry with it the aura of causality. When we say someone has a habit, such as cigarette smoking, we are offering a description of repetitive behavior. The same is true when we refer to "habits of mind." For instance, we might choose "persistence." By doing that we would be saying that Bryon persists in working to a solution for a problem unlike Jerry who gets frustrated and quits.

   In many ways, it would be possible to use the concept "habit" in much the same way as using "trait" in its descriptive sense. The problem with habit however is twofold. First, habitual behavior is characteristically unconscious behavior; I do not choose to engage in habitual behavior—I simply do it as though I am an automaton. Indeed, the first step in many recommended processes for eradicating an undesirable habit is becoming conscious that I act repeatedly in a particular way and I am asked to keep a record of what I habitually do, that is become conscious of my behavior.

   Second, habit, in its typical use, refers to fairly narrow and isolated behavioral acts such as smoking, folding one's arms across his chest, tapping his foot, tapping her pencil. Costa (2005) and his colleagues may represent "responding with wonderment and awe" as a "habit of mind" but in everyday speech this is an extraordinary use of habit. We would more likely say that Hilda habitually talks about the beauty of sunsets or George habitually points to the mysteries of language development.

The Attractiveness and Dangers of Using Disposition in Accreditation and Regulation of Teacher Education

In her book on dispositions in early childhood, Lilian Katz (1993) contrasts the concept of disposition with most of the candidates for replacing attitudes that we have described above. She then undertakes a formal definition of disposition, but first she notes, "Though the term disposition is used in some of the psychology literature, definitions of it are rarely offered." She concludes after an extensive survey of the psychology literature that "in sum, usage of the term disposition is ambiguous and inconsistent. Only one attempt to define the construct psychologically has been found, namely that by Buss and Craik (1983) as act frequencies constituting trends in behavior" (p. 3)

So why would the leaders in teacher education and certification like those leading NCATE and managing teacher certification at the state level act to replace "attitudes" with "dispositions" which is typically used ambiguously and inconsistently?

The attractiveness of the concept disposition appears to lie precisely in this ambiguity and inconsistency. For teacher educators and the profession of education the concept "disposition" has not been a part of the conventional vocabulary used by teacher educators even though it appeared in Dewey's and Arnstine's writing. It had, for all practical purposes, no history, no abstract or practical meaning. It has been, and perhaps remains, for teacher educators an empty linguistic vessel. Introducing the term, disposition, then is likely to spur exploration of how better to prepare educational personnel since no one knows for sure what they are to do or how to do it. Disposition does have the advantage of being associated with behavior, with actual behavior and not merely intention or belief, and therefore is supportive of the emphasis on performance that the accrediting and certification agencies were emphasizing. In short, it has the advantage of stimulating development of teacher education in a performance-based direction.

Yet there are dangers in essentially pushing educators to attribute specific meanings to the term disposition and then assessing whether candidates in professional education programs possess them. The push appears to come from a desire of both NCATE and state teacher certificating authorities to assure the public that teachers prepared by institutions of higher education are in fact competent and effective. This desire was heightened by the appearance of A *Nation at Risk* (National Commission on Excellence in Education, 1983); this federally funded publication sharply criticized the condition of teacher education in the United States: "The teacher preparation curriculum is weighted heavily with courses in 'educational methods' at the expense of courses in subjects to be taught."

It went on to recommend that "persons preparing to teach should be required to meet high educational standards, to demonstrate an aptitude for teaching, and to demonstrate competence in an academic discipline. Colleges and universities offering teacher preparation programs should be judged by how well their graduates meet these criteria" (p. 30). This report produced ample progeny that also criticized the preparation of educational personnel. In fact, the Fordham Institute, along with several other groups, continues to point to deficiencies in teacher education. Recently the Fordham Institute published *Better Leaders for America's Schools: A Manifesto*; sample bullet points from the Executive Summary suggest the tone of the document:

- Despite a surplus in many places of people "certified" for administrative positions, our schools too often are not being led by qualified men and women.
- A certified administrator is not necessarily a qualified leader (Thomas B. Fordham Institute, 2003, p. 13).

In response to these attacks on teacher education, NCATE and state teacher certification bodies are essentially left to argue that their role is to enhance the quality of teacher education. As a result leaders of these entities are virtually forced to make claims such as the one Arthur Wise, Director of NCATE (2000) makes: "As more institutions meet NCATE's national professional standards, more qualified teacher candidates will be available, since candidates from accredited institutions pass licensing examinations at a higher rate than do those from unaccredited institutions or those with no teacher preparation" (p. 2).

A significant part of providing "qualified teacher candidates" is to assure that they possess the required dispositions. Therefore NCATE (2002) and the several states that have adopted NCATE-like standards, have stipulated that each institution must develop a conceptual framework and this framework must outline "the dispositions that the faculty value in teachers and other professional school personnel" (p. 13). One of the rubrics spelling out an acceptable level of compliance with one of the NCATE standards stipulates that "candidates are familiar with the dispositions expected of professionals. Their work with students, families, and communities reflects the dispositions delineated in professional, state, and institutional standards" (p. 16). Finally, another standard requires that the institution "systematically assesses the development of appropriate professional dispositions by candidates" (p. 19). These standards and their explicit and implicit requirements represent significant pressure on institutions and their faculties to develop an understanding of what a disposition is, what dispositions an effective educator should exhibit, and finally to assess whether candidates in the institutions' programs possess these dispositions.

The danger of this push is illustrated by the collapse of an earlier and similar effort by teacher educators to take a leading role in assuring the public that the graduates of teacher education programs were competent and that judgments about graduates were free of racial bias. In the late 1960s and 1970s, the concept of Performance Based Teacher Education (PBTE) swept across the country. Many states and institutions adopted an approach that focused on predefined, stipulated sets of "competencies" that teacher education programs would teach or otherwise instill in their candidates. Candidates were expected or required to demonstrate these "competencies" particularly in student teaching and other internship settings.

Midway through the seventies, Paul S. Pottinger (1976) observed that:

> Performance-based teacher educators are trying to instill public confidence in teachers' competence by empirically validating specific behavioral objectives. Research, theory, and development, however, have not kept pace with the social, political, and legal requirements that are being imposed. (p. 30)

For Pottinger (1976), the social demand for accountability in the preparation of professional educators had outrun the capacity of educators to devise systems that would actually deliver the desired accountability. Pottinger suggests that PBTE failed because of its allegiance to what he terms the "tyranny of reliability." That is, many of its proponents held that "moecularizing global behaviors into subunits is theoretically sound" or that "this reductionism makes behavior more amenable to objective observation, which, *ipso facto*, solves the problem of reliability" (p. 36).

Pottinger's (1976) warning about the difficulties PBTE faced—which could be supplemented by reference to a host of other observers and writers—suggests that including "dispositions" among the goals of teacher education and insisting on "scientific," particularly reductionist, assessment of them may lead to similar difficulties.

With these possibilities in mind, we now turn to addressing some of the fundamental questions about the concept, dispositions.

WHAT IS A DISPOSITION?

A history of the concept, dispositions, properly begins with Aristotle and his discussion of virtue in *Nicomachean Ethics*. Here he outlines his view that everyone has the potential to live a moral life and in which he "describes ethical virtue as a 'hexis' ('state' 'condition' 'disposition')—a tendency or disposition, induced by our habits, to have appropriate feelings" (Kraut, 2005). The key concepts here are the notions of potential and of disposition or tendency. That is, an individual person may or may not mature as a virtuous person and even if he/she does, he/she may from time to time engage in nonvirtuous acts because of a tendency to behave in a certain way under certain conditions. These two notions are fundamental to describing the nucleus of the concept, dispositon. This is well represented in lines from a soliloquy by Friar Lawrence in *Romeo and Juliet:*

> Virtue itself turns vice, being misapplied,
> And vice sometime's by action dignified.
> Within the infant rind of this small flower
> Poison hath residence, and medicine power;
> For this, being smelt, with that part cheers each part;
> Being tasted, slays all senses with the heart.
> Two such opposed kings encamp them still
> In man as well as herbs- grace and rude will;
> And where the worser is predominant,
> Full soon the canker death eats up that plant. (Act II, Scene 3)

As Joseph Malikail (2003) notes,

> *"Grace"* and *"Rude Will"* (Friar Lawrence's words) are both *dispositions* of character. Good or bad actions may correspond to a *disposition*, indicative of a state of character. *Hexis, habitus* or disposition is a general term for a person's readiness to act in a certain way. It finds expression in acts of particular virtues or vices like honesty, generosity, cheerfulness, jealousy or cruelty. (p. 8)

Malikail elaborates our understanding of disposition as used by Aristotle when he says, "The Greek word *Diathesis*, in Latin *Dispositio*, means to put things in a certain order. Ordering or arranging implies relating one thing to another; evidently a disposition has parts" (p. 8).

In short, Aristotle lays the groundwork for a discussion that continues in philosophical circles to this day though at times his parentage is not immediately evident. His parentage is evident however in the passage I quoted from Dewey earlier in this chapter. Dewey was writing in the early decades of the twentieth century; by the mid-century and the development of a new kind of philosophy, particularly in England, new ways of thinking about and using the concept of dispositions appeared. In his book, *Concept of Mind*, Gilbert Ryle (1949) attacks what he calls the "ghost in the machine." His avowed purpose is to attack the Cartesian dualism of mind and body. His essential argument is that in thinking about the mind and the body, many, if not most philosophers, have made a "category-mistake," that is, they have treated the mind and the body as though they are terms belonging to the same logical category. According to Ryle, volitional physical activity is not caused by volitional acts of the mind.

The question Ryle (1949) faces is how to talk about mind and body. He resolves this question by arguing that having a mind means that a person is disposed to behave in certain ways; that is, we are disposed to behave in certain patterns under given circumstances. That is all that is happening; there is no need for an explanatory mechanism that causes these behaviors. It is important to understand that Ryle is interested in "talk" about minds and behavior. What he accomplishes in his argument is to render "talk" of mind into "talk" of behavior and physical activity. For him there is no mind to explain away in any event. Ryle might be said to hold the mind as dispositional.

Dispositions, for Ryle (1949), are a way of explaining how behavior occurs without having to invoke a causal relationship between mind and body. Dispositions are attributions that we make about people after witnessing their behavior. Take for example a teacher who frequently asks students higher-order questions. Each time the teacher asks such a question, we witness an episode. After watching several of these episodes, we might describe the teacher as disposed to asking higher-order questions. In making these statements we do not need to invoke the notion of mind to explain some mysterious connection between the teacher thinking about asking such questions and then doing it. Rather, we simply observe and then say that she is disposed to asking higher order questions.

Donald Arnstine (1967) in his *Philosophy and Education: Learning and Schooling* is a direct descendant of Ryle when he argues that learning is the process of acquiring and changing particular kinds of dispositions. While he does not explicitly offer a definition of dispositions, Arnstine views dispositions as attributes that we ascribe to people and things. When he speaks of dispositions, like Ryle, he is speaking of one way that we talk about others—we use dispositional statements. This is clear from the following passage:

> A disposition, then, is not some sort of a thing or mysterious unobservable property of a thing; rather it is a concept that has it use in predictive statements. To ascribe a disposition to something or to someone is to say he has a tendency to behave in certain ways when certain conditions are realized. Ascribing a disposition, then, allows for the making of a prediction (although it may also be used as a sort of explanation. (p. 32)

In addition to making clear that dispositions are ascriptions made by observers and not innate qualities of a thing or a person, Arnstine (1967) helpfully describes what he terms, "the openness of dispositional concepts:"

The grounds on which dispositional statements are made and the ways they are verified point up another property of such statements which is of special importance when we consider the dispositions of people (whose behavior is less precisely determinable than that of inanimate objects). It is just because the exercise of a human disposition may take so many different forms that singular events are inadequate either as bases or as verifications of dispositional statements. Cruelty, for example, is a dispositional concept, but it has no single or uniform set of exercises. (p. 35)

Arnstine continues:

It is for these reasons that, in ascribing dispositions, we often aim at greater precision of communication by specifying the object of the disposition, the manner of its exercise, and the conditions under which it is most likely to be exercised. Still, it is never possible fully to specify all the conditions for the exercise of any disposition, since this would call for a crystal ball that afforded exact knowledge of the future. (p. 35)

DISTINGUISHING THE DISPOSITIONAL FROM THE NONDISPOSITIONAL

There are several ways of conceptualizing the question of distinguishing the dispositional from the nondispositional and each of these responses can be given twists and turns making the responses complex and varied. Here are some possible and simplified responses to this question:

1. The question is meaningless. We cannot distinguish the dispositional from the nondispositional because everything about human behavior is, in fact, dispositional. This position holds that there is nothing about human being X's behavior that is predictable in any real sense. Put another way, all behavior is conditional and potential—which particular behavior someone engages in depends at least partially on the interaction of the individual or thing with the environment. This is essentially the position underlying the work of Buss and Craik (1983) in their article titled, "The Act Frequency Approach to Personality." Following Hampshire's (1953) view of dispositions, they argue for a concept of disposition that is essentially a category of behavior attributed to an individual after the individual has engaged in a sufficient number of actions falling within the parameters of the category, say generous.

2. We cannot distinguish the dispositional from the nondispositional because everything about human behavior is, in fact, nondispositional. This position would hold that for all of our talk about

behavior, for all of our attempting to explain why I or someone else exhibits "x" instead of "y" behavior, it is in any event all a matter of brain chemistry. To allege meaningful control over this chemistry is to believe in fairy tales. This is a thoroughgoing materialist position in which dispositions are identified with states of mind that have their source in the biological and chemical structures and activities of the brain.

3.   The dispositional is based on categorical properties, that is, unchanging aspects of our makeup. Here the argument has to do with finding the "ground" for the disposition. In the case of working with teachers, we might say that every teacher has a "temperament." Talk about temperament usually assumes that aspects of one's temperament are the result of heredity, neural, and hormonal factors. Following Chess and Thomas (1986), aspects of temperament might be labeled as "activity, regularity, initial approach/withdrawal, adaptability, intensity, mood, persistence/attention span, distractibility, and sensory threshold" (pp. 273-281). Thus, just as the fragility of glass may in fact rest on the peculiar molecular structure of glass, so the disposition of generosity may in fact rest on the initial approach/withdrawal aspect of one's temperament. Those holding this view take the position that there is some kind of innate aspects of one's makeup that are permanent. They may become distorted, deformed, or hidden but they are in fact always present in one. Dispositions—that is propensities to act in particular ways—flow out of this innate stratum.

The question of separating the dispositional from the nondispositional not only arises when we address issues of assessing dispositions but it is implicitly addressed by the authors of several chapters in this book. Katz and Raths (1985), for instance, have throughout their writings on dispositions followed Buss and Craik's (1983) formulation of dispositions. On the other hand, Parker Palmer (1998), whose contribution is described in this book by Sally Hare, speaks of a "true self" and founds much of his work on the notion of "identity." His is no simple notion of identity. He describes identity in part as "an evolving nexus where all the forces that constitute my life converge in the mystery of the self" (p. 13). Nevertheless he holds that there is a core of the self from which dispositions flow. Other authors in this book take positions along the continuum whose ends are represented by Katz and Raths and by Palmer.

IDENTIFYING DISPOSITIONS

Another question focuses on the nature of dispositions themselves. We might frame the question as follows: Are the number of significant dispositions related to educators infinite? Are there criteria that might be applied to separate the important dispositions from the nonimportant? And once significant dispositions have been identified, is it possible that we have only identified supradispositions that are in turn made up of subdispositions?

NCATE standards and state rules and regulations now require institutions to identify and assess dispositions. To some, it appears that these standards put them in the position of Diogenes. First they must generate a list, long or short, of dispositions and then go hunting for individuals who exhibit those dispositions or test individuals who volunteer to see if they manifest the chosen dispositions. There are, however, no suggested criteria for which of an apparently infinite number of dispositions should be selected. Ritchhart (2002) provides us some guidance when he discusses the problems associated with identifying critical thinking dispositions: "As our cursory examination of these lists of thinking dispositions indicates, developing an ideal list is no easy task. It is often difficult to keep the list focused solely on thinking and not to veer off into other values" (p. 26). This appears to be the case in teacher education as well.

One of the major issues facing teacher educators is distinguishing between dispositions that are desirable in any person in the workforce or even casual acquaintances—punctuality, honesty, effective listening—and those dispositions that appear to be more specifically related to "educating." As I have read lists of dispositions generated by teacher education institutions, I have often thought that the lists represent the kinds of attributes faculty members want in their associates. All this is to say that there is no apparent plumb line to assist in identifying dispositions. Given the focus of NCATE on the effect of candidates and graduates on the learning of pupils they teach, it would seem that one candidate for being a plumb line is "facilitating student learning." Another is candidate is "being a good employee and a good colleague."

One of the assumptions underlying the requirements promulgated by NCATE and several states appears to be that there are a limited number of such dispositions that can somehow be identified as critical to being an effective educator. But the identification of a particular disposition might in fact result in the further identification of several derivative dispositions. In his discussion of bravery, Mumford (1998) says that "bravery provides us with an example of a disposition which is a complex of subdispositions" (p. 8) He goes on to show that bravery presupposes fear or knowledge of the danger in which one is acting. A person acting without fear or knowledge of the potential danger of acting can hardly be called brave. Mumford observes that "bravery is a complex of … two subdispositions: a particular disposition to represent certain but not all situations as fearful and a disposition to the right response toward fear" (p. 8). There are also derivative dispositions such as the following: hunting for a specific book might be taken as derivative of the disposition to want to learn about Swift and wanting to learn about Swift might be taken as a derivative of a more fundamental disposition that we could call curiosity. The question, then, is at what level does the identification of dispositions begin or stop.

Another assumption about dispositions is that they function in the same way in all or most education setting. This assumption, which is as old as teacher education, continues to be suspect since there appear, at least in a cursory review, sufficient differences among teaching, say, kindergarten, eighth grade social studies and twelfth grade calculus to require differing dispositions. If the NCATE standards and state rules are intended to cover all certificated educational professions including administration and school service personnel, the differences in the roles and responsibilities suggest that the list is likely either be short and very general or to be very long and differentiated in response to roles and responsibilities.

Then there is the matter of what constitutes effective teaching, effective administration and so on. Parker Palmer (1998) reports that

> listening to those stories [of students telling about their good teachers], it becomes impossible to claim that all good teachers use similar techniques: some lecture nonstop and others speak very little; some stay close to their material and others loose the imagination; some teach with the carrot and others with the stick. (p. 10)

If Palmer is correct difference rather than similarity seems more likely when "good" teaching is closely examined—at least in techniques used. On the other hand, study after study, consultant after consultant claims to have isolated the "characteristics" of effective teachers and leaders. Are these characteristics the same as "dispositions" or are they mere labels of certain patterns of action that are so highly aggregated that the differences get washed out?

DISPOSITIONS: CAUSES OR DESCRIPTIVE STATEMENTS?

Mumford (1998) observes that "dispositions are posited as explanations of past events and grounds for the prediction of future events." He goes on to wonder "what exactly their role is in the production of such events and whether they have any role at all to play in explanation"

(p. 11). In other words, the question is what kind of statement are we making when we ascribe a disposition to someone or something. Are we asserting that the disposition inheres in the person or the thing so that it serves as a cause? Or are we simply summarizing a number of observations about the person or the thing behaving in similar ways on a number of occasions, as Katz and Raths would do? Put another way, the question is whether dispositions are reducible, eventually, to properties or to occurrences. If they are properties, they "belong" to the person; if they are occurrences they are simply generalized statements about how persons are acting.

This question has been asked in other ways. For instance, McCarthy (1993) in her discussion of dispositions associated with critical thinking argues that viewing critical thinking as a disposition associated with an action creates an infinite regress because critical thinking is the disposition to engage in ... (a disposition).... An alternative view is to think of critical thinking as a disposition that is a necessary condition for someone to be a critical thinker—that is it inheres in the person. In this view, what we might call the realist view, holds that dispositions refer to "capacities, or call them powers, abilities, tendencies or propensities of systems." They are "not mere descriptions, stating empirical generalizations" but are the "stable properties of a system that describe how a system acts or interacts, given a situation of certain triggering conditions" (Vanderbeeken & Weber, 2002, p. 43). In this view, dispositions exist in the thing itself, may exist without manifesting themselves, and can be used to explain behavior. In this approach a disposition is not the same as its manifestation.

This question has significant implications for how assessments are designed and how nurturing and development (as well as elimination) of dispositions proceeds. Pottinger (1976), for instance, argues that "unobservable but measurable generic and causal linking variables of behavior are equally if not more critical than observable behaviors for defining and measuring competence" (p. 39). On the other hand, if dispositions represent a statement aggregating several episodes of a certain behavior, then, the observable is all that is available and there is no need to move beyond the descriptive in assessment and beyond the modification of behavior in nurturing dispositions.

EXPLORING EDUCATOR DISPOSITIONS

The remainder of this book is divided into three parts.

   i.   Theoretical Perspectives:

This section addresses five different perspectives toward dispositions. A chapter is devoted to each perspective and each chapter presents the the-oretical underpinnings for the perspective and offers guidance regarding the programmatic and assessment implications for the perspective.

- Breese and Nawocki-Chabin base their contribution on the work of Bandura in the area of social cognition. They will argue that behav-ior is a manifestation of dispositions. In addition, they will propose integrating Bandura's theoretical approach with the analytical tools that have been developed by Boyatzis.

- Wasciscko proposes using perceptual psychology as a theoretical construct of understanding educator dispositions. He outlines the work of Arthur W. Combs and his associates in identifying the aspects of persons effective in the helping professions: their char-acteristic perceptions of self, other people, the nature of helping, important purposes of helping, and, the world in general. He then proceeds to show how the work of Combs can be applied to the task of identifying, developing, and assessing educator dispo-sitions.

- Oja and Reiman suggest the usefulness of adopting a developmental perspective in thinking about the nurturing and assessment of educator dispositions. They adopt a three faceted view of teacher development: (1) conceptual which they base on the work of David Hunt; (2) ego development based on the work of Loevinger; and (3) moral development based on Kohlberg and his progeny.

- Freeman argues that dispositions manifest themselves in particular places at particular times and as a result it is virtually impossible to identify a priori the dispositions that enable to an educator to be effective. He proposes that instead of focusing on dispositions as concepts or objects, attention should be given to viewing disposi-tions as process. He elaborates the notion of "reasoned eclecticism" and proposes that it is a metadisposition that will serve educators most effectively because it responds to specific place and time.

- Hare bases her reflection on the work of Parker Palmer, arguing that teachers must focus on personal identity and integrity. She explores the notion of teacher formation, seeing the development of teacher dispositions as following a series of discernments about the self in relationships to the role of teacher.

ii.   Experiential Perspectives on Educator Dispositions

This section presents the two perspectives offered by differing research approaches to educator dispositions.

- Raths, who along with Katz originally proposed that dispositions be incorporated into teacher education, reviews their contributions to the development of the concept of dispositions and then reports regarding their successes in using ratings of dispositions in the evaluation of both individuals and programs.
- Peterson presents research involving graduates of an alternative certification program. She reports on an analysis of the dispositions regarded as essential by these graduates to succeed as teachers in schools serving predominately at-risk students. Peterson also examines the dispositions these graduates said they had to develop or change in order to be successful in the context of schools and teaching.

iii.   Persisting Issues Raised by Dispositions

Two of the most troublesome issues related to the concept of educator dispositions are how to assess the adequacy of the dispositions manifested by an individual educator and how to assist individuals in developing or reducing the power of dispositions.

- Diez (2002) observes that a "number of significant problems with assessment as related to licensure continue to dog the credibility of the process. Most important, while the standards describe teaching as a set of highly complex tasks, much of what currently passes for teacher testing follows a reductionist model—looking not so much at what's important but at what's easy to measure" (p. 13). She then analyzes the problems created by three approaches to assessment of dispositions: reductionism, superficiality, and disconnectedness. Her contribution ends with proposals about how the assessment of dispositions can have integrity and contribute to the development of teacher education candidates.
- Diez, in a chapter based on Freeman's outlines, addresses the issue of how to work with individual candidates in developing the dispositions required of educators. Her intent is to address the possibility that working with dispositions requires, in the words of Katz and Raths, "to act as surrogate clinical psychologists." She summarizes the major principles of the emerging field of "coaching" and suggests how implementing these principles in the context of working with candidates avoids many of the problems with approaches designed to "fix" candidates. She reports on her experience in

coaching candidates in a nationally acclaimed teacher education program.

- Stooksberry closes the volume with a proposal for dialogue in teacher education concerning three issues pertaining to the topic, "dispositions": their definition, their development in teacher education programs, and their assessment. Stooksberry's essay rehearses the principal ideas found in the collection of essays here and challenges the field to respond productively to the inevitable dialogue that this book will surely prompt.

NOTES

1. The appearance of dispositions in this document can be probably be attributed to Raths serving as a consultant to the Minnesota Task Force.
2. By e-mail, I asked Linda Darling-Hammond for help in understanding how the concept of dispositions was so quickly adopted. In a response, she said that "the term dispositions was widely used when I became involved in teacher education standard setting in the early 1990s" (personal communication, August 21, 2003).
3. The process by which this occurred is not mysterious. To avoid the legal difficulties of substituting NCATE standards for duly promulgated state rules and regulations, many of these states simply adopted NCATE standards, or paraphrases of them, as rules and regulations.

REFERENCES

Arnstine, D. (1967). *Philosophy of education: Learning and schooling.* New York: Harper & Row.

Burke, K. (1945/1969). *A grammar of motives.* Berkeley: University of California Press. (Original work published 1945)

Buss, D. M., & Craik, K. H. (1983). The act frequency approach to personality. *Psychological Review, 90,* 105-126.

Chess, S., & Thomas, A. (1986). *Temperament in clinical practice.* New York: Guilford.

Cook, D. (1992). Psychological impact of disability. In R. M. Parker & E. M. Szymanski (Ed.), *Rehabilitation counseling basics and beyond.* Austin, TX: PRO-ED.

Costa, A. L., & Kallick, B. (2005). *What are the habits of mind.* Retrieved January 21, 2005, from http://www.habits-of-mind.net/on

Covey, S. (1989). *The 7 habits of highly effective people.* New York: Simon & Schuster.

Darling-Hammond, L., Gendler, T., & Wise, A. E. (1990). *The teaching internship: practical preparation for a licensed profession.* Santa Monica, CA: Rand.

Dewey, J. (1922) *Human nature and conduct: An introduction to social psychology.* New York: Modern Library.

Diez, M. E. (2002). The certification connection. *Education Next, 1*(2), 8-15.

Hampshire, S. (1953). Dispositions. *Analysis 14,* 5-11

Interstate New Teacher Assessment and Support Consortium. (1992). *Model standards for beginning teacher licensing and development.* Washington, DC: Council of Chief State School Officers.

Judicial Administration Division Lawyers' Conference (1987) *Guidelines for Reviewing Qualifications of Candidates for State Judicial Office.* Chicago: American Bar Association. Retrieved February 5, 2005, from http://court.nol.org/manual/aba.htm

Katz, L. G., & Raths, J. D (1985). Dispositions as goals for teacher education. *Teaching and Teacher Education, 1,* 4, 301-307.

Katz, L.G. (1993). *Dispositions: Definitions and implications for early childhood practice.* Retrieved July 17, 2003, from http://ceep.crc.uiuc.edu/eecearchive/books/disposit.html

Kraut, R. (2005). Aristtole's ethics. *Stanford Encylopedia of Philosophy.* Retrieved February 27, 2005, from http:plato.standford.edu/entries/artistotle-ethics

Malikail, J. (2003) Moral character: hexis, habitus, and habit. *Minerva—An Internet Journal of Philosophy, 7.* Retrieved March 17, 2005, from http://www.ul.ie/~philos/vol7/

McCarthy, C. (1993). Why be critical? (or rational, or moral): on the justification of critical thinking. Philosophy of Education: Proceedings of the Forty-Eighth Annual Meeting of the Philosophy of Education Society. Ed. by Alexander, H., Arcilla, R & Bogdan, D. Place unknown: Philosophy of Education Society.

Mumford, S (1998). *Dispositions.* New York: Oxford University Press

National Commission on Excellence in Education. (1983). *A nation at risk: The imperative for educational reform. A report to the nation and the secretary of education.* Washington, DC: United States Department of Education.

National Council for the Accreditation of Teacher Education. (2000, May 15). Groundbreaking teacher preparation standards to be used beginning next year, NCATE press release.

National Council for the Accreditation of Teachers. (2002) *Professional Standards for Accreditation of Schools, Colleges, and Departments of Education.* Washington, DC: Author.

Palmer, P. J. (1998). *The courage to teach: exploring the inner landscape of a teacher's life.* San Francisco: Jossey-Bass.

Pottinger, P. S. (1976). Techniques and criteria for designing and selecting instruments for assessing teachers. In B. Levitov (Ed.), *Licensing and accreditation in education: The law and the state interest.* Lincoln, NB: Study Commission on Undergraduate Education and the Education of Teachers.

Ritchhart, R. (2002). *Intellectual character: What it is, why it matters, and how to get it.* San Francisco: Jossey-Bass.

Ryle, G. (1949). *The concept of mind.* London: Hutchinson.

Schirato, T., & Webb, J. (2002). Bourdieu's notion of reflexive knowledge. *Social Semiotics, 12*(3), 256.

Task Force on Teacher Education. (1986). *Minnesota's Vision for Teacher Education: Stronger Standards, New Partnerships.* St. Paul, MN: Task Force on Teacher Education, Minnesota Higher Education Coordinating Board and MBOT.

Teglasi, H. (1995). *ERIC Digest: Assessment of temperament.* Greensboro, NC: ERIC Document Reproduction Service No. ED389963.

Thomas B. Fordham Institute. (2003). *Better leaders for America's schools: A manifesto with profiles of education leaders and a summary of state certification practices.* Washington, DC: Author.

Thurstone, L. L. (1928). Attitudes can be measured. *American Journal of Sociology, 33*, 529-554.

Vanderbeeken, R., & Weber, E. (2002). Dispositional explanations of behavior. *Behavior and Philosophy, 30*, 43-59.

Wise, A. E. (2000, Spring). Perfomanced based accreditation: Reform in action. *NCATE Quality Teaching*, 1-2.

CHAPTER 2

THE SOCIAL COGNITIVE PERSPECTIVE IN DISPOSITIONAL DEVELOPMENT

Lee Breese and Rita Nawrocki-Chabin

As educators nurture, observe, and provide feedback to preservice teacher education candidates, all the papers, projects, lesson plans, and clinical evaluations culminate in one pivotal question: "Would we want that candidate teaching our (grand)sons and (grand)daughters?" If we answer "yes," we would applaud the high school teacher who effortlessly determines the longitude and latitude of London and the elementary teacher who expertly describes the food chain of rural Wisconsin. We would enthusiastically acknowledge the teacher who embraces cooperative learning and PowerPoint slides to facilitate his content goals. But we would want more. We would prize a teacher whose dispositions (see Appendix for a definition of dispositions and other key terms) toward teaching and learning compelled him to know each of his students' strengths, areas for growth, inclinations, and aversions; who honors student culture and prior knowledge, and who commits to the develop-

Dispositions in Teacher Education, pp. 31–52
Copyright © 2007 by Information Age Publishing
All rights of reproduction in any form reserved.

ment of the whole student (not just his cognition) to inform instruction leading to learning.

Leading educational organizations (Interstate New Teacher Assessment and Support Consortium [INTASC], 1991) and accrediting bodies (National Council for Accreditation of Teacher Education [NCATE], 2002) acknowledge the importance of dispositions. Schools of education across the country have developed a myriad of rubrics, checklists, scales and interview protocol providing testimony to the accrediting gods that their candidates have the requisite dispositions that complement knowledge and skills. If this educational heart of teaching is as important as content mastery and pedagogy, then in order to strengthen the necessary interconnectedness among knowledge, skills, and dispositions, teacher education programs must address the systematic development and assessment of dispositions.

What then are the teacher dispositions undergirding caring, trusting, relationships that impel students to ask questions, take risks, enjoy learning? Where does respect for the learning style of each learner originate? Can teacher educators structure strategies that allow candidates to examine the dispositions they bring into a teacher education program and to develop or further cultivate dispositions that secure those student-teacher relationships and perspectives toward teaching and learning that result in thriving classroom communities? Some teacher educators have proposed curricula for nurturing teacher dispositions that create student-centered learning. Purkey and Novak (1997) integrate invitational learning theory into practice as one avenue to approach school-wide and individual relationship building. Invitational learning emphasizes that attending to "people, policies, places, practices, and programs" (p. 3) sends clear messages that students are "able, valuable, responsible" (pp. 41-47) participants in school life, ultimately impacting positive student engagement. In an invitational school, for example, students exercise ownership for classroom rules, teachers honor learning diversity through a variety of instructional strategies, and programs like peer helpers and before school sports leagues meet the identified needs and interests of students. Invitational learning further delineates both the empowering and deleterious effects of teacher dispositions on classroom climate and student learning, emphasizing the need to nurture the positive. In another approach, Nodding's (1986) ethic of care includes a four-stage process of modeling, dialogue, practice, and confirmation by which teachers can cultivate nurturing environments. McCombs (1998) identifies research that demonstrates improved motivation and learning when teachers care about and attend to the unique needs of each learner. Similarly, Marzano (2003) reiterates the importance of student-teacher relationships in a classroom management context.

Nearly a century ago Dewey (1916) referred to dispositions as "habits of thought" which are influenced by both the intentionally devised habits and the unconscious reactions to the environment (p. 231). Katz (1995), referring to dispositions as styles, stable habits of mind, traits, and characteristic ways of responding, carefully explains that each of these has a connection to dispositions (pp. 49-54). Katz' discussion of dispositions particularly emphasizes the deliberate nature of dispositions: "A disposition is a pattern of behavior exhibited frequently and in the absence of coercion, and constituting a habit of mind under some conscious and voluntary control, and that is intentional and oriented to broad goals" (p. 63). Spencer and Spencer (1993) describe student centered orientation, a competency composed of dispositions, as positive expectations of students demonstrated by indicators of positive regard, the view that students are capable of change, and student initiated modifications of learning that are consistent with the student's learning objectives. Drawing on the work of Bandura (1977, 1997), Bandura and Walter (1963), and Boyatzis (1982), we define dispositions as intellectual and emotional investments in events, situations, and people. Preservice and in-service educators develop positions toward teaching and learning that direct their work with students, parents, and colleagues. Dispositions are made manifest through intentional, practiced behaviors that can be challenged, developed, and enhanced even as they denote behavioral tendencies that endure over time. Because dispositions are not visible, analysis of dispositions must rely upon the actions of the teacher in the classroom. Behaviors signaling effective teacher dispositions are indicators of competence in actual performance over time.

THEORY, LANGUAGE, AND REFLECTION

In our ongoing work with preservice teacher education candidates, we have found that Bandura's (1997) social cognitive approach offers a coherent vehicle to address dispositional development. Adding Boyatzis' (1982) language and self assessment (Alverno College Faculty, 2000) to observational learning affords candidates a practical model to explore, analyze, change, and nurture their and others' dispositions toward teaching and learning. The dispositions we seek to explore and nurture are those which build communities of learners, honor diversity, and promote effective student engagement such as positive regard for students and a commitment to do what it takes to help each learner succeed.

Bandura's Social Cognitive Perspective

According to Bandura (1997), modeling and reinforcement are the chief factors influencing behavior development. His modeling theory presented in four stages provides insight into how behavior, in this case preservice teacher education candidate behavior, can be nurtured or changed over time. In stage one, attention to modeled behavior, the candidate is aware of appropriate and positive teacher behaviors such as the use of proximity in classroom management or the choice of reflective teaching as an effective instructional strategy. Retention of appropriate behavior, stage two, encourages the candidate to remember and recall those behaviors as she observes her cooperating teacher in a field placement, analyses a case study and discusses readings or exercises in a classroom context. In stage three, reproduction of behavior, the candidate replicates, for example, a particular classroom management or instructional strategy in a role play or field experience. The final stage, motivation and reinforcement, propels the candidate to practice and refine the behavior. Our role as teacher educators is to structure opportunities for candidates to examine the relationships among teacher behaviors, their impact on teaching and learning, and the dispositions such behaviors signal to students, colleagues, administrators, and parents. We believe such opportunities will synchronize the deliberate choice of effective dispositions and their consequent behaviors. Key here is Bandura's emphasis on self assessment. Although instructor, cooperating teacher, and peer feedback all contribute to constructive analysis and growth, optimal knowledge and progress and the consequent drive to perfect a given behavior resides in the individual candidate's capacity to recognize and critique her own behavior.

We have witnessed countless examples of candidates initially struggling through the reasons behind both stellar and "I'll-never-do-that-again" lessons. As professors and mentor-coaches, we ask the reflective questions that draw out those reasons. Over time, sustained practice in self assessment allows candidates to become their own best critics. No longer the necessary crutch, we instead affirm the candidate's successful analysis of her own work and encourage her to set appropriate goals in ongoing course and field work. A powerful component in the learning process, self assessment mirrors, sometimes with brutal clarity, the effect of intended behavior. Mentkowski and Associates (2000) affirm the development and ramifications of self assessment:

> Students develop confidence that they can transfer their knowledge and abilities to new settings through performances, when they see themselves do it. Knowing what they can do across settings leads to self-regard in that

learners appreciate their own ways of doing things. Similarly, self reflections and individual development interact as students actively engage the breadth and diversity of approaches and views they have encountered (p .233)

As educators, regardless of instructional level, we also know the price-less effect of internal motivation (McClelland, 1987). As Bandura (1997) champions self analysis, he completes his four-part modeling theory with the individual assuming primary responsibility for behavior development. When a teacher education candidate, indeed any educator, is cognizant of positive teaching behaviors, reflects and grows from them, part four of the modeling theory, motivation and reinforcement, channels toward self effi-cacy, the internal conviction that I have the knowledge, skills, and disposi-tions, for example, to engage reluctant readers, dialogue effectively with challenging parents, and question policy and practice not in the best interest of students or the school community.

Boyatzis' Language

Whereas Bandura's theory describes the process of observational learn-ing, grounded in self-efficacy striving, that guides self-directed develop-ment of dispositions, Boyatzis (1982) provides the candidates with guidelines for analyzing the nature of their present dispositions and the development of future dispositions. The explicit language of Boyatzis enables students to scaffold their analysis into a common language to accurately describe self-observation and goal setting. Boyatzis describes the relationship of specific actions or behaviors that denotes dispositional skills, self-image/social roles, and traits/motives as ways to discover per-ceived goals necessary to performing the functions of a competent teacher in the following manner:

1. *Skills*—Skills are the ability to demonstrate a system and sequence of behavior related to attaining a performance goal
2. *Self-Image and Social Roles*—Self-image is both the concept of one-self and the evaluation of self. Social roles refer to a set of accept-able and appropriate social norms for the social group to which a person belongs.
3. *Motives and Traits*—A motive is a recurrent concern for a goal or condition that drives, directs, and selects behavior and traits are the characteristic ways a person responds to an equivalent set of stimuli. Both exist at the conscious and unconscious levels. (pp. 28-34)

Although dispositions may initially exist at both the conscious and unconscious level, motivations drive behaviors consistent with the candidate's current understanding of the social roles of an effective teacher. For example, if a candidate commits to honoring diversity in student learning, she will filter that motive through her concepts of the social role of an effective teacher. Reaching for consistency between motivation and behavior to honor diversity will guide her choices of skills. Acting on that motive confirms the social role of an effective teacher who meets the learning needs of all her students. Thus, she might choose to teach math from a minimum of three perspectives (skills) in order to reach all of the learning styles within her classroom. With access to this language framework, students can examine their reasons behind the dynamic interaction of the components of their perceived dispositional development which "drives directs, and selects behavior of the individual" (McClelland, 1987, p. 112). Maintaining a dispositional knowledge of these areas is essential to performing as a competent teacher, but it also gives preservice teachers a language to use for reflection: "Peeling away the metaphorical layers of dispositions may enable future teachers to begin to conceptualize the reasons for the actions that demonstrate a disposition and move to the higher levels of agency that question the effects of their actions" (Breese & Nawrocki-Chabin, 2006, p. 51).

Reflective Practice in Observational Learning

The power of reflective practice has increasingly moved to the forefront of the educational process (Mentkowski & Associates, 2000). For Dewey (1916) the recursive action-reflection process is critical to authentic learning. We engage in some experience, some social interaction, some learning; but the full import of that encounter for present learning and adaptation to future experience and problem solving remains incomplete unless we reflect on the how and why of that experience. Bandura's (1977) studies of social learning further reinforce the role of reflection in developing behavior. Rather than seeing behavior as either the product of one's internal conviction or entirely socially determined, he projects behavior as "a continuous reciprocal interaction of personal and environmental determinants" (pp. 11-12). Modeled behavior mediated by an individual's cognitive process, that is, reflection, results in behavioral decisions—hence the prominent role of self regulation in social learning theory: "At the highest levels of development, individuals regulate their own behavior by self-evaluation," an intrinsic reinforcement of behavior (pp. 101-105). The reflective practitioner in an educational setting can enhance performance through sustained observational learning complemented by self-assessment.

In the Alverno College environment, self reflection assists students to succeed. The success of students relies on the ability "to assess performance with the help of criteria, and to reflect on their learning" (Alverno College Faculty, 2000, p. 4). Since the College supports explicitly and consistently developed self-assessment, this ability is a coherent part of the learning framework and includes the following components:

- Students reflect on learning
- Describe learning in qualitative terms
- Synthesize learning
- Make sense of it
- Evaluate learning (p. 8)

All students are accorded multiple opportunities over time to self-assess their performance. In one beginning preservice teacher class, for example, candidates videotape performances in a classroom and use that videotape as the basis for self- and peer assessment of the dispositions demonstrated in a single classroom taping session. As the process unfolds over time, candidates begin to recognize the relationship between self-assessment and reflection:

> Self-assessment is usually concerned with the making of judgments about specific aspects of achievement often in ways which are publicly defensible (e.g., to teachers) whereas reflection tends to be a more explanatory activity which might occur at any stage of learning and may not lead to a directly expressible outcome. All self-assessment involves reflection, but not all reflection leads to self assessment. (Brew, 1999, p. 160)

Alverno College uses a developmental framework for self-assessment involving observing, interpreting/analyzing, judging, and planning. Each student is encouraged to form the habit of observing carefully and analyzing observations before leaping to judgments. For example, preservice teachers in one section of their first education course carefully observe teacher behaviors in the film *Dead Poets Society* (the attention component in Bandura's ([1997] observational learning). Then they produce a narrative analyzing the dispositions demonstrated by the actions of the teachers over time in the video (the retention component). In the field component of the class, candidates intentionally practice (reproduction component) behaviors that signal effective dispositions toward teaching and learning. Finally candidates analyze their performance from multiple perspectives and set dispositional goals for their next teaching opportunity as well as for ongoing class work (motivation component). However, the components of reflective practice previously presented are not always sequentially followed in learning situations, making it possible for students to move into and out of positions on the continuum, but still meet the criteria for competency. Self monitoring is the sign of an advanced ability to assess oneself and focuses on the development of judgments concerned with publicly defensible aspects of achievement. Because self-assessment and reflection are integral to learning at Alverno, highlighting their use in observational learning was a natural fit as we began a precise focus on dispositional development in preservice teachers.

INITIAL STUDY

With Bandura's (1997) observational learning model, Boyatzis' (1982) language, and commitment to self assessment, we had the components to study, practice, and reflect on dispositional awareness and growth. We began with four successive semesters, focusing on one section of preservice teachers in their first education course (Breese & Nawrocki-Chabin, 2006). Each semester added further modeling and analysis of dispositions as we realized the importance of attention and retention in observational learning. Students grappled with their own definition of dispositions, read about dispositions, role played classroom scenarios and viewed professional teaching videos as well as portrayals of teachers in film, analyzing teacher behaviors for the underlying dispositions toward teaching and learning. In all semesters, preservice teachers videotaped their own instruction in a field setting, analyzed their own and a partner's performance, and conducted peer conferences.

Over time, our understanding of using criteria to guide students in their self-assessment of dispositional growth has expanded to include feedback from the instructor as well as peer-feedback and candidate self-assessment. To assist in reaching further dispositional growth, we utilized the college-wide electronic portfolio, the Diagnostic Digital Portfolio (DDP) in which both the candidate and the instructor responded to the 5-minute video clip using identical criteria. For example, candidates used Boyatzis' language to effectively discuss the connections between behaviors and underlying dispositions. Candidate self assessment and instructor feedback remained as a permanent electronic record for the candidate's ongoing analysis of her development over time. The use and analysis of multiple materials in multiple settings over time extended candidates' opportunity for reflection and consideration of the fluid dynamics present in each classroom context (Hammerness, Darling-Hammond, Grossman, Rust, & Schulman, 2005).

KEY OBSERVATIONS

The previous study and current work with all levels of candidates using Bandura's (1997) observational learning, Boyatzis' (1982) language, and self assessment has surfaced four key observations in approaching dispositional development with preservice candidates: (1) having dispositions, (2) self awareness, (3) agency in shaping dispositions, and (4) dispositions others perceive. Candidates benefit first from recognizing dispositions in others and in themselves. Next, they develop the capacity to connect their teacher behaviors to underlying dispositions, being especially aware of the disconnect that can occur between a behavior and a disposition. Then, candidates assume personal agency in their ongoing development. Finally, how others regard a candidate's disposition and how a candidate regards others' dispositions further informs agency and efficacy of a candidate's self-concept.

Having Dispositions

Recognition of dispositions in others was introduced in the classroom before preservice teachers were asked to analyze their own dispositions. Recognizing separate skills and behaviors proved most accessible in candidates' initial observations. For example, acting as principal and colleagues in a class role play activity, candidates analyzed the dispositions of a disillusioned, cynical teacher and those they displayed in their interactions with her. In their written reflection about the experience, many seemed to struggle with the dispositions they demonstrated as they tried to give advice to the troubled, antagonistic teacher. As one candidate reflected, she found difficulty aligning her motive with her displayed behaviors:

> I am a little concerned that my assessment of Jane's [disillusioned teacher] current teaching stance appears to be negative. I could have spent a little more time but it was difficult to match empathy with discomfort toward her. How will I make this meeting inviting to her by using this letter? I selected skills and strategies clearly designed to help guide Jane back to effective teaching, but when we did the role play, I started by saying that I could see she had a problem and my body language was stiff. This disposition did not set the right tone. I think her attitudes were hard to deal with.

During the beginning phase of dispositional analysis, many candidates observed themselves demonstrating a skill like wait time, and were able to identify the behavior but not identify the disposition it might represent. Early on in each semester, many of the preservice teachers stopped with a one-dimensional description of a skill, for example, smiling, without looking at the relationship between the skill and their own social role expectations. Fewer still were able to connect a trait or motive to this basic skill. However, as self-awareness grew through greater exposure to dispositional manifestations in the field and classroom, participants developed a differentiated analysis of their dispositional signals. For example, one preservice teacher discussed how she smiled but at the same time assumed an unfriendly stance. She noticed she was bending over a student's back; thus, the child could not even see her smile. She questioned the dispositional message and decided that there must be consistency between the disposition (motive in this case) and the skill. By the end of the semester many candidates not only observed how a particular disposition was part of their (Boyatzis') self-image, but also went beyond a narrow focus on themselves by considering the effects of this disposition on students. For example, one candidate analyzed a set of dispositional behaviors, their combined impacts on her students, and subsequently developed an abstract understanding of how to improve:

> I smiled, nodded, and made eye contact with each student in my group. I felt comfortable and I wanted them to feel comfortable with me. I thought that then they would put out the effort to do the work that I was going to give them. [Here the student anticipated the effect of her behavior.] From now on I will try to improve my dispositions by using many positive nonverbal signals to send the message that they [students] are important.

Of course, classrooms are complex environments. Not all students will respond the same way to teacher dispositions. However, the above candidate does recognize that her repertoire must include multiple, effective nonverbal behaviors to respond to the diversity in her classroom.

Another preservice teacher reflected on her behavior in a way that demonstrated how her positive self-image connected to an awareness of how her social role utilized skilled teaching behaviors to communicate an intended message:

> This was very exciting to me; I was teaching! I carefully planned the lesson for a small group, but then my cooperating teacher wanted me to teach the skill to the whole class of students with many ESL children. I prepared the cards for each student to read because I wanted them to all participate in the game. When I presented the lesson, I continuously scanned the whole classroom and looked at students individually as they responded to my questions as part of the game. I made certain to call on every student and guide their answers so they would succeed. I believe they thought that I showed respect and interest in them through this behavior because they

were very attentive and involved in the lesson. My disposition was that their successful learning was important to me.

Self-assessment results in Bandura's self-regulated behavior and the motivation to continue behavior that positively impacts student engagement and learning.

Self-Awareness

Occasionally, preservice teachers found a clash between the disposition they wanted to signal and the behavior itself. As she observed her video clip for the electronic portfolio and began the written analysis, one preservice teacher simply was not able to find the potential or actual results that she expected; and she expressed frustration in her analysis. For example, the subject of curriculum adaptation led to a discussion of how curricular choice, a skill to be developed, could send unintended dispositional messages. Her cooperating teacher usually rendered curricular choices, and the preservice teacher wanted to work collaboratively with her. When the candidate began teaching this particular lesson, she discovered one student who struggled with cursive writing, a requirement of the cooperating teacher. The candidate reflected on the best course of action to display her strong disposition that each student has different learning needs, and that she was "willing to do what it takes to ensure he will be successful in achieving the objectives of the [social studies] lesson." She believed that if her lesson were engaging and focused, her message of interest and concern for the subject and the student's participation would lead to a "high level of enthusiasm for the discussion with no coaching." The candidate allowed the student to write only the correct word in cursive rather than the entire sentence as the latter choice would have effectively frozen the student in failure. Reliance on previous teaching experience (Bandura's retention and reproduction) and what she imaged as the effective classroom teacher (Boyatzis' social role) supported her reflective analysis and subsequent action. Her initial concern emerged because she felt a disconnect between her inner motive and the requirement of the cooperating teacher's curriculum. After receiving feedback that discussed only the behavior and after guided reflection on the connection between motivation, habit, and behavior, she questioned her ability to control and develop effective curriculum that would impact the message she wanted to send. She realized that a single skill cannot send the whole dispositional message and reflected that this dispositional awareness would enable her to work on consistency between her motive and delivery.

Agency in Shaping Dispositions

Within the framework of dispositional analysis and growth, preservice teachers were expected to develop a sense of their own agency and control. Through each classroom modeled activity, reflection, self-assessment, and feedback, candidates expressed more agency and a firm belief in their own ability to develop productive teachers dispositions that surfaced in effective teacher behaviors An example of this growing sense of agency came as preservice teachers reflected on their language use in a classroom, a behavior that most believed indicated attention to student learning while maintaining a steadfast focus on the individual student's need for acceptance from a teacher. In written analysis, they often reverted to the communications terms with which they were familiar, particularly tone of voice and pitch, without focusing on the actual words they used and the possible effects of those words on their students. One analyzed her language use as, "fluctuation in tone of voice impacts greatly how well students are listening to the teacher," ignoring completely the impact of the words themselves. Yet, during her peer conference this same preservice teacher noted that "poor language choices could lead students to interpret your dispositions differently than you want to portray, making awareness of what is said and how it is said very important in assisting children to recognize my disposition toward them and their learning." Furthermore, she discussed how even when her disposition was one of respect for all students in the classroom, the simple choice of referring to girls as "you guys" was offensive to one girl, the opposite of her intention. The student withdrew from class participation. As a result, the candidate set a goal of not using "you guys" as a reference to students because it could indicate a preferential disposition for boys. This preservice teacher reinforced her analysis by extending past discrete behaviors and located the natural connections between dispositions and social roles. Such connections led to a greater depth of understanding and application reaching Boyatzis' self-image layer. Another student easily saw connections between language usage and classroom practices, implicitly acknowledging her agency to change and develop self-image to what she believes will assist learning in her classroom:

> Tone of voice and classroom practice are two [dispositional behaviors] I am going to begin to work on. I am going to specifically focus on talking slower and explain directions with more detail for younger students. I am also going to begin working on adjusting my voice tone when I want their attention or to stop misbehavior. As I walk around the class speaking to students, I will make a conscious effort not to turn my back to any of the students.

However, as she integrated these areas, she nevertheless missed the impact dispositional behaviors could have on the learning of the class. In later peer discussions, she discovered that her motives were associated with controlling the behavior of some students who seemed disengaged during her presentation.

The capacity for dispositional growth surfaces as candidates move through their program and perform in a variety of clinical settings. Because of the nature of a small college, some candidates could be informally observed and address dispositions as we encountered them in other classes and assessments. For example, as candidates self assessed their own lessons or participated in the ED 220 assessment interview, opportunities to examine their dispositions also arose. ED 220, a one-on-one interview with an education faculty member, explores candidate growth in selected WI Standards for Teacher Development and Licensure. One candidate responded to dispositions associated with Standard 6 (Communication). Her goal, "appreciation of their environment and that of others," was motivated by a strong wish to affirm diversity of learning styles in each student. She addressed her image of an effective teacher and the skills she must display in her ED 220 reflective writing by using Boyatzis' three levels and combining those with invitational learning techniques:

> The dispositional motive (Boyatzis' motive) of this unit was that of appreciating diversity within each learner and [his/her] ability to learn and demonstrate different things within strengths and weaknesses. As an effective teacher (Boyatzis' social role), I aimed to help them develop their own self-confidence. I did not want any of my students feeling as though they could not achieve certain goals. Therefore, I tried to present goals in a manner that was inviting and nonthreatening. I prepared a list of positive responses to the lesson for my own use (Boyatzis' skills). Once they tried the activity, I provided them with positive feedback that encouraged them to continue moving forward.

We grappled with how this more advanced candidate would choose to respond to dispositional growth. Generally, she seemed to express an enthusiastic sense of agency arising out of her abilities to reflect upon dispositions in terms of motives, social roles of effective teachers, and skills.

Candidates who accessed the language and framework of dispositional development appeared more confident in the self assessment process. Students in their beginning class were often nervous about their initial field teaching experiences. However, some of the threat of getting up in front of students seemed to dissipate as they delved into their own dispositional messages. This analysis enabled candidates to identify problem areas and talk about needed growth. One student referenced "turning her back on students at the board" and the possible message of disengagement. As she discussed her behaviors, she decided that she could become more professional by using the dry-erase board for a shorter period of time or preparing her list before the students even entered the room. Throughout the discussion she made clear references to her commitment to growth and change as a result of analysis of her own dispositions. She never questioned her own ability to change and improve. Not only did students use analysis as a catalyst for development, they expected to change some of their dispositional behaviors that did not match with their motives and image of the social role of an effective teacher.

Dispositions Others Perceive

An unexpected result emerged from candidate peer conferencing. Through analysis of videotapes, written reflections, and classroom observation, we ascertained the power of peer conferencing, not only for disposition analysis, but also for the support and validation of preservice teachers' current level of development. It seemed to be a time for collaborative analysis of both what was observable and what was possible. One preservice teacher noted, "I feel that the peer conferencing not only helps to hone your teaching skills, but it also provides feedback that is essential to your growth as a professional. Another perspective is almost always a useful learning tool." Gaining another's perspective seemed to assist preservice teachers' critical analysis of their own dispositions. Preservice teachers overwhelmingly viewed the peer conference as a nonthreatening experience enabling them to extend dispositional reflection to the self-image layer.

Candidates also showed an instinctive understanding of the concept of *intentional* dispositions and the possibility that intentional dispositions could begin with self-knowledge. One student articulated her thoughts by discussing the peer conference as a method of assisting her with developing new teaching strategies, clarifying some of her positive dispositions, and guiding her growth in self-knowledge. She explained that she knew the importance of invitational language from her course work. But, to her peer assessor, she seemed uncomfortable in front of her small class of three, not showing her usual friendly manner. Thus, she appeared to be less than inviting to her students. During the peer conference, this preservice teacher expressed surprise that her personal discomfort with an awkward teaching situation was so visible. Although her peer assessor found many positive dispositions, this hint of discomfort led to a reflection about discovering a common meaning for dispositions, new strategies for teaching, clarification of positive dispositions, plus ways of reaching the same outcome through different dispositional behaviors. They each agreed that the peer conference "helped me to know myself as a teacher."

Although some of the preservice teachers seemed hesitant to discuss their dispositional goals in the peer conferences, almost all candidates directly confronted the dispositions they felt needed work on the electronic portfolio. For example, one discussed the disparity between her message and her behavior before she set a goal:

> One of the things I noticed in my video clip was that my [behavior] sent a different message than I intended. For instance, I did not smile a lot at the beginning of my lesson, and my facial expression seemed serious. My vocal quality sounded a little stale at times. I felt as though I was sending the message that I didn't care, the total opposite of what I was feeling. I would like to work on this because even though my lesson plan was inviting and motivating my speech and body language [were] not. The [behaviors] should match the message.

Another candidate discussed a dispositional behavior that would suggest "discussion is important to me." She recognized the potential message of "valuing the students' ability to evaluate and articulate" opinions but she also recognized the need to work on developing the behaviors as a package. She noted this was a goal of hers because she saw herself thank students for their input and move quickly to "get through" the lesson, defeating some of the purpose of her positive dispositions according to her analysis.

Efforts toward becoming a reflective practitioner should include feedback from multiple perspectives in order to articulate a plan for development of effective dispositional growth. Thus, the instructor feedback on the 5-minute video selection becomes an important part of the cycle. For this particular preservice teacher, instructor feedback gave further impetus to her growth decisions:

> You clearly demonstrate your application of the principles of dispositional growth when you discuss the role of the teacher in sending appropriate messages to students through dispositional [behaviors]. You demonstrate a clear connection between the behaviors and motives of the teacher and the responses of the students. Of particularly positive note, you include the awareness of your own growth by setting a reasonable and attainable goal.
>
> You set a goal of getting the *whole* class involved in the lesson. I too noticed that the table in the back of the room, out of your direct vision when standing at the overhead, seemed to be less engaged than the others. Perhaps, you could have moved away from the overhead, in their direction. In addi-

tion, some directed wait time as you moved around the room could have brought the group into the learning circle and completed your projection of the positive disposition that learning is for *all* students. Consistency between the disposition you want to display, your image of effective teaching, and the skills you choose to display dispositions can help send a constant message to all the students in the room.

Another set of partners, first grade and seventh grade preservice teachers, observed how they both smiled and walked around the room to display the disposition that the teacher does care. However, as they viewed these similar behaviors in their video clips, they concluded that that these behaviors would not necessarily engage student leaning. Both agreed the directions given were not as clear as they should have been and impacted engagement more than walking among students. Although both expressed a plan of even better preparation, neither appeared comfortable enough to actually set a specific personal goal for growth during the peer conference. Such an impasse highlights one of the challenges of the social cognitive perspective for dispositional growth. Preservice teachers can identify behaviors they observe and often astutely analyze consequent effects in the classroom (the attention and retention components of observational learning). However, in order to assess changing or developing dispositions, candidates must be aware of initial underlying dispositions. Absolute clarity between dispositions, which cannot be observed, and behaviors reflecting dispositions must be articulated repeatedly in order for preservice teachers to reflect upon changes in dispositions. Only then can Bandura's reproduction phase of observational learning complemented with self-assessment intentionally shape dispositions others perceive and provide the ongoing self regulation that drives effective teaching and learning.

As one of these candidates analyzed her dispositions based on the 5-minute electronic video clip, she discussed some specific goals in dispositional growth and synthesized patterns of behavior in the same articulate manner as the peer conference. However, she also discussed modifications in her dispositions. She noted that "at times I'd ask a question and then turn away or focus my attention elsewhere as the student answered." She felt any student might interpret the behavior as "the teacher doesn't care about an answer; therefore, I don't need to pay attention." As a result of this analysis, the preservice teacher found an area for dispositional growth: "I would like to be more conscious of paying full attention to the responses of all of the children so that they all understand that they are an important part of the class."

Some candidates early on recognized the social role of teachers and used self-assessment to further motivate, self regulate dispositional development:

I did what teachers do in a classroom. I gave children choices and allowed them to be as creative as they can be. I created a warm and inviting approach to my students. Through experience, I know that I will get a chance to analyze more dispositions along the way [in] my teaching field and I will continue to look at myself in the mirror.

In addition to feedback from peers and instructors, candidates who have encountered dispositional analysis in a number of courses confidently developed an increasingly sophisticated critical eye toward their and others' dispositions. One such candidate acknowledged her own need for proficiency in all aspects of teaching and articulated the importance of dispositions:

I realize that I am a student myself, with further learning and development as part of my process as a future educator of children. I do know that teaching has caused me to reassess my way of demonstrating my dispositions. Since I am still learning the skills to educate, I try very hard to think outside my own box [image of the role of effective teachers] to discover different ways to present concepts appropriate to the ages and multiple intelligences of the students that I am fortunate enough to teach. I am open to the suggestions of my cooperating teachers and instructors because I know that the ultimate winners in this overall process will be my future students. I know that my teaching skills will always require reassessment.

Although this candidate clearly expressed dispositional perceptions, for us, there was always the question of whether or not our future teachers would recognize dispositional balance in themselves and others. The question was answered by a student completing her final field before student teaching, when she expressed concerns about her cooperating teacher's dispositions, citing her personal discomfort with some of the teacher's behaviors. In reflective writing, she delineated her perception of some poorly matched motives, ineffective teaching (social role), and skills. In an incident at school, the teacher had laughingly warned two students not to sit on the lab tables near any experiments that were hot. However, she said nothing to the remaining students. Then, in an aside to the candidate, the teacher predicted that these students would not pass this time either. As the class progressed, the teacher sat on a lab table herself and talked with several of the students about the golf team while one of the students burned a hole in his pants from sitting too close to the experiment. In a manner the candidate perceived as very angry, the teacher berated the class and told them they had failed the lab experience.

After discussion and reflection, the preservice teacher came to the conclusion that her cooperating teacher was not really intending to send such a mixed message to her students, but that her motivations for learning were not aligned with her own behavioral images of what the role of a teacher should be. Frustrated by her observations, the candidate nonetheless learned from that experience and made a commitment to her own dispositional awareness and growth:

> I will be flexible and caring in classroom behaviors when I sense students need more clarification. I realize that not all teachers are proficient in recognizing and changing dispositional behaviors, so I will not judge them, but instead I will continually use my ability to hone my skills and talents, set objectives for myself that will make me effective, and continue to learn from my students (who inevitably will become my best teachers).

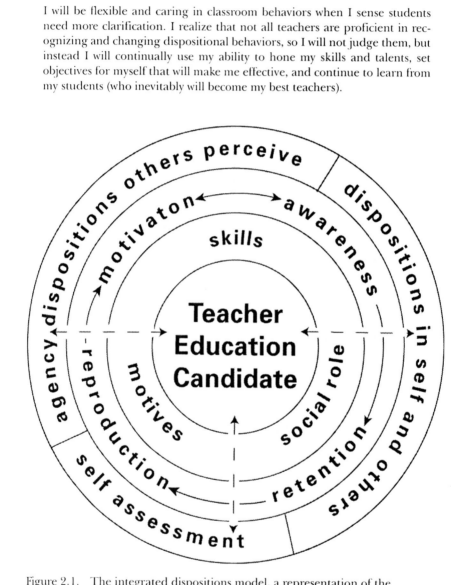

Figure 2.1.   The integrated dispositions model, a representation of the relationships among Bandura's observational learning, Boyatzis' language, and the authors' key understandings.

Important and powerful, dispositions are nonetheless elusive because unlike observing how a teacher uses positive reinforcement or structures collaborative learning, dispositions can only be inferred through the behaviors that manifest them. Dispositions are dynamic, constantly developed and reinforced. We are committed to the belief that teacher behaviors can be nurtured. Bandura (1997) offers an accessible framework for dispositional development. Boyatzis' (1987) language allows candidates to analyze their and others' dispositions. Self assessment completes the developmental triad.

To capture and extend the ideas of these three components, we have conceptualized The integrated disposition model (see Figure 2.1). The teacher education candidate, the core of our model, is our raison d'etre as teacher educators. We begin with the assumption that teacher education candidates have little to no knowledge of dispositions and their impact on teaching and learning. Working outward, the next ring reflects Boyatzis' language allowing candidates to distinguish behaviors from dispositions, recognize teacher roles in the classroom, understand how motive relates to social roles, and generate behaviors consistent with motives and social roles. A secure language allows preservice teachers to access Bandura's four-part observational learning model, the next ring. In the initial stages of awareness and retention, candidates can identify both the behavior and some of the social roles of an effective teacher. As they practice skills associated with their evolving conceptualization of effective teaching, motives that initiate their behaviors become a key element in the dispositional process. If a candidate values student learning and determines more focused time on task would reach that goal, she will filter that motive through what she thinks is the role of an effective teacher and select skills consistent with that image.

The reproduction stage of Bandura's model enables candidates to practice effective teacher behaviors they have observed. Self assessment, a component of this stage, allows the candidate, over time, to become adept in judging to what extent her behaviors lead to success in the classroom and are congruent with her dispositions. In addition, self analysis continues to affirm or challenge the candidate's image of herself as an effective teacher. In the final stage, the more success the candidate experiences, the more motivated she is to practice and refine those behaviors effective in her classroom. Self-efficacy emerges as a natural outgrowth of success. The two-way arrow connecting motivation and awareness signals how greater self efficacy leads to a heightened awareness of dispositions and their manifestation through behaviors.

The outer circle represents our perspective of dispositional analysis and development that begins with recognition of dispositions in self and others using Boyatzis' language and Bandura's model. Self assessment represents the single most powerful component leading to agency. And agency promotes risk taking, a willingness to put students first, and confidence in the myriad of decisions made in the classroom. Commitment to self assessment, already embedded in Bandura, must be given equal priority with the observational model and the language of dispositional analysis. Finally, candidates with agency become sophisticated judges of their own dispositional behaviors and develop confidence in their analysis of peer behaviors manifesting dispositions. In addition, feedback others provide serves the crucial function of directing attention toward an external reading of behaviors and their objective effects. The two-way arrows from the teacher education candidate through each ring evidence the integrated nature of the model. Bandura's observational learning and our key understandings are interpreted through the language of Boyatzis', and the language is accessible at any stage of any ring.

Teaching is not just what happens in a classroom; at its best and at every level, teaching is a scholarly activity for the benefit of others (Shulman, 1989). In our ongoing teaching we will continue to strategically infuse disposition discussion, analysis, practice, and reflection in practice into the teacher education program. Working with our colleagues, we will further develop strategies for developing dispositional awareness so that we can enable preservice teachers to move to a more sophisticated practice and analysis of their own dispositions. Together, we hope to create a shared language that further articulates and encourages this profoundly powerful heart of teaching.

APPENDIX: GLOSSARY OF TERMS

Criteria

Criteria are standards for performance. The translation of broad outcomes into specific criteria provides a more complete description of what the outcome might look like in practice. Criteria are often developed or adapted collaboratively by students and faculty, always available to students before the assessment, reviewed by students as they prepare for the assessment, and used again as students self assess their performance (Alverno College Faculty, 2000, pp. 70-71).

Dispositional Analysis

The ability to reflect and respond to the connections between a recognized belief, attitude, motive, or trait as it is mediated by self-image of an effective teacher. Dispositional analysis explains the reasons for choosing classroom behaviors and the resulting message that students receive.

Dispositional Behavior

A behavior, either verbal or nonverbal, that projects a particular disposition. For example, wait time is a nonverbal behavior that demonstrates consideration for students who need processing time before responding.

Dispositional Growth

This term represents an increase in knowledge about and recognition of the development of dispositions selected by the teacher to make teaching and learning more effective.

Dispositional Knowledge

In our work, the ability to recognize, reflect upon, and apply information and observations about dispositions as expressed through Bandura's theory and Boyatzis' language.

Dispositional Message

Communication resulting from teacher behaviors. For example, through verbal and nonverbal behaviors and instructional practice, a teacher can intentionally or unintentionally send messages to students that learning diversity is either valued or unimportant in a given classroom.

Dispositions

Intellectual and emotional investments in events, situations, and people. Preservice and in-service educators develop positions towards teaching and learning that direct their work with students, parents, and colleagues. Dispositions are made manifest through intentional, practiced behaviors that can be challenged, developed, and enhanced even as they denote behavioral tendencies that endure over time.

REFERENCES

Alverno College Faculty. (2000). *Student self assessment at Alverno College.* Milwaukee, WI: Alverno College Institute.

Bandura, A. (1977). *Social learning theory.* Englewood Cliffs, NJ: Prentice-Hall.

Bandura, A. (1997). *Self-efficacy: The exercise of control.* New York: Freeman.

Bandura, A., & Walter, R. H. (1963). *Social learning and personality development.* New York: Holt, Rinehart and Winston.

Boyatzis, R. E. (1982). *The competent manager: A model for effective performance.* New York: Wiley.

Breese, L., & Nawrocki-Chabin, R. (2006). Reflective practice that nurtures disposition. *Academic Exchange Quarterly, 10(3),* 49-53.

Brew, A. (1999). Towards autonomous assessment: Using self-assessment and peer assessment. In S. Brown & A. Glasner (Eds.), *Assessment matters in higher education: Choosing and using diverse approaches* (pp. 159-171). Buckingham, England: Society for Research into Higher Education and Open University Press.

Dewey, J. (1916). *Democracy and education.* New York: The Free Press.

Hammerness, K., & Darling-Hammond, L., Rust, F., & Shulman, L. (2005). The design of teacher education programs. In L. Darling-Hammond & J. Bransford (Eds.), *Preparing teachers for a changing world: What teachers should learn and be able to do* (pp. 390-441). San Francisco: Jossey-Bass.

Interstate New Teacher Assessment and Support Consortium. (1991). *Model standards for beginning teacher licensing and development: A resource for state dialogue* (Working Draft). Washington DC: Council of Chief State School Officers.

Katz, L. (1995). *Talks with teachers of young children: A collection.* Norwood, NJ: Ablex.

Marzano, R. J. (2003). *Classroom management that works: Researched-based strategies for every teacher.* Alexandria, VA: ASCD.

McClelland, D. C. (1987). *Human motivation.* New York: Cambridge University Press.

McCombs, B. L. (1998). Integrating metacognition, affect, and motivation in improving teacher education. In M. Lambert & B. L. McCombs (Eds.), *Reforming schools through learner-centered education* (pp. 379-408). Washington, DC: APA.

Mentkowski M., & Associates. (2000). *Learning that lasts.* San Francisco, CA: Jossey-Bass.

National Council for Accreditation of Teacher Education. (2002). *Professional standards for the accreditation of schools, colleges, and departments of education.* Retrieved from http://www.cate.org/2000/unit_stnds_2002.pdf

Noddings, N. (1986). Fidelity in teaching, teacher education, and research for teaching. *Harvard Educational Review, 56(4),* 496-510.

Purkey, W. W., & Novak, J. M. (1997). *Inviting school success: A self-concept approach to teaching, learning, and democratic practice* (3rd ed.). New York: Wadsworth.

Shulman, L. S. (1989). Toward a pedagogy of substance. *AAHE Bulletin, 41(10),* 8-13.

Spencer, L. M., & Spencer, S.M. (1993). *Competence at work: Models for superior performance.* New York: Wiley.

CHAPTER 3

THE PERCEPTUAL APPROACH TO TEACHER DISPOSITIONS

The Effective Teacher as an Effective Person

M. Mark Wasicsko

INTRODUCTION

Ask people to describe the qualities of a teacher who had a significant positive impact on their lives and they invariably relate such things as: "she believed in us, made us feel worthwhile and had high expectations of us." "He was enthusiastic, had a great sense of humor and had an infectious excitement for the adventures of living and learning." "She spooned out freedom and responsibility in equally plentiful doses." "Under his watchful eye I blossomed that year." And so on.

When describing their best teachers, people frequently struggle with words to express the deeply meaningful and personal relationship that existed and the life-altering impact it had. Asking thousands of students, friends, and acquaintances about their most effective teachers led to the conclusion that *it is not so much what the teacher knows or does rather it is who*

Dispositions in Teacher Education, pp. 53–89
Copyright © 2007 by Information Age Publishing
All rights of reproduction in any form reserved.

the person is that makes all the difference. It is particular human qualities or dispositions in combination with, and shining through, their knowledge and skills that allow some teachers to transform many students' lives. Over 5 decades of being a student, then a teacher, and now a teacher educator has led the author to the realization of the paramount importance of educator dispositions when it comes to fostering meaningful and lasting learning. The perceptual model described herein offers a means by which dispositions associated with highly effective teachers can be defined, understood and, more importantly, applied to the educator preparation process.

Three basic questions regarding teacher dispositions will be explored in this chapter: (1) what are dispositions?, (2) why use a perceptual approach for understanding and applying dispositions?, and (3) how should dispositions be used in educator preparation programs?

WHAT ARE DISPOSITIONS?

The term "dispositions" as it relates to teachers is undergoing a vernacular evolution much like what happened with "discipline," "quality," "assessment," and "highly qualified." At present there are almost as many different definitions of dispositions as there are institutions preparing teachers. However, most institutions have discovered that, while crucial and essential elements to teacher effectiveness, dispositions are difficult to define and operationalize in programs to prepare teachers.

As illustrated in Figure 3.1, current definitions of dispositions tend to fall along a continuum ranging from specific, observable behaviors to inferable personality traits and typically include one or more of the following elements:

- *Teacher behaviors*—Observable activities of candidates during class activities or with children, including behaviors such as writes and speaks Standard English, punctual, smiles, neat/orderly appearance, and so forth.
- *Teacher characteristics*—Attributes or tendencies of candidates that are persistently demonstrated, such as tolerance of differences, open-mindedness, patience, enthusiasm, critical thinking, and so forth.
- *Teacher perceptions*—Core attitudes, values, and belief systems that lie beneath teacher behaviors and teacher characteristics, such as self-concept, seeing students as able, a people-centered orientation, and so forth.

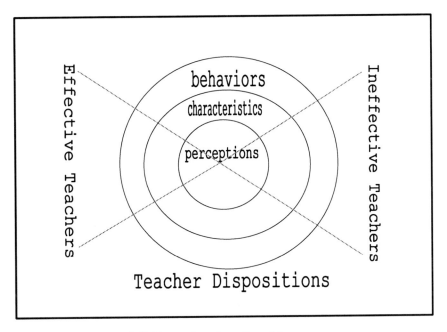

Figure 3.1.   Current definitions of teacher dispositions.

Important information about teacher dispositions may be acquired from observable and measurable behaviors (obtained from observations, behavioral inventories, checklists, etc.), from personality characteristics (using rubrics requiring moderate inference), or from candidate core values, beliefs or perceptions (using higher inference clinical-type assessments). Each approach to dispositions presents its own unique advantages and challenges. For example, having a definition of dispositions that focuses on specific teacher behaviors might provide for more "objective" assessment but may have less predictive value or lead to an unwieldy compendium-type check list of desired but insufficient behaviors. Drilling down into the core of the personality to the values or perceptions level could lead to a more manageable number of variables and more predictive value, but will require the use of high inference measurement tools. No matter which approach is adopted, a key factor that frequently limits the functionality of the model is having valid and reliable measurement strategies and tools.

By applying research findings and professional judgments, the sectors in Figure 3.1 can be populated with behaviors, characteristics, and/or perceptions that have varying degrees of correlation with either effective or ineffective teachers as well as those that seem unrelated to effectiveness.

Given sufficient time, valid assessment methods and tools, and enough sampling, most approaches can provide helpful information about candidate dispositions.

The optimal operational definition of dispositions is a construct that is clear, useful, and easily understandable by students and faculty, flows from (or is at least complementary to) a program's mission or value statements, and is based on a strong theoretical and research foundation. Many less than satisfactory attempts to operationally define dispositions result from fuzzy constructs that overlap with content knowledge and pedagogical skills, contain too many and/or overly complex elements that would make valid and reliable assessment nearly impossible, or lack a sufficient research base or assessment tools. A further difficulty frequently encountered comes with limiting the definition to a reasonable number of variables with a clearly defined scope. A straightforward way to avoid many of these pitfalls is to apply Ockham's Razor and limit the scope to as few elements as necessary and restrict the definition of dispositions to encompass only elements that can not be categorized as knowledge or skills. This interest in parsimony led to the adoption of a dispositions model based on the perceptual psychology of Arthur W. Combs (1949), and elaborated by others (Combs et al., 1971, 1974a, 1974b, 1976, 1994).

The major focus of Combs' (1949) research was on the human qualities (he called them perceptions) of teachers and other helping professionals that permitted some individuals to facilitate greater than average positive change in students, clients, and other individuals with whom they interact. From this perspective, the primary goal of the teacher preparation program is to increase the personal effectiveness of candidates by facilitating the amalgamation of dispositions (personal values, attitudes, and beliefs), professional and content knowledge, and skills so that completers become effective, integrated teaching instruments for carrying out the purposes of schools and society. If the process is successful, program completers would have integrated their dispositions, knowledge and skills so thoroughly that the majority of their interactions with students (both intentionally planned lessons and spontaneous learning opportunities) would lead to increased learning, growth and development. Figure 3.2 depicts the progression of candidates through the program in the perceptual dispositions model.

This conceptualization keeps the three components (knowledge, skills, and dispositions) somewhat distinct thus allowing for the use of preexisting conceptual framework components for knowledge and skills but still recognizing that the "effective teacher" is a union of all three. For the sake of brevity and focus, this chapter concentrates only on the dispositional element of the conceptual framework. However, the effective teacher

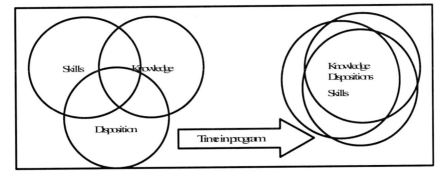

Figure 3.2.   Progression of candidates through the perception disposition model program.

must possess a breadth and depth of content and professional knowledge as well as the pedagogical skills necessary for facilitating meaningful student learning and growth.

Following is an all too brief overview of the basic tenants of Combs' theory. (In the perceptual dispositions model the terms perceptions and dispositions are used interchangeably.) Combs, a contemporary and colleague of Abe Maslow and Carl Rogers, postulated that (a) people behave according to how the world appears to them; (b) behaviors are symptoms of underlying perceptions (Combs used the terms attitudes, values, and beliefs synonymously with perceptions); (c) core perceptions are formed over a lifetime and change slowly; (d) behavior can be understood if one can determine how people perceive themselves, their world, and their goals; and (e) one understands others' perceptions by "reading behavior backwards"—a high-inference, clinical skill analogous to active listening that can be taught and used with a high degree of validity and reliability (Combs, Soper, Gooding, Benton, Dedrick, & Usher, 1969).

Over the course of 40 years, Combs and many others explored the implications of a perceptual psychology for understanding and improving the education professions. Many of the studies investigated the perceptual characteristics of teachers who were able to significantly and positively affect others' lives. In these studies effectiveness was determined using various methods: evaluation of teachers by pupils, peers, and administrators; qualification for national honors for outstanding teaching; and assessment of student product outcomes (e.g., test scores on achievement tests). Results of these studies point to at least four general areas of perceptions that can serve to differentiate effective from ineffective teachers. The four areas are: (1) perceptions about self, (2) perceptions about other people, (3) perceptions about the purposes of teaching, and (4) general frame of reference. The implication for teacher preparation is clear: there are a reasonable number of identifiable perceptions/dispositions associated with teacher effectiveness that can and should be taken into account in teacher preparation programs.

Table 3.1 summarizes the research from the Florida studies in the helping professions (Combs et al., 1969).

The four general areas, as well as the factors within each area, were distilled from an intensive review of the literature. Four of the 12 perceptual factors were chosen to be the dimensions for the dispositions construct in the perceptual dispositions model. The choice of the four factors was based on availability of training procedures and materials for assessment as well as ease with which novice raters could be trained to understand and use the factors.

A brief descriptive summary of the four areas of dispositions used in the perceptual dispositions model follows.

Disposition about self—Effective teachers have a natural ability to identify with virtually all students including those with diverse abilities and backgrounds. They have positive yet realistic self-perceptions exhibited by their "can do" attitudes and usually expressed by a belief that they can help almost any student. Further, they recognize that they do not "teach classes," but rather "teach students," one at a time, by making personally meaningful connections between what is important to the students and the subjects being taught. Not surprisingly, ineffective teachers show difficulty identifying with and teaching some students, frequently have doubts about their ability to deal with situations they encounter, and tend to be less optimistic and upbeat. The studies, summarized in Table 3.1, found positive relationships between the inferred self-concepts[1] of teachers and student achievement as well as significant differences between the perceptions of effective and ineffective teachers.

Disposition about other people—Effective teachers have positive dispositions about students. In the perceptual studies, effective teachers were found to see others in a more realistic and positive way. They differed from ineffective teachers in that they generally perceived others as dependable, able, and worthy. Eight studies compared teachers' perceptions of others and all eight found significant differences between effective and ineffective teachers (see Tabe 3.1).

Dispositions about the purpose of teaching—The research indicates that teachers' beliefs about the purposes of education and teacher effectiveness are related. Effective teachers take a larger view about the purposes of education believing that things such as making long-term, positives changes in students' lives and fostering good citizenship are more important than a single grade or homework assignment. They see the larger

Table 3.1. Florida Studies in the Helping Professions (1969)

PERCEPTUAL ORIENTATION	COMBS & SOPER (1963) Counselors	O'ROARK (1976) School Couns.	JENNINGS (1973) Resident Assist.	GOODING (1964) Elem. teach.	VONK (1970) In-Service Teach.	BROWN (1970) Young Educators	KOFFMAN Classroom Teach.	ASPY & BUHLER (1975) Teachers	DEDRICK (1972) Jr. Coll. Teach.	USHER (1966) Coll. Teach.	DOYLE (1969) College Teach.	CHOY (1969) Coll. Teach.
PERCEPTION OF SELF												
IDENTIFIED-UNIDENTIFIED*	S	S			S	S	S	S		ns	S	
ABLE-UNABLE			S	S				S	S	ns	S	
POSITIVE-NEGATIVE				S		S		S		ns	S	S
PERCEPTION OF OTHERS												
ABLE-UNABLE*	S		S	S			S		S	S		
DEPENDABLE-UNDEPENDABLE	S	S		S			S			S		
WORTHY-UNWORTHY	S		S	S		S	S		S	S		
PERCEPTION OF PURPOSE												
LARGER-SMALLER*	S			S	S							
FREEING-CONTROLLING	S		S	S	S	S			S	ns		
REVEALING-CONCEALING	S		S	S	S	S				ns		
FRAME OF REFERENCE												
PEOPLE-THINGS*	S	S	S	S								
INTERNAL-EXTERNAL	S	S							S			
OPENNESS-CLOSEDNESS (TO EXPERIENCE)					S						S	

S = Significant
ns = Not significant
Blank = Not tested
* Definitions used in perceptual dispositions model

issues rather than the more immediate and less important ones, and seem to constantly ask themselves, "How will my students be better 10 years from now because of what we are doing today?" Ineffective teachers, on the other hand, tend to focus on the mundane, short-range, non-personal aspects of teaching.

General frame of reference—The research tells us that effective teachers are people-oriented rather than thing-oriented; spend a good deal of effort building positive relationships with their students, colleagues, and the community; and have a service orientation.

The perceptual model purports that there are few if any specific behaviors or methods that are necessary conditions for effectiveness. The perceptual theorist, in contrast to behaviorists, would argue that specific behaviors are not predictable but whole classes of behaviors can be understood from the viewpoint of the person exhibiting the behaviors. For example, if a teacher's core belief is that all students are able and have the capability to learn, this belief will manifest itself in the vast majority of her intentional and unintentional behaviors which will, in turn, be evident to students. An interesting case in point is the apparent paradox of two stern, highly demanding teachers—one venerated by students and the other reviled. Both teachers used similar teaching methods, gave difficult tests and mountains of homework, yet one was loved by students who worked hard to meet the demands and the other was sabotaged at any opportunity. One explanation for this difference is the contrast between the teachers' dispositions: one teacher was tough on students because she believed they were able and needed to be challenged to their maximum potential while the other was tough because she believed that students who were not kept busy would make her life miserable. In the end, both were correct. While many of the teachers' behaviors were similar, the dispositions were different and most students had no difficulty reading the behaviors backwards to the underlying intentions or dispositions behind the behaviors. In the fast moving, spontaneous, human environment called a classroom, meaningful learning happens when the teacher facilitates an alignment of favorable and frequently unplanned conditions—students feel able and valued, material has personal meaning and utility, and the presentation is interesting and challenging.

In summary, the perceptual dispositions model (Table 3.2) defines dispositions as the core perceptions (values, attitudes, and beliefs) exhibited by teachers that permit them, when combined with significant knowledge and skills, to be effective in facilitating learning, growth and development in virtually all the students with whom they interact.

**Table 3.2.   Perceptual Dispositions Model:
Effective Teacher as an Effective Person**

Perceptions of self as <u>identified</u> with a broad range of students rather than unidentified.
Perceptions of students as <u>able</u> to deal with the problems they face rather than unable.
Perceptions of purpose in terms of <u>larger</u> implications rather than <u>smaller</u> insignificant outcomes.
A frame of reference that focuses on <u>people</u> concerns rather than things.

WHY USE A PERCEPTUAL APPROACH FOR UNDERSTANDING AND APPLYING DISPOSITIONS?

In the fall of 2000, in preparation for a 2003 NCATE visit, the faculty at a large, regional, comprehensive teacher preparation institution decided to make an intentional, research-based implementation of a dispositions construct the foundational element of the program's conceptual framework. A core element in this initiative was the assessment and use of dispositions as a key component in the admission process.

The motivation to use dispositions as the core element in the conceptual framework came initially from the anecdotal and observational realizations that a small but significant number of candidates who were "dispositional mismatches" for teaching careers—those who could not seem to connect with students, were unsuccessful in student teaching, and were frequently the most difficult and litigious students—had characteristics that were usually identifiable by faculty in introductory courses. These students were usually bright, had little difficulty with content mastery, and could at least mimic appropriate teaching strategies. However, their dispositions were very resistant to change over the course of the program. Additionally, it was observed that alternative career exploration strategies that typically worked with most students, such as class and individual discussions, career counseling, and self-reflection, proved ineffective in dissuading these individuals from pursuing teaching careers. These observations, in alignment with many psychological theories, suggested that dispositions that take a lifetime to form are unlikely to change easily and sufficiently in the relatively short time period of a teacher preparation program for this relatively small number of students. Consequently, it was decided that teacher candidates should possess a minimal level of required dispositions at the time of admission to the program and that dispositional screening should be an important consideration just as are other requirements such as GPA, criminal records checks, and standardized test scores.

The perceptual dispositional model has appeal because, in addition to the theoretical and research base cited above, it is <u>straightforward</u>

and easily understood by students and faculty and has a readily *available research-based assessment tool* that, while not easy to master, provides highly valid information that can be used for predictive purposes. The model also has a broad range of applicability including use in admissions processes with traditional, master of arts in teaching and alternative route students, for designing curricular experiences to enhance dispositions, for professional development and personal improvement, as well as serving as criteria for hiring faculty (Wasicsko, 1978, 2004, 2005a, 2006).

Straightforward and Easily Understood Approach—As indicated above, the theoretical premise upon which the perceptual model is based is relatively straightforward and intuitive—effective teachers are effective people. Perceptual theory advances the idea that since behaviors are caused by the underlying perceptions/dispositions, knowing someone's dispositions offers predictive power for a whole range of behaviors related to teacher effectiveness. For example, if one of a teacher's core dispositions is that students are basically able and can learn at high levels, the teacher's behaviors—from lessons to methods to assignments and even casual conversations—will reflect this belief. These same core dispositions allow most actions of effective teachers' to be perceived by students as empowering and therapeutic no matter if the actions are part of a carefully planned lesson or a reaction to an immediate situation that is spontaneously converted into a teaching moment.

A Research-Based Assessment Tool—The research studies by Combs and others used one or more of the perceptual/dispositional scales in Table 3.1 with highly skilled raters to assess subject dispositions. In these studies the scales were used to assess subjects' dispositions in classroom observations, interviews, and written vignettes (called human relations incidents) about teaching or helping experiences. In addition to finding significance in differentiating effective from ineffective teachers, a high positive correlation was found among the perceptual factors. For example, a person scoring high on ability to identify with diverse learners tended to be people rather than thing oriented. This same relationship existed among the other scales and in virtually no instance did a person rate very high on one factor and very low on another. This leads to the hypothesis that in the highly effective person all the traits are integrated and interrelated and, for the sake of parsimony, allows for the use of fewer dimensions for assessing a person's dispositions without sacrificing validity. This also has implication for developing curricular experiences to positively affect dispositions: experiences that facilitate positive change in any one area may have a corresponding positive effect on the others.

Wasicsko (1977b) studied the ability of raters learning to score the 12 perceptual factors and found that they acquired the ability to use four factors more rapidly than the others. The four factors, one in each area, were:

1.   Perceptions of self as <u>identified</u>.
2.   Perceptions of others as <u>able</u>.
3.   Perceptions of purpose in terms of <u>larger</u> implications.
4.   A frame of reference that focuses on <u>people</u>.

These four perceptual factors were chosen as the scales, shown in Table 3.3, upon which dispositions would be rated in the perceptual dispositions model. Each scale is made up of a pair of definitions separated by a seven point 7-Likert scale with the dispositions of effective teachers on one end (7) and those of ineffective teachers on the other (1). When assessing dispositions the scales are added together to get a composite score ranging from 4 on the low, ineffective end and 28 on the high or effective end.

Prior to using the perceptual scales for either research or screening purposes, raters are provided with systematic training and must demonstrate acceptable proficiency. The typical training consists of face-to-face sessions that covers the theoretical background for the perceptual dispositions model, presents detailed descriptions of each of the scales illustrated with numerous examples, and provides group and individual practice on the perceptual scales using candidate-written vignettes about teaching or helping situations in which they have been involved (these are described in more detail later in the chapter). The minimal acceptable level of proficiency to use the scales is an 80% interrater agreement with professional raters on a 13 item posttest. Similar training may be obtained through a set of self instructional materials followed by a posttest to determine interrater agreement.[2]

When the perceptual rating scales were used in the process of implementing this model in an institution's teacher education program, it was found that faculty could understand and then use the scales for decisions regarding candidate admission, as guides for curricular experiences intended to improve dispositions, and, as an added bonus, in the faculty search process. Further, and probably more important, it was found that the majority of students enrolled in career exploration and foundations courses could use and understand the dispositions scales to make accurate self-reflections about their "fit" in an education career.

The most common ways to collect information about dispositions are through written human relations incidents (HRIs) or journals, by direct observation of teaching or helping situations, and through interviews. HRIs can be collected in application materials, as classroom assignments,

Table 3.3.   Perceptual Rating Scale

PERCEPTION OF SELF

IDENTIFIED	UNIDENTIFIED
The teacher feels an oneness with all people. S/He perceives him/herself as deeply and meaningfully related to persons of every description.	The teacher feels generally apart from others. His/her feelings of oneness are restricted to those of similar beliefs.

7   6   5   4   3   2   1

PERCEPTIONS OF OTHERS

ABLE	UNABLE
The teacher sees others as having capacities to deal with their problems. S/He believes others are basically able to find adequate solutions to events in their own lives.	The teacher sees others as lacking the necessary capacities to deal effectively with their problems. S/He doubts their ability to make their own decisions and run their own lives.

7   6   5   4   3   2   1

PERCEPTIONS OF PURPOSE

LARGER	SMALLER
The teacher views events in a broad perspective. His/her goals extend beyond the immediate to larger implications and contexts.	The teacher views events in a narrow perspective. His/her purposes focus on immediate and specific goals.

7   6   5   4   3   2   1

FRAME OF REFERENCE

PEOPLE	THINGS
The teacher is concerned with the human aspects of affairs. The attitudes, feelings, beliefs, and welfare of persons are prime considerations in his/her thinking.	The teacher is concerned with the impersonal aspects of affairs. Questions of order, management, mechanics, and details of things and events are prime considerations in his/her thinking.

7   6   5   4   3   2   1

or as part of a journal or portfolio assignment. The instructions to write an HRI used in most of the perceptual research and for the implementation of the model at the regional institution are provided in Table 3.4.

Below are two examples of HRIs written by teachers (presented exactly as written) followed by scores and rationales from trained raters. For these HRIs the interrater agreement among professional raters (within one point plus or minus on the 7-point scale) was 100% indicating high confidence in assessing the dispositions of the writers. These are provided to illustrate the use of two of the scales and the process by which raters are taught and are not meant to serve as training for using the scales. System-

Table 3.4. The Human Relations Incident

I would like you to think of a significant past event that involved yourself in a teaching or helping role with one or more other persons. That is, from a human relations standpoint, this event had special meaning for you. In writing about this event, please use the following format:

FIRST Describe the situation as it occurred at the time.

SECOND What did you do in the particular situation?

THIRD How did you feel about the situation at the time you were experiencing it?

FOURTH How do you feel about the situation now? Would you wish to change any part of
it?

atic training is necessary for the valid use of these scales for program purposes. When being trained to use the perceptual scales, raters are asked to follow four steps:

(1) <u>Carefully</u> examine the perceptual definitions.

ABLE	*UNABLE*
The teacher sees others as having capacities to deal with their problems. S/He believes others are basically able to find adequate solutions to events in their own lives.	The teacher sees others as lacking the necessary capacities to deal effectively with their problems. S/He doubts their ability to make their own decisions and run their own lives.

The beliefs one holds about others, whether accurate or false, affect behaviors toward them. Therefore, it is imperative that teachers believe people are basically able to cope with their problems. Children cannot learn to solve problems unless given a chance to try. If a teacher believes students to be able, the stage is set for positive growth and successes.

(2) Read the human relations incident, keeping the definitions in mind.

EXAMPLE 1

Today on the playground, John, one of my children, broke his glasses. This was not my day for playground-duty so I did not see what happened. Three conflicting reports were told to me. The children were running after the ball, John was sitting on the ground with his glasses beside him and Henry stepped on them. This was the first report. The second report was that Henry had hit John and broken the glasses. The third report was that John had become angry and had hit Henry over the head, breaking the glasses. The boys were very boisterous. I asked the boys to take their seats—all except John.

John was in tears and would not talk. I suggested that he take his seat and come talk with me when he felt like it. Some time later John came to my desk and said, "I'm ready to tell you. I got mad at Henry for getting the ball and hit him. I had my glasses in my hand and they got broken." I smiled at him, thanked him and asked him to tell his mother. I believe this was the way I should have handled the situation.

(3) How would a person who saw others as "able" describe the situation? Unable? How must a person <u>perceive</u> to behave in the manner just described? Reread the perceptual definitions and make your rating on the scale provided.

ABLE	*UNABLE*
The teacher sees others as having capacities to deal with their problems. S/He believes others are basically able to find adequate solutions to events in their own lives.	The teacher sees others as lacking the necessary capacities to deal effectively with their problems. S/He doubts their ability to make their own decisions and run their own lives.

<u>7   6   5   4   3   2   1</u>

(4) Compare your ratings with those of the professional raters.

ABLE   7   X   5   4   3   2   1   UNABLE

The teacher showed trust in the coping ability of children. She believed that the children, if it were left to them, would tell her the truth. She relates that John was told "to take his seat and come talk to me when he felt like it." A teacher who saw people as unable may have pulled rank and demanded the truth before they took their seats. Instead, the teacher acquired the needed information, demonstrated respect for the student's ability, and may have created a learning situation for John and the entire class.

EXAMPLE 2

(1) Carefully examine the perceptual definitions.

(2) Read the human relations incident, keeping the definitions in mind.

LARGER	*SMALLER*
The teacher views events in a broad perspective. His/her goals extend beyond the immediate to larger implications and contexts.	The teacher views events in a narrow perspective. His/her purposes focus on immediate and specific goals.

I had about 30 first graders for an art lesson of paper designs. The students needed a lot of assistance and demonstrations because this project was new to them. One student did just the opposite of the assignment and I responded with shock and said "What are you doing?" I felt irritated and wondered how the child could be so dumb. But now I think that I hurt the child's self confidence and that in the future I should handle the situation more calmly, since art is highly self-interpretive.

In the same first grade class, I was pinning notes on students to go home. Out of the corner of my eye I saw one boy take two pins and hide them in his pocket. This boy is a discipline problem so I figured he might use these pins in a destructive way. I got very angry and shouted at the boy to return them. His eyes got large and he returned one. I got even angrier because he gave me only one. I thought he thought he was fooling me by giving one back. I could not paddle him so I yelled at him even louder, although we were face to face. He returned the last pin. I told him to sit down. He did and covered his face with his hands. Since then he has followed my directions a little more closely. I try to give him extra duties such as passing out things to make him feel useful. Still, yelling like that is more an emotional than reasonable way to handle a discipline problem.

(3) How would a person with a larger purpose act in a similar situation? Smaller? How must a person perceive to behave in the manner just described? Reread the definitions and make your rating on the scale provided.

LARGER	*SMALLER*
The teacher views events in a broad perspective. His/her goals extend beyond the immediate to larger implications and contexts.	The teacher views events in a narrow perspective. His/her purposes focus on immediate and specific goals.

<u>7   6   5   4   3   2   1</u>

(4) Compare your ratings with those of the professional raters.

LARGER   7   6   5   4   <u>3   X   1</u>   SMALLER

The teacher's purposes are directed at the immediate situations: trying to get through the lesson, even at the cost of personal belittlement of the students. The goals appear to be to control students' behavior with little or no concern for long-range implications. The teacher does not reflect on the larger implications—what effect will this have on the student's life or even why the pins were taken. Thus, the raters concluded that the perceptions of the purpose of teaching are smaller.

The same set of perceptual scales can be applied to student (or faculty) interviews through the use of carefully crafted questions to gauge candidate dispositions. The best questions will be ones that are unconventional, unanticipated and get people off their rehearsed scripts. The goal is to engage people in conversation about things that interest and enliven them and then infer their core dispositions by carefully listening to their answers. Following are two examples of questions that can be adapted for student or faculty interviews. Once again, the reliable and valid use of the scales with such questions is dependent in part upon the inferential skills of the raters.

- How would your friends (students or colleagues) describe you to others?
- Tell about a situation in which you helped a person or taught a significant lesson

Of the three methods for collecting information on dispositions the interview presents unique opportunities and challenges. Interview questions can provide open-ended alternatives to the HRI that can get at the root of a person's core dispositions. In interview situations, just as with HRIs, the utility and validity of the perceptual model come from rigorously adhering to the use of the scales and avoiding three common pitfalls: (1) assuming there are "looking-fors," specific behaviors, or catch phrases that are indicative of all effective or ineffective teachers (in fact there is no right or wrong answer to questions such as these), (2) judging the candidate response based on the answer the interviewer would provide ("I would or wouldn't have done it that way"), and (3) being distracted by the candidates presentation, appearance or charisma. The interviewer would use the same perceptual scales used with HRIs to rate core dispositions.

The third and probably the best venue for collecting dispositional data is direct observation of candidates in teaching/helping situations. Once again, the same scales are employed with which to infer dispositions. A skilled rater using the perceptual scales can make reasonably accurate assessment of dispositions by observing a 1-hour teaching session.

HOW SHOULD DISPOSITIONS BE USED IN AN EDUCATION PROGRAM?

There are at least three ways that a dispositions model should be applied to teacher preparation programs. First, dispositions information should be used as admission criteria. This use stirs considerable debate among faculty especially with regard to ethical and legal considerations. Second, dispositions should be part of the intentional and systematic effort to enhance candidates' performance as they progress through a program. How this is accomplished depends on the definition chosen, overall conceptual framework, assessment tools, and so forth. Third, the conceptual framework in general and dispositions specifically should be used to hire full- and part-time education faculty. It seems only reasonable that the faculty instructing future teachers should exhibit the dispositions that program completers are supposed to possess. While all of these are important issues, the remainder of the chapter will focus on the issue that has stimulated the most controversy—dispositions as admission criteria.

Dispositions as Admission Criteria

One of the most difficult situations faced by teacher educators is encountered when students who clearly lack the dispositions necessary to be effective teachers meet all other admission requirements. Most teacher educators will admit that they recognized a "dispositional mismatch" for some students very early in the program but did not have adequate tools (procedural and/or legal) to counsel them out of the program or deny them admission. When persistent, as they so frequently are, these students can become the moral and legal dilemmas who reach the end of the program with passing marks but are deemed marginal or unsafe to practice.

It is the view of the author that teacher educators have an ethical responsibility to encourage and admit candidates who have the dispositions (then be sure they acquire the knowledge and skills that will foster growth and learning in students) and not to admit those who cannot <u>demonstrate</u> that they possess the minimal level of needed elements. Allowing people to invest years and significant resources preparing for a career for which they are ill suited is a tragedy eclipsed only by the possibility of their entering the profession and negatively impacting the lives of students over the course of a 25 year teaching career.

Arguments for using dispositions in admission decisions have theoretical as well as practical roots. Most teacher educators agree that some elements related to effective teaching are more easily taught to candidates than others. The continuum in Figure 3.3 illustrates this.

There is good evidence that *content knowledge* is among the easier elements to teach (as well as measure) and *warmth* among the hardest to teach. Many question whether it is possible to teach the elements on the right hand side of the continuum or if it is reasonable to think that major changes in these characteristics can happen during the course of a 2-4 year program. General tenets of perceptual and behavioral psychology also support these concerns. From a perceptual psychological perspective, perceptions/dispositions are formed over a lifetime and are resistant to change. (There are exceptions to this rule usually accompanying significant and frequently traumatic life events in which rapid change can occur, obviously not a methodology to be used in teacher preparation programs!) A similar axiom comes from behavior psychology with the observation that behaviors take about as long to extinguish as they took to be

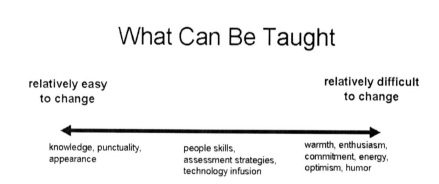

What Can Be Taught

relatively easy
to change

relatively difficult
to change

knowledge, punctuality,
appearance

people skills,
assessment strategies,
technology infusion

warmth, enthusiasm,
commitment, energy,
optimism, humor

Figure 3.3.   Effective teaching more easily taught to candidates than others.

acquired. The fact that people can and do change cannot be disputed. The essential questions programs must answer are how much change is reasonable to expect in the time and with the resources allotted. And, more importantly, should candidates be admitted with the hope that they will change sufficiently so as not to be detrimental to future students' learning, growth, and development.

Fortunately, the actual number of candidates whose dispositions should preclude their admission is relatively small. The magnitude can be approximated by the number of candidates who are unsuccessful (or at least should not pass) their field experiences. In most open admission institutions the percentage of students in this category might range from 3 to 5%. However, while small in number these individuals account for a significant portion of the angst of the faculty, absorbs considerable time and resources from the academic and legal administration, and reflects poorly on programs with P-12 colleagues. The task for teacher educators is to create a dispositional admission plan with a good measure of predictive validity that is humane, fair, and that will stand up to legal challenges.

Just as in the case of other admission requirements such as GPA or standardized test scores, candidates who cannot demonstrate the minimal level of acceptable dispositions should be <u>deferred</u> until such time as they can supply such evidence. (Note that the use of the term "deferred" is critical and intentional here.) <u>Denying</u> (as opposed to deferring) a student admission to a program can lead to a legal request to provide evidence that the candidate does not meet the criteria followed by a request for a prescription for meeting the criteria. Experience tells us that it is much more difficult for an admission committee to provide evidence that someone is "emotionally unstable" or "socially immature" with sufficient precision to stand up to the most rigorous legal scrutiny than it would be for a questionable student to obtain a letter from a certified psychologist verifying that s/he is not a threat to himself or others. On the other hand, deferring a candidate until such time as he/she can demonstrate that the criteria are met leaves the burden of proof with the candidate and avoids or delays the thorny issue of passing judgment on a person's ability to change and someday meet the criteria. The perceptual model requires students to provide evidence that they possess the minimal dispositions prior to admission just as they are required to have evidence that they have the needed GPA or test scores.

Due to the differing nature of graduate and undergraduate initial teacher preparation programming (e.g., age of students, opportunity to get to know students prior to requests for formal admission, etc.) two slightly different strategies are used for assessing dispositions at admission. The following discussion looks separately at undergraduate admission and admission to the master of arts in teaching (MAT) program.

The admission process in the undergraduate program employs the following three steps: (1) self-assessing and self-selecting, (2) mentoring and counseling, and (3) admitting or deferring. The three steps were integrated into the freshman and sophomore foundations courses Introduction to Education (a freshman level, large lecture, 1-hour, pass-fail, orientation to careers in education course) and foundations of education (the typical 3-hour sophomore level introductory education course). These two courses were open to all university students and did not require admission to the teacher education program. It was deliberately decided that students should have knowledge about teaching careers, opportunities to reflect on their strengths and weaknesses in relation to teaching, and P-12 classroom and field experiences prior to making a decision to request admission to the teacher education program.

Self-Assessing and Self-Selecting

Perceptual theory purports that people are generally able to make good decisions about career fit if they are given adequate information and an opportunities for self-reflection. The experience gained from having over 2000 students complete the introductory course confirms this assumption. The introductory, 1-hour, career exploration course was devised to provide students with basic information about education careers; a "peek into P-12 classrooms" early field experience; significant information about the knowledge, skills, and dispositions necessary to become an effective teacher; and guided self-reflections about the dispositions associated with the best teachers. The course objectives included the following:

1. Identify the qualities of and expectations for effective teachers.
2. Make reflective judgments about personal dispositions, goals, interests, and abilities as related to a career in teaching.
3. Demonstrate communications skills necessary for teachers.
4. Understand admission to teacher education requirements and procedures.
5. Understand requirements for teacher certification.
6. Become aware of career opportunities in education.
7. Develop an awareness of the diverse and exceptional populations in schools.
8. Effectively engage in using technology for completing all assignments.

9. Successfully complete P-12 classroom observations at each level and with special populations.

10. Decide whether a career in teaching is a good "fit" worthy of further exploration.

To help students assess their "fit" for a teaching career, four dispositions reflection assignments were developed and tested in the introductory course. Copies of these are included in the Appendix. The student-generated responses to the assignments were not used to assess students for admission to the program. Rather, their responses were used by the students for their self-reflection/self-assessment and for inclusion in their portfolio should they enter the teacher preparation program.

Assignment #1- The Human Relations Incident (HRI)

To serve as material for self-reflection at the end of the course, the students' first assignment was to write about a teaching or helping situation using the following prompt: Think of a significant event that involved you in a teaching or helping situation. The event you describe should be one that has personal meaning for you. It would be helpful if you describe what happened and your feelings about the situation. Include as much detail as possible when answering the following questions: (1) Describe the situation as it occurred at the time. (2) What did you do in that particular situation? (3) How did you feel about the situation at the time you were experiencing it? (4) How do you feel about the situation now? (5) What would you change, if anything?

Assignment #2- My Favorite Teacher

This assignment is used to focus on the characteristics of a teacher who the students remember as having made a significant impact on their lives. To facilitate student reflection on the qualities of effective teachers, and later as a part of the self-reflective assessment, students were asked to write an essay about their favorite teacher using the following instructions: Who was your favorite teacher? What is the first characteristic that comes to mind when you think about your favorite teacher? Describe a specific event that stands out in your mind that happened with that teacher. How did your favorite teacher treat you?

Assignment #3 - Effective Educators' Dispositions

Ethically, students deserve to know the criteria upon which they will be assessed for admission and program completion including the dispositions criteria. Assignment #3 sought to train students to use the disposition assessment scale (Figure 3.4) with which they were to be assessed for admission and upon completion of the program. The assignment provided students with training to help understand the dispositions scales followed by practice in scoring sample student- and teacher-written HRIs similar to the ones they had written in Assignments #1. Each sample HRI was followed by the professional rater's score and a rationale for the rating. Finally, students scored two HRIs without being provided a rationale or rating to gage their proficiency on using the dispositions scales.

Assignment #4- Reflecting on Personal Dispositions

This was the culminating activity in the introductory course. Students used their responses to assignments 1-3, the course lectures, classroom observations, and course materials to self-assess their "fit" for a career in teaching. The assignment consisted of a series of self-reflection questions that aligned with the four dispositional areas. The majority of students were able to make useful and accurate judgments about their decision to pursue or not pursue a career in teaching.

Mentoring and Counseling

The second course in the admission sequence, Foundations of Education, was a fairly typical foundations course that included embedded dispositions related assignments. The course included lectures, reflective exercises, and a field placement involving tutoring a special needs P-12 student. The course instructors, proficient with the dispositions scales, helped mentor and guide students with continued self-assessment and, in those few cases of severe dispositional "mismatch," alternative career counseling. By the end of the course the instructors had a good assessment of the students' capabilities and potential for a career in teaching.

In addition to assigning a course grade, instructors were required to assess each student's dispositions and indicate on a written recommendation form if evidence was presented that the student had the minimal level of dispositions required for admission. If sufficient evidence was accumulated during the course, the instructor could recommend the student for admission and the admission committee could waive an interview. It was possible for a student to pass the course (to have sufficient knowledge) but not demonstrate the needed level of dispositions. If the evidence supplied by the student was not clear and compelling for having the required dispositions, the student went to the admission committee for an interview using, once again, the same dispositional scoring criteria. If the admission committee did not find evidence of having the minimal level of dispositions in the interview, the student was deferred and could try to bring other evidence for a re-interview at a later date.

PRELIMINARY RESULTS—UNDERGRADUATE

Almost 2000 undergraduate students completed the introductory course by the fall of 2005. Preliminary analysis indicated that students could understand the dispositions scales; they could make accurate use of the scales in assessing written HRIs; they were able to make accurate self-assessments regarding their dispositional fit for a career in education; and they were able to make decisions to continue or not continue to pursue admission based on their self-assessment.

One of the most interesting findings was that a small number of students who scored the lowest on the dispositions scales (determined by trained raters blindly scoring the four assignments) had the most trouble accurately self-assessing their dispositional fit. In these cases, and even when presented with evidence to the contrary, these students continued to insist that they had the required dispositions in significant amounts and would be effective teachers. These students also had the greatest difficulty using the dispositions scales in Assignment #3 and had difficulty with making reflections in Assignment #4. Should further analysis confirm these preliminary results, serious doubts are cast on the efficacy of open admission to teach education programs and on the reliance on self-deselection for careers decisions for applicants who do not possess the desired dispositions. In all likelihood these would be the students who become problematic once admitted into the program and cause the practical, ethical, and legal issues at the end of the program. Follow-up studies to test this hypothesis are underway.

As was expected, students receiving high dispositions scores made more accurate self-assessments and could more accurately rate HRIs in Assignment #3. They also made more realistic decisions about careers in teaching even though some of them opted out of teaching in favor of careers in other helping professions. Most students scored in the middle of the dispositions scales and made reasonable judgments about their career choices. Approximately 65% of the students taking the first, introductory course indicated that they planned to continue on to the second course and to pursue admission to teacher education.

The efficacy of mentoring and counseling students regarding their dispositional fit in the second course (Foundations of Education) had mixed results dependent upon the course instructor. When the instructor was adequately trained on the scales and committed to implementing the dispositions screening program, it worked to either help mismatched students pursue other options or led to students being deferred by the admission committee. In cases where the instructors lacked training or commitment, some mismatched students slipped into the program. This presents a most interesting dilemma, the implications of which remain to be seen: Can a model for dispositions be created and successfully implemented if the faculty are not committed to the model or cannot demonstrate the dispositions themselves?

GRADUATE ADMISSION PROCESS

Due to significant differences between an undergraduate program and a MAT/alternative certification graduate program, the three-step admission approach used with the undergraduate program was reinterpreted. Under the stipulations of No Child Left Behind (NCLB), degreed candidates seeking teacher certification can enter a classroom as a "highly qualified teacher" upon enrolling in an alternative route to certification program with little or no coursework completed. This "fast-track" possibility places an additional burden on teacher education faculty to make well-informed decisions about the dispositions of a candidate at admission and/or in a time period as brief as one semester. For these reasons, the admission or deferral process (Step #3 for undergraduates) became the *first* step in the MAT program.

The undergraduate dispositions admission process was established prior to admitting the first MAT cohort; therefore, the undergraduate model was adapted to fit the needs of the graduate program. In the graduate program, the first step—self-assessing and self-selecting—takes place independent of teacher education faculty. Applicants are encouraged to self-assess their dispositions prior to application through completion of Assignment #1- "The Human Relations Incident" and Assignment #2- "My Favorite Teacher" (described above). These two essays are requirements in the total admission process. The essays, along with an admission interview, are scored by the MAT admission committee using the perceptual rating scale. Applicants were assigned a dispositions score from 4 to 28 corresponding to the sum of ratings on the 4-Likert scales of 7 points each (see Figure 3.4). The dispositions score is a critical part of the admission process that is considered along with previous education, GPA, graduate exam scores, and PRAXIS II content area exam scores. After admission, the MAT candidates are encouraged to continue to self-assess their dispositions, using the perceptual dispositions model. A small number of applicants that have met all other academic requirements have been deferred admission based upon unsatisfactory evidence of required dispositions.

Initially, a minimum dispositions score of 14 appeared appropriate, as this score represents the median of the possible score of 4–28. But the minimum score was increased to 18 prior to admission of the third cohort for two reasons. First, unlike the undergraduate program, the MAT program only had the capacity for a specific number of new students and the number of applicants was growing thus enabling faculty to become more selective in the admission process. Second, the faculty examined dispositions scores from the first two cohorts, noting that dispositions of those admitted with scores in the range of 14-16, while in most cases acceptable, were having more difficulty demonstrating the desirable dispositions.

PRELIMINARY RESULTS—GRADUATE

Eighty-four MAT candidates, in the first two cohorts, were admitted using a minimum disposition score of 14. The lowest disposition score from the first 2 years was 14 (on a 28 point scale). This candidate, along with two candidates that each scored 15, experienced significant problems related to disposition their during field placements. One of these three candidates accepted a teaching job under the temporary "alternative" certification, experienced considerable problems in the classroom, and resigned before the mid-term. On the other hand, several candidates who accepted teaching positions that received scores of 18 or higher proved to be excellent teachers.

Beginning with the third cohort, the minimum disposition score of 18 was adopted. Since the adoption of 18 as a minimum score, 242 candidates have been admitted and three applicants that met all academic criteria were deferred because of lack of evidence regarding desirable dispositions. Preliminary results indicate that the perceptual dispositions model screening process has been a success for MAT admission. Since setting the minimum score at 18, MAT program faculty have not been faced with the problems associated with serious dispositional mismatches. The mean score of the candidates that have been accepted in all cohorts is 24.6 (on a 28-point scale). Plans are in place to survey the principals of MAT graduates in order assess the relationship between the disposition scores and the performance of graduates in the classroom. A preliminary survey of the principals for a small portion of the 2002 cohort provides anecdotal evidence that a correlation may exist, but these results were based upon a small sample and further study is needed.

The essential role of assessing dispositions for admission into an alternative certification program is to prevent applicants from entering a program that allows them to very quickly enter a classroom as a teacher-of-record. The perceptual dispositions model has proved to be an effective method for an MAT/alternative certification program. Even with effective dispositions screening, one must remember that though candidates may seem to have the dispositions for a career in teaching, these candidates may discover, upon entering the classroom, that teaching is not the career that they envisioned. This may be a mentoring issue, the subject of further investigation.

CONCLUSIONS

In this chapter, three basic questions regarding educator dispositions were explored: (1) what are dispositions, (2) why use a perceptual approach for understanding and using dispositions, and (3) how should dispositions be used in educator preparation programs.

From the perceptual vantage point, dispositions are best defined as those core values, beliefs or perceptions that cause behavior and allow some educators to affect student learning, growth and development more positively than others. Of particular interest are those dispositions that seem to permit some educators to facilitate transformative change in a good number of the students they teach.

The implications for educator preparation programs are several (1) dispositions that form over a lifetime should be taken into account in the candidate admissions and selection process, (2) intentional efforts to enhance dispositions should be integrated throughout the teacher preparation program, (3) teacher candidates should demonstrate that they possess dispositions associated with effective teachers prior to program completion, and (4) teacher education faculty should possess the dispositions expected of program completers.

The perceptual dispositions model shows promise for solving some of the critical pragmatic and procedural issues surrounding admitting teacher candidates with the dispositions associated with effective teachers. It appears that the perceptual dispositions model provides students with opportunities to make accurate self-assessments regarding career fit and faculty with the means of admitting candidates with the necessary dispositions while deferring candidates who can not demonstrate the required dispositions. Preliminary results indicate that undergraduate students can understand the definition of dispositions in the perceptual dispositions model and, with the notable exception of students with severe "dispositional mismatch," can make accurate self-assessments about "fit" for teaching careers by using structured self-reflective tasks. Further, teacher education faculty can use the dispositional scales to make judgments about dispositions for both undergraduate and graduate admissions processes IF they understand and are committed to the dispositions model. (This begs the question if faculty can be committed to and use the dispositions model if they do not possess the dispositions themselves and to the bigger question of whether the same dispositions required of students should be required of all faculty.) The next step in developing the perceptual dispositions model will be longitudinal studies to track program completers and determine correlates between candidate dispositions and student learning, growth, and development.

APPENDIX

The four assignments contained in the Appendix were developed to help students self-assess their dispositions prior to requesting admissions to the teacher preparation program. The materials are copyrighted but may be used for noncommercial purposes in the preparation of educators and other helping professionals. The materials are also available on the Web site of the National Network for the Study of Educator Dispositions.

> Assignment #1—The Human Relations Incident (HRI)
> Assignment #2—My Favorite Teacher
> Assignment #3—Effective Educators' Dispositions[3]
> Assignment #4—Reflecting on Personal Dispositions

INTRODUCTION TO EDUCATION—ASSIGNMENT ONE[4]

The Human Relations Incident (HRI)

Background—The goal of this class is to help you to think about education careers and find answers to questions such as: "What are the characteristics associated with effective teaching?" And "Do I have the attributes that will allow me to become an effective educator?"

Being an educator is not for everyone. Just as certain talents and interests are needed to become an accountant, nurse, fire fighter, or engineer, there are essential characteristics for becoming an effective educator. Most experts agree that the essential ingredients for being effective teachers include: a significant knowledge base, teaching skills, and dispositions. This course will focus on what education careers are like and about the *dispositions* needed to be an effective educator. Our main goal is to help you discover if you have "the dispositions to teach."

Assignment—For this assignment you will describe a situation in which you interacted with one or more other people in helping or teaching role. The event you describe does not need to be a formal teaching situation. It may be something that happened on the spur of the moment, with a friend or relative, and so forth. What you write will become part of your portfolio (the materials you will prepare for admission to the education program should you decide to pursue a teaching career) and will also be used in a study being conducted to better understand the process by which educators are prepared. Most importantly, however, you will use what you write later to help you decide if an education career is right for you. So, take your time and answer as thoroughly as possible. Please use the following instructions:

> *Think of a significant event that involved you in a teaching or helping role with one or more persons. The event you describe should be one that has personal meaning for you (something that interested you, something that made you wonder, something that made you feel good, something that just did not work out as you had hoped, etc.). It would be helpful if you describe feelings about the situation. Include as much detail as possible when answering the following questions:*

>> *Describe the situation as it occurred at the time.*
>> *What did you do in that particular situation?*
>> *How did you feel about the situation at the time you were experiencing it?*
>> *How do you feel about the situation now?*
>> *What would you change, if anything?*

INTRODUCTION TO EDUCATION—ASSIGNMENT TWO

My Favorite Teacher

Background—A good place to start a search for the characteristics of good teachers is with our own schooling experiences. When people are asked to recall what they remember about their favorite teachers—the ones they credit most with helping them succeed in life—the responses are remarkably similar: "She was much more than just a teacher; she was a friend." "He really enjoyed teaching and cared about students." "She looked for the good in each of us." "She believed in me and never embarrassed me in front of the class." "He could teach us something and make it fun." "She liked me as a person." "She held our interest with her lively, humorous manner and her thorough knowledge of the subject." Sound familiar?

Almost everyone's recollections about their favorite teacher fall into three broad categories: (1) the best teachers treated students as able, worthy human beings and capable learners, (2) they made learning personally meaningful, and (3) they were knowledgeable about and genuinely interested in what they were teaching. Because they possessed these characteristics our favorite teachers were able to make lasting changes in our lives. As a matter of fact, you are probably exploring the possibility of an education career because of the personal impact one of these teachers had on your life. If you plan to be an educator and want to be a favorite teacher to your students, you will have to develop and enhance these same kinds of traits in yourself.

Assignment—Hopefully, each of us has had teachers who have made a significant positive impact on our lives. Think about all the teachers you have had and choose your favorite, the one who helped you most to get to where you are today. Once again, what you write will be used as part of your portfolio, our study and with your career exploration.

To help you remember and describe this teacher, please answer the following questions:

Who was your favorite teacher?

What is the first characteristic that comes to mind when you think about your favorite teacher?

Describe a specific event that stands out in your mind that happened with that teacher.

How did your favorite teacher treat you?

INTRODUCTION TO EDUCATION—ASSIGNMENT THREE

Effective Educators' Dispositions

"Dispositions" is used to describe the attitudes, perceptions and/or beliefs that form the basis for behavior. Not surprisingly, there is a significant body of research indicating that teachers' dispositions about students, about teaching, and about themselves, strongly influence the impact they will have on student learning and development. In this assignment you will see if you can identify the dispositions (they are called *perceptions* from here on) of individuals by reading human relations incidents (HRI). Before beginning, a brief description of four areas of perceptions that are associated with effective educator is presented.

Perceptions of self as IDENTIFIED—A person's self-perceptions (also called their self-concept) are probably the most important factor relating to educator effectiveness. Simply stated, effective educators are confident in their ability to help people learn and they believe they have "what it takes" to handle the problems they confront. Another self-perception of effective teachers is the ability to *identify* with diverse individuals and groups. The best educators proactively find ways of individualizing learning environments to take into account individual, racial, cultural, and generational differences.

Perceptions of other people as ABLE—Effective educators see people in essentially realistic and positive ways. They see students as generally dependable, able and worthy. Effective educators believe that when students are provided with the opportunity, they will more frequently than not do what's right, that students usually have the ability to cope and deal with their own problems and can be trusted.

LARGER perceptions of purpose—The best educators see their job in a larger context as one of releasing a student's inner potential to become whatever her talents and interests might permit. They are concerned with how students will develop and behave, not only in class today or this year, but tens of years from now. They see their jobs as helping students grow into good world citizens and the kinds of neighbors we all want to live near.

PEOPLE oriented frame of reference—All educational situations involve both people and things. The best educators know that to make learning meaningful and useful, they must deal with the human aspects - the feeling, beliefs and attitudes of students. So good teachers listen to students' problems, try to make their classes challenging and non-threatening, display a sense of humor and realize that good teaching means that students grow not only in the quantity of knowledge but in their mental health as well.

What follows are human relations incidents written by pre or in-service teachers. The descriptions above have been condensed into a briefer definition (called rubrics) on which you are to rate the perceptions of the writer. Use the following steps for making your ratings:

1. Carefully read the perceptual rubric. When necessary, go back and reread the description above.
2. Read the HRI, keeping the rubric in mind. Ask yourself how the writer must perceive to have described the situation this way.
3. Reread the definitions and decide where on the scale the writer's perceptions lie.

For this assignment you will read 10 HRIs and see if you can get a "feel" for the perceptions associated with effective educators. To complete the assignment you will test your ability to rate perceptions on 2 HRIs.

NOTE: THIS ASSIGNMENT HAS BEEN TRUNCATED AFTER ONE EXAMPE DUE TO LENGTH BUT IS AVAILABLE ON THE NNSED WEB SITE.

Example 1: PERCEPTIONS OF SELF AS IDENTIFIED

1. <u>Carefully</u> examine the perceptual definitions.

IDENTIFIED	*UNIDENTIFIED*
The educator feels a oneness with all people. S/He perceives him/herself as deeply and meaningfully related to persons of every description.	The educator feels generally apart from others. His/her feelings of oneness are restricted to those of similar beliefs.

Effective educators feel closeness to people of every description, independent of race, creed, or national origin. This does not mean they are friends with everyone, but rather that they have the capacity to understand and feel a compassion for all people. The feeling of identification is familiar to everyone. The joy over the accomplishments of loved ones, the excitement over a team's victory, and even the sadness over the tragedies of friends and neighbors exemplify this identification. Some of the greatest figures in history have developed this feeling of oneness or identification to such an extent that all humankind has been included.

The opposite is seen in people who never come to share meaningful experiences with another human being. Most people fall somewhere between these extremes. Effective educators perceive a greater identification between themselves and all students, regardless of beliefs and background. This is an essential quality for effective teaching.

2. Read the human relations incident, keeping the definition in mind.

He was extremely poor but just as proud. He needed help but the problem was how could we help him without hurting him? Jerry (fictitious name) was a very good math student in on of my seventh-grade classes. He made good grades, but he started going to sleep every day in class after he finished his work. At first, I just let him sleep, thinking that it was a temporary thing. However, it occurred more and more often. I confided in his homeroom teacher and we became real snoopers. She went into his locker every day for a week and discovered that all he had for lunch every day was bread with margarine spread on it. Next we went to the principal. We offered to buy his lunches but the principal said no. He called in the school nurse and she investigated the home situation. She found conditions quite critical and as we had suspected, the children were suffering from malnutrition. Jerry was just too tired to stay awake all day and since math seemed to be his easiest subject, he chose that class in which to sleep. Well, the outcome was that the principal offered Jerry a job in the lunchroom for free lunches. Jerry accepted and does not know to this day that two teachers were "snoopy." He stopped sleeping in class almost immediately. He is now a senior in high school and is still in the accelerated math program where I placed him at the end of the seventh grade.

How would a person perceive in this situation if s/he were identified with others? Unidentified? How must a person <u>perceive</u> to behave in the manner just described?

3.   Reread the definitions and make your rating on the scale provided.

IDENTIFIED	*UNIDENTIFIED*
The educator feels a oneness with all people. S/He perceives him/herself as deeply and meaningfully related to persons of every description.	The educator feels generally apart from others. His/her feelings of oneness are restricted to those of similar beliefs.

<u>7 6 5 4 3 2 1</u>

4.   Compare your ratings with those of the professional raters.

The professional raters scored this person a <u>6</u>. (Hereafter, the professional raters' score will be denoted by an X on the appropriate number of the scale.) A score of <u>5</u>, <u>6</u>, or <u>7</u> would have indicated agreement with the trained raters. (Hereafter, the range on the scale indicating agreement with the professional raters will be boxed in.)

IDENTIFIED <u>7 X 5</u> 4 3 2 1 UNIDENTIFIED

A perceptual rating must be independent of personal likes and dislikes. From an external point of view, rummaging through a student's locker, and even his lunch, might elicit a personal evaluation of "dislike" for those involved. This may appear to violate our beliefs and philosophies. However, when the intent and perceptions of the person involved are understood, a different opinion may be reached. It is dangerous to focus on behavior taken out of context. After setting aside personal external evaluations of behavior, decide how the person involved perceives. Where do his perceptions lie on a perceptual continuum? Personal likes and dislikes cannot, of course, be ignored. But it is possible to recognize them and hold them in abeyance when examining the perceptual factors.

The evidence in the example indicates a person who identifies well with other people. This person shows a high regard for the feelings of students and a sense of accomplishment in the success of students. A less identified educator might have felt his concern was to teach math and not get involved in the personal problems and feelings of students. There appears to be personal pride and satisfaction, which comes with identification, when the teacher says, "He is now a senior in high school and is still in the accelerated math program where I placed him at the end of the seventh-grade."

Some information about identification comes from the nature of the incidents the person chooses to relate. Are the incidents student-centered or self-centered? Generally like him or unlike him? Here again, the example shows an identified person who relates to others in meaningful ways.

INTRODUCTION TO EDUCATION—ASSIGNMENT FOUR[5]

Reflecting on Personal Dispositions

The major purposes of this course are to provide you with information about some of the characteristics associated with educator effectiveness and give you an opportunity to reflect on the "match" between you and a career in the education professions. This assignment has two parts consisting of sets of questions on which you are to think and respond.

Part 1 - Effective Educator Characteristics—Please answer the following questions in your own words. (One or two sentences are adequate.)

1. How do effective educators perceive themselves?
2. How do effective educators perceive others?
3. How do effective educators perceive the teaching task?
4. What general orientation (people vs. things) do effective educators have?

Part 2—Self-Assessment

We now come to the most difficult task in this course, the self-assessment. You have written an Human Relations Incident, thought about the effective teachers you have had and assessed the qualities that help people become effective teachers. Now it is time to reflect on your own dispositions. To complete the task you will need to go back and reread the HRI you wrote at the beginning of the course then answer the following questions.

Perceptions of Self as IDENTIFIED

IDENTIFIED	*UNIDENTIFIED*
The educator feels a oneness with all people. S/He perceives him/herself as deeply and meaningfully related to persons of every description.	The educator feels generally apart from others. His/her feelings of oneness are restricted to those of similar beliefs.

1.   How do you perceive yourself? What evidence do you have that you identify with people? How will these perceptions affect your ability to become an effective educator?

Perceptions of Others as ABLE

ABLE	*UNABLE*
The educator sees others as having capacities to deal with their problems. S/He believes others are basically able to find adequate solutions to events in their own lives.	The educator sees others as lacking the necessary capacities to deal effectively with their problems. S/He doubts their ability to make their own decisions and run their own lives.

2.   How do you see others? What evidence do you have that you perceive other people as basically able to learn and grow? How will your perceptions of others affect your career as an educator?

LARGER Perceptions Of Purpose

LARGER	*SMALLER*
The educator views events in a broad perspective. His/her goals extend beyond the immediate to larger implication and contexts.	The educator view events in a narrow perspective. His/her purposes focus on immediate and specific goals.

3. What are your perceptions about the purpose of education? What evidence do you have that you are interested in long-term positive results for students? How will this affect your ability to be successful with students?

PEOPLE Oriented Frame of Reference

PEOPLE	THINGS
The educator is concerned with the human aspects of affairs. The attitudes, feelings, beliefs, and welfare of persons are prime considerations in his/her thinking.	The educator is concerned with the impersonal aspects of affairs. Questions of order, management, mechanics, and details of things and events are prime considerations in his/her thinking.

4. What is your general frame of reference and how will this affect your teaching? What evidence do you have that you prefer the people aspects of education over the things? How will this affect your ability to be an effective educator?

5. Reflect on your answers to the above. Is a career in the education professions a good match for you? If yes, at what level do you think you would be best suited? If no, what did you learn about yourself that helped you with your decision? Be specific with your answers, using examples from your reflections, class information, and/or field experiences.

NOTES

1. Inferred self-concept is a measure of self-concept based on evaluations (inferences) of the subject's self-perceptions made by trained perceptual raters.

2. As one might deduce, the biggest impediment to using the perceptual methodology is the fact that training must be provided by an expert trainer. This has historically limited the use of the methodology to groups trained either by Combs or individuals he trained. To help overcome this limitation, self-instructional materials were developed with Combs as part of the author's doctoral research. The materials were originally tested with a variety of audiences including superintendents. The materials were found to enable users to accurately assess the perceptual characteristics of educators (Wasicsko, 1977a). A recently revised version titled *Assessing Dispositions—A Perceptual Psychological Approach* is available for downloading from the Web site of the National Network for the Study of Educator Dispositions (www.educatordispositions.org).

3. Assignment #3 is shortened to include only the first of 10 HRIs that are used to train students to use the dispositions rubrics upon which the student's admission will ultimately be based. The complete assignment is available at the NNSED Web site.
4. The following materials are copyrighted by the National Network for the Study of Educator Dispositions (NNSED) and may be duplicated for use by NNSED members.
5. This assignment was truncated here to save space. It is available at www.teacherdispositions.org.

REFERENCES

Aspy, D. N., & Buhler, K. (1975). The effect of teachers' inferred self concept upon student achievement. *Journal of Education Research, 47*, 386-389.

Brown, R. G. (1970). *A study of the perceptual organization of elementary and secondary outstanding young educators.* Unpublished doctoral dissertation, University of Florida.

Choy, C. (1969). *The relationship of college teacher effectiveness to conceptual system and perceptual orientation.* Unpublished doctoral dissertation, University of Northern Colorado.

Combs, A. W., & Snygg, G. (1949). *Individual behavior: A perceptual approach to behavior.* New York: Harper & Row.

Combs, A. W., & Soper, D. W. (1963). The self, its derivate terms and research. *Journal of Individual Psychology, 14*, 64-67.

Combs, A. W., & Soper, D. W. (1969). The perceptual organization of effective counselors. *Florida studies in the helping professions.* Social Science Monograph #37. Gainesville: University of Florida Press.

Combs, A. W., Soper, D. W., Gooding, C. T., Benton, J. A., Dickman, J. F., & Usher, R. H. (1969). *Florida studies in the helping professions* (Social Science Monograph #37). Gainsville: University of Florida Press. Retrieved 2005, from http://www.fieldpsychtrust.org/florida_studies.pdf

Combs, A. W., Avila, D. L., & Purkey, W. W. (1971). *Helping relationships, basic concepts for the helping professions.* Boston: Allyn & Bacon.

Combs, A. W. (1974a). Humanistic goals of education. In I. D. Welch, F. Richards, & A. C. Richards (Eds.), *Educational accountability: A humanistic perspective.* San Francisco: Shields.

Combs, A. W. (1974b). Why the Humanistic Movement needs a perceptual psychology. *Journal of the Association for the Study of Perception, 9*, 1-3.

Combs, A. W., Blume, R. A., Newman, A. J., & Wass, H. L. (1974). *The professional education of teachers: A humanistic approach to teacher preparation.* Boston: Allyn & Bacon.

Combs, A. W., Richards, A. C., & Richards, F. (1976). *Perceptual psychology: A humanistic approach to the study of persons.* New York: Harper & Row.

Combs, A. W., & Gonzalez, D. M. (1994). *Helping relationships: Basic concepts for the helping professions* (4th ed.). Boston: Allyn & Bacon.

Dedrick, C. V. (1972). *The relationship between perceptual characteristics and effective teaching at the junior college level.* Unpublished doctoral Dissertation, University of Florida.

Doyle, E. J. (1969). *The relationship between college teaching effectiveness and inferred characteristics of the adequate personality.* Unpublished doctoral Dissertation, University of Northern Colorado.

Gooding, C. T. (1964). *An observational analysis of perceptual organization of effective teachers.* Unpublished doctoral dissertation, University of Florida.

Jennings, G. D. (1973). *The relationship between perceptual characteristics and effective advising of university housing para-professional resident assistants.* Unpublished doctoral dissertation, University of Florida.

Koffman, R. G. (1975). *A comparison of the perceptual organization of outstanding and-nrandomly selected teachers in "open" and traditional classrooms.* Unpublished Doctoral Dissertation, University of Massachusetts.

O'Roark, A. (1976). *A comparison of perceptual characteristics of elected legislators and public school counselors identified as most and least effective.* Unpublished doctoral dissertation, University of Florida.

Usher, R. H. (1966). *The relationship of perceptions of self, others, and the helping task to certain measures of college faculty effectiveness.* Unpublished doctoral dissertation, University of Florida.

Vonk, H. G. (1970). *The relationship of teacher effectiveness to perception of self and teaching purposes.* Unpublished doctoral dissertation, University of Florida.

Wasicsko, M. M. (1977a). *A research based teacher selection instrument.* East Lansing, MI: National Center for Research on Teacher Learning. (ERIC Document Reproduction Service No. ED193193)

Wasicsko, M. M. (1977b). Improving teacher selection using perceptual inference in the teacher selection process. East Lansing, MI: National Center for Research on Teacher Learning. (ERIC Document Reproduction Service No. ED193195)

Wasicsko, M. M. (1978, April). *Selecting invitational teachers: The use of perceptual data in the teacher selection process.* Paper presented at the American Education Research Association Conference, Toronto, Canada. (ERIC Document Reproduction Service No. ED152719)

Wasicsko, M. M. (2004, October). The 20-minute hiring assessment: How to ensure you're hiring the best by gauging educator dispositions. *The School Administrator, 61,* 40-42.

Wasicsko, M. M., Callahan, C., & Wirtz, P. (2004). Integrating dispositions into the conceptual framework: Four a priori questions. *The Kentucky Counseling Association Journal, 23,* 24-29.

Wasicsko, M. M. (2005a, February 18) Hiring for the fourth factor. *The Chronicle of Higher Education, 51,* C2.

Wasicsko, M. M. (2005b). Assessing educator dispositions: A perceptual approach. National Network for the Study of Educator Dispositions. From www.educatordispositions.org

Wasicsko, M. M. (2006, September/October). Determining dispositions to teach, *Principal, 86, 51-52.*

CHAPTER 4

A CONSTRUCTIVIST-DEVELOPMENTAL PERSPECTIVE

Sharon Nodie Oja and Alan J. Reiman

What are the relationships between teacher judgments and teacher professionalism? How can constructivist-developmental theory inform our understanding of teacher judgments? What criteria will teacher education programs use as they decide how to allocate faculty time and limited resources for the optimal design of programs that can show change in teacher candidates' knowledge, performance, and disposition? How can educators create significant and progressively more complex learning experiences for future teachers that prompt growth in professional judgments and actions? What pedagogies should a teacher educator use to facilitate an open discussion about moral issues regarding race and equity that supports diverse views while encouraging perspective taking? What considerations should a mentor teacher consider as she assists a cohort of new teachers who are feeling overwhelmed with their new responsibilities?

Challenges such as these, about which even experts disagree, are called ill-structured problems (Wood, 1983). These types of professional problems are characterized by two prominent features: they cannot be defined

Dispositions in Teacher Education, pp. 91–115

with a high degree of completeness, and they cannot be solved with a high degree of certainty. In the last 25 years, we have investigated how educators come to understand and make judgments as they are engaged in complex new experiences that are ill-structured. As well, we have investigated how relatively modest but intensive professional development programs can be designed to foster growth in teacher performance and teacher conceptual, ethical, and ego judgments. These programs are guided by a set of seven developmental design principles that we refer to as the integrated learning framework (ILF). The ILF emphasizes the importance of designing progressively more complex (and ill-structured) new experiences that encourage teachers to learn as they teach and assist others to learn.

There are two central messages of this chapter. The first message is that dispositions are best understood within the context of teachers' thoughtful, responsible, and professional interpretation, judgment, and action. The second message is that constructivist-developmental research in the domains of conceptual judgment, moral judgment, and ego judgment can offer important insights and implications for program design and assessment, because the evidence describes the nature and process of persons' interpretations, judgments and related actions in ill-structured professional contexts.

As you read this chapter, you will find that our characterization of professional judgment relates teachers' interpretations, problem-solving, and professional actions based on three judgment domains. Also, because teacher professionalism involves social purposes and responsibilities, any characterization of teacher professional judgment must be morally grounded (Shulman, 1998). Thus, our work is strongly influenced by research in moral psychology.

In the sections to follow, we review theoretical assumptions, describe three judgment domains and their assessment, introduce design principles for fostering the growth of judgments, and propose implications for teacher education programs.

DEFINITIONS AND THEORETICAL BACKGROUND

How are we defining professional judgments within the constructivist-developmental tradition? Extending the work of Raths (2000), we interpret dispositions as attributed characteristics of a teacher that represent dominant and preferred trends in teachers' interpretations, judgments and actions in ill-structured professional contexts (Reiman & Johnson, 2003). Ill-structured refers to problems for which there is no one right answer. In effect, the experts disagree, thus there is a dilemma as to how to respond. Our definition is not intended to suggest that teacher decision making only involves judgments about ill-structured problems in the classroom. However, teachers' interpretations and judgments about ill-structured classroom problems represent a promising lens through which to better understand dispositions.

Our brief overview of constructivist-developmental theory responds to three questions. What are the central assumptions of the theory? What domains of cognitive development are particularly germane to a discussion of teacher dispositions? And what does research evidence tell us about relationships between development across the domains and teacher performance and teacher content knowledge? In our response to each of these questions, we describe the potential relationship to our definition of teacher judgments.

Theoretical Assumptions

Our work has evolved out of a small group of theoretical models of late adolescent and adult intellectual, ego, and moral development. Our early work was grounded in the cognitive-developmental tradition of Harvey, Hunt, and Schroder (1961), Kohlberg (1969), Loevinger (1976), Mead (1934), Perry (1970), Piaget (1965), Selman (1980), and Sprinthall and Thies-Sprinthall (1983). Our more recent work and research has much in common with more constructivist-developmental perspectives of Fischer and Pruyne (2002), King and Kitchener (2004), and the social-cognitive perspectives of Mentkowski and Associates (2000) and Rest, Narvaez, Bebeau, and Thoma (1999).

These theoretical approaches share (a) the underlying assumption that meaning is constructed, (b) the emphasis on understanding how individuals make meaning from their experiences, (c) the assumption that development and learning occur as people interact with their environments, and (d) the assumption that construction and reconstruction of meaning occurs through assimilation and accommodation and affective dissonance. These theories also share the view that persons' meaning making is described in developmental terms. The organizing principles, reasons, and affect people use in interpreting their experiences are described as becoming more complex, integrated, and principled over time. Such development does not occur automatically. Rather, growth depends on interactions within social environments that both support and challenge growth (Oja & Reiman, 1998; Windschitl, 2002). This view has much in common with Vygotsky's zone of proximal development (Vygotsky, 1978).

Reasoning

In contrast with Kohlberg (1969) however, we do not claim cross-cultural universality. And we endorse King and Kitchener's (2004) concept of a complex rather than simple stage model of development. King and Kitchener have raised questions about the "simple stage" model first outlined by Kohlberg. Their longitudinal samples ($n = 1,995$) suggest that although adolescent and adult reasoning has stage-like properties, it does not evolve in a lock-step, one-stage-at-a-time fashion. In comparison, the "complex stage model," first described by Rest (1979), suggests that although a person may rely heavily on a stage of reasoning while attempting to resolve an ill-structured problem, a limited number of statements and conclusions by the person will be consistent with a prior stage of reasoning and a small number of statements may be consistent with a more advanced and more-complex stage.

Performance

A second theoretical model that has affected our thinking about ILF research is Joyce and Showers (1995) coaching model and Fischer and Pruyne's (2002) skill theory. Joyce and Showers described and assessed the coaching process as it unfolds in professional development contexts. They identified four key conditions for reflective coaching. They include rationale, demonstration, guided practice in the laboratory setting, and coaching in the field setting. A key finding is that coaching in the field setting is required if one is to achieve "executive control" of complex new instructional models.

Fischer and Pruyne (2002) identified seven skill levels that emerge between ages 2 and 30. These skill levels represent two tiers, the representational and the abstract tier. The representational tier encompasses an individual's ability to manipulate concrete representations, objects, people, or events; while the abstract tier includes an individual's ability to integrate, manipulate, and reason about skills or performances using abstract reasoning and judgments. More complex developmental plateaus require the ability to abstract and correspond to Fischer and Pruyne's theory of abstract levels of skills. The most important influence of Fischer and Pruyne's work is their assumption that no skills and related understanding of subject area can exist independently of the environment and the developmental levels of an individual. Tasks that one can perform without support reflect a person's "functional level" while tasks that require assistance to perform reflect a person's "optimal level." The space between the functional and optimal levels represents the developmental range.

As this brief summary suggests, the assumptions of constructivist-developmental theory emphasize that meaning is constructed. As educators, it is important to understand how persons are making meaning from experience. Change may be automatic, but development is not automatic. Development occurs when there is optimal interaction with the environment. Further, our approach emphasizes a complex stage model and offers important theoretical links between developmental change and performance. In particular, we summarized the theory of Fischer and Pruyne (2002) who describe functional and optimal levels of performance. We now turn to three judgment domains that have been of particular interest to us. These three domains include the conceptual/reflective, self/ego, and moral/ethical domains. We will briefly describe each domain, review methods of assessing the domain, and then summarize evidence linking the judgment domains to teaching performance and teacher content knowledge.

Investigating Development Across Three Judgment Domains

Our ILF research has investigated developmental change of educators across three partially interdependent judgment domains: conceptual/reflective, self/ego, and moral/ethical. We view these domains as the fulcrum of good teaching. Let us examine the domains more closely.

The first domain (conceptual/reflective) surfaced from the longitudinal research of Hunt (1976) and King and Kitchener (1994). This domain supports our view of the teacher as epistemologist (reflective thinker), and teachers' epistemic assumptions are associated with how they approach complex and ill-structured tasks.

The extensive basic research of Loevinger (1976) on ego development frames our view of the teacher's professional judgment needing to be emotionally and socially mature. Being able to care, to provide empathy, and to balance one's own needs with the needs of others is a feature of a mature and integrated ego.

Finally, the painstaking research of Rest et al. (1999) with moral judgment frames our view of the teacher as principled and caring decision maker. The moral domain includes four components: teacher ethical sensitivity, teacher ethical judgment, teacher ethical motivation, and teacher character. These four components have been outlined in contemporary research in moral psychology (Lapsley, 1996; Lapsley & Narvaez, 2004; Rest et al., 1999). Let us take a closer look at each of these judgment domains.

Conceptual/Reflective Judgment

Conceptual complexity and reflective judgment can be defined as the development of more complex modes of epistemological understanding.

For example, if we asked a teacher to describe her professed epistemology (stated assumption about knowledge, its certainty, and learning) and then observed the teacher as she enacted her epistemology, we would have an insight into the degree of congruence between the teacher's epistemological interpretations, judgments, and instructional actions. Miller (1981) and King and Kitchener (1994) found that a person's reasoning and epistemic assumptions in the conceptual/reflective domain mature from stereotypes and clichés toward constructed meaning, toward recognition of individual differences in attitudes, interests, and abilities and increased tolerance of paradox, contradiction, and ambiguity. Teachers at more complex conceptual/reflective levels have a greater tolerance for diverse learners and greater empathic communication with learners (Miller, 1981 review of 60 studies). These teachers employed more problem-posing with learners (Peterson, Fennema, Carpenter, & Loef, 1989) and were able to accommodate more student perspectives (Newmann, 1993).

Many studies of teacher conceptual complexity have used the paragraph completion method (PCM) (Hunt, Butler, Noy, & Rosser, 1978; Miller, 1981), also known as the conceptual level (CL) test. This test assesses conceptual level, defined as both cognitive complexity (discrimination, differentiation, and integration) as well as interpersonal maturity (increasing self-responsibility) (Hunt et al., 1978). A person scoring at a higher conceptual level is more structurally complex, more capable of responsible actions and, most important, more capable of adapting to a changing environment than is a person at a lower conceptual level (Hunt, 1975, p. 187). The preferred form of the PCM contains five sentence stems and the person is asked to write at least three sentences on each stem. Two of the sentence stems elicit a person's views about structure: "What I think about rules" and "When I am told what to do." Two more stems focus on uncertainty: "When I am not sure" and "When someone does not agree with me." The fifth stem elicits views on authority: "When I am criticized." Scores range from 0 to 3 in increments of .5. Scoring rules are laid out in the PCM manual and there are numerous practice stems to help a scorer reach high scoring reliability. However, Hunt et al. (1978) and associates acknowledged that the PCM, as presented in the scoring manual, is "not sensitive in detecting developmental change at higher levels" (p. 42).

Another method to measure growth in the intellectual domain is the learning environment preferences (LEP) questionnaire (Moore, 1989). The LEP is an objective instrument based on Perry's (1970) scheme of intellectual development. The LEP prompts people to choose among descriptions of ideal learning environments from a list of 13 items for each of five domains: view of knowledge/learning, role of the instructor, role of the student/peers, classroom atmosphere/activities, and the role of evaluation/grading. Scores are reported as a conceptual complexity index (CCI). The tests can be scored by the Center for the Study of Intellectual Development, headed by William Moore. For more information see the Web site www.perrynetwork.org.

An interview method we used to investigate growth in the reflective judgment domain is the reflective judgment interview (RJI) (King & Kitchener, 1994). The RJI consists of four ill-structured problems, a standard set of interview questions, and probe questions. One can be certified to be an RJI interviewer and to score transcribed interviews. The interviewer's goal is to elicit answers that will indicate the person's functional stage of reflective judgment. Reflective judgment is defined as bringing "closure to situations that are uncertain" by evaluating "beliefs, assumptions, and hypotheses against existing data and against other plausible interpretations of the data" (King & Kitchener, 1994, pp. 6-7). The term reflective is used to mean the thinking and reasoning of persons at the higher stages in the reflective judgment model. The model consists of seven stages: stages 1, 2, and 3 form the prereflective period, stages 4 and 5 are the quasi-reflective period, and stages 6 and 7 represent reflective judgment. Research with the RJI indicates that many college students score at the prereflective stage 3 and that the development to the quasi-reflective stage 4 is a major cognitive shift during the undergraduate experience.

Some scholars have argued that teachers' ways of making meaning from their experiences must be accounted for in educational reform (Spillane, Reiser, & Reimer, 2002). In effect, how a teacher understands and implements curriculum is shaped by the individual's cognition, epistemic assumptions, and context. As an example, work in mathematics education continues to show relationships between teachers' conceptual judgments and how they teach mathematics (Schoenfeld, 1992). Teachers' views of the nature of their subject, and their perception of the purpose of education, are framed within the conceptual/reflective judgment domain.

Ego Maturity

Ego maturity is defined here as the development of more complex, differentiated, and integrated understandings of the self and others; the development moves away from manipulative, exploitive, self-protective attitudes toward self-respect, mutual respect, and identity formation. We found teachers with advanced ego maturity used a wider variety of coping behaviors in response to school pressures, employed a larger repertoire of group process and change strategies, and were very self-reflective and highly effective in collaborative action research groups (Oja, 2000; Oja & Ham, 1984; Oja & Smulyan, 1989).

The Washington University sentence completion test (SCT) is a measure of ego maturity and assesses changes in a person's judgments about intrapersonal and interpersonal relations. The SCT is a semiprojective test based on Jane Loevinger's (1976) theory that characterizes ego as a combination of personality, individuality, and method of facing personal problems in life. The test consists of 36 sentence stems. The response to each stem is independently rated as one level of ego maturity: E-2 Impulsive, E3 Self-Protective, E-4 Conformist, E-5 Self-Aware, E-6 Conscientious, E-7 Individualistic, E-8 Autonomous, and E-9 Integrated. In a pooled sample of over 1,000 male and female participants, from school-aged to middle-aged, including college students and others, Hy and Bobbitt (1991, as cited in Loevinger, 1998) reported that ego E-levels ranged from E-2 to E-9, with most cases at E-5 and E-6, typical of the college-aged. In a study of 55 experienced teachers that were involved in a program to learn new skills related to individualizing instruction, supervising peer or cross-age teaching, and contracting with students for behavior change, Oja and Sprinthall (1978) reported an average ego level of E-6. In a study of 28 experienced cooperating teachers involved in collaborative action research on the mentoring of student teaching interns, the average ego level was E-7 (reported in Oja, 2000). The scoring manual (Hy & Loevinger, 1996) provides numerous practice items so a rater can reach high levels of reliability. Hy and Loevinger note that the theory of ego development shares many characteristics with conceptual judgment reasoning (e.g., cognitive complexity and interpersonal maturity) described by Hunt and associates (1978).

An interview measure of ego maturity is based on Robert Kegan's (1982, 1994) theory of development that subsumes concepts like identity development, self-esteem, and locus of control. His theory focuses on the Self as a system that actively makes meaning, and through this process, becomes more complex over time. At different stages the Self is embedded in, "subject" to, and noncritical of certain ways of making meaning, but can reflect on or make "object" previous ways of making meaning. A person's developmental Self stage can be assessed through an hour long clinical interview using a manual that describes indicators for five different developmental stages and the four transition points between every two stages (Lahey, Souvaine, Kegan, Goodman, & Felix, 1987). Katharina Fachin-Lucas (1999) used this assessment in a mentoring study in which 39 college sophomores (many interested in teaching as a career) mentored sixth grade at-risk preadolescent girls weekly for the duration of a semester.

A related measure of teacher ego maturity is described in Robert Selman's most recent book (2003) that is based upon his theory of the growth of interpersonal understanding and 30 years of research with elementary students, and, in the last 10 years, with teachers. His work delineates developmental levels of interpersonal action and extends his theory beyond an individual's social perspective taking to the coordination of social perspectives in discourse and action. He charts how particular individual differences in personal meaning actively maintain gaps between interpersonal understanding and interpersonal competence. He suggests how these personal meanings, once understood, might become the levers for releasing latent maturity. Part III of his 2003 book discusses his preliminary theory about teachers' levels of social awareness and a developmental chart of teachers' professional reflection. Selman's theory may be helpful to teacher development programs interested in focusing on teacher dispositions related to a developmental domain of interpersonal understanding.

Moral/Ethical Judgment and Action

The moral domain includes teacher ethical sensitivity, teacher ethical judgment, teacher ethical motivation, and teacher character. Chang (1994) summarized over 20 studies of teachers' moral reasoning. Two studies in Chang's review are representative of Chang's findings. First, a case study by Johnston and Lubromudrov (1987) found that teachers using higher levels of moral reasoning encouraged students to participate in making classroom rules, and these teachers were more willing to help students understand the reasoning for the rules. Second, Oser's (1992) experimental study found that teachers using advanced moral reasoning were more likely to encourage students to take multiple perspectives; these teachers were more inductive in their teaching and more learner-centered.

The defining issues test (DIT) by James Rest (1986) is an objective measure of moral judgment. Moral judgment is defined as a "psychological construct that characterizes the process by which people determine that one course of action in a particular situation is morally right and another ... is wrong. Moral judgment involves defining what the moral issues are, how conflicts among parties are to be settled, and the rationale for deciding on a course of action" (Rest, 1994, p. 5). Given an ethical dilemma, a person will rate and rank a series of twelve statements in terms of their importance in resolving the dilemma. Using the patterns of the ratings and rankings, the test is scored to determine "estimates of the relative strength of three moral schemas: personal interest maintaining norms, and postconventional moral reasoning (Rest et al., 1999, p. 6). Rest et al. (1999) provide evidence that postconventional reasoning is linked to community involvement ($r = .31$), civic responsibility ($r = .44$), and respect for human rights. The tests can be mechanically scored for a small fee at the University of Minnesota Center for the Study of Ethical Development. The results are reported as percent scores in each of the three schema. Experimental studies investigating change in moral development scores often focus on the change in the percent of postconventional thinking, called the p-score. Case studies like Johnson and Reiman (2005) present scores in all three schema for each of the mentor teachers and student teachers.

Postconventional moral reasoning has been associated with greater racial ethical sensitivity. A more qualitative measure of moral/ethical judgment is the Racial Ethical Sensitivity Test (REST) (Brabeck et al., 2000) which has five scenarios on video with scenes of racial or gender intolerance in schools. Participants choose two out of five scenarios and respond to a semistructured interview. Raters use a scoring rubric to rate between six and nine issues for each scenario discussed by the participant. The scores on the two scenarios are then averaged for each participant to create a composite score ranging from 1-3, where a 3 represents high ethical sensitivity. In a sample of 22 teacher candidates, Maher (2005) found three clusters of scores; he labeled the cluster of scores from 0-1.36 as low, the mid range of scores was 1.37 to 1.63, and high scores were over 1.63. Maher found that teacher candidates scoring at the higher levels of the REST conducted more balanced conferences with caregivers in clinical settings.

Does Development in the Three Judgment Domains Make a Difference in Professional Performance?

The research in all three domains shows a consistent predictive relationship between more complex reasoning and performance. In the domain of conceptual complexity, Miller's (1981) meta-analysis of over 200 studies is a comprehensive review of content and predictive validity supporting the idea that teachers at more complex conceptual levels need less structure in professional development experiences, tend to be more tolerant of ambiguity, tend to be more responsive to learner needs and to adjust instruction accordingly, and tend to justify their decisions based on evidence from multiple sources. The relationships are very consistent. Likewise, as noted earlier, studies of relationships between teaching and ego and moral maturity indicate consistent positive relationships. However, the correlations tend to be at moderate levels (.30 - .50).

Summarizing our discussion up to this point, we have reviewed the assumptions of constructivist-developmental theory, identified three judgment domains that have been investigated extensively, reviewed established assessment systems[1] for these judgment domains, and reviewed some of the evidence showing relationships between reasoning and performance for each of the three domains. We now turn to the question of how to promote judgments in the three domains. Specifically, we summarize seven program design principles that we and our associates have investigated over the last 25 years. We will describe the seven design principles and then summarize research evidence related to the principles.

DESIGN PRINCIPLES FOR APPLICATION TO EDUCATIONAL SETTINGS

Teacher professional education, like many other fields, needs a practice-based theory that can help us understand dispositions and guide curriculum and pedagogy within our professional education programs (Ball & Cohen, 1999; Diez, 1999; Murray, 1996). A number of researchers have begun to test the theoretical conditions described earlier by Sprinthall and Thies-Sprinthall (1983) as a teaching and learning framework that involves components for an instructional repertoire and conditions for growth. We refined the framework to seven applied design principles that integrate new learning with constructivist-developmental growth and call it the integrated learning framework (ILF).

The Integrated Learning Framework

Building Trust and Respecting Contexts

Educators must contextualize learning and instruction by accounting for the experiences of colleagues or preservice teachers who are taking on new and expanded professional roles. This condition includes acknowledging prior knowledge and experience and developing rapport with learners (e.g., students and teaching colleagues). Building collaborative and trusting relationships fosters not only the teachers' professional skills but their social, reflective, and ethical development as well.

Complex New Roles and Helping Experiences

When teachers engage in complex new roles in schools and classrooms, the experience (action) can cause "knowledge disturbances" (Reiman & Thies-Sprintall, 1998, p. 79) as one encounters information or concepts that differ from one's prior knowledge. Analysis and reflection (inquiry) spurs the Piagetian interacting processes of assimilation and accommodation in relation to the immediate new experiences. Learning to interpret, moment by moment, how students, or a novice colleague, are constructing meaning from a planned experience can be an important catalyst for transformation in one's thinking and performance. Complex new roles and experiences cause conceptual disequilibrium which spurs reconsideration of professional judgments. Helping another colleague while learning new competencies (e.g., mentoring) or working collaboratively (e.g., action research) also tends to bolster the potential for learning and development, since in the Vygotskian sense, one can perform at a developmentally more advanced level when others provide assistance and coaching.

Guided Inquiry.

Guided inquiry includes both self-assessment and reflection through carefully planned activities, ongoing discussions, and dialogue journals that encourage self-assessment of one's performance. These assessment and reflection activities are guided by a "more capable other." Our stance is that inquiry is the central role of a practicing teacher, and it should be the central role of the teacher educator. Inquiry becomes a professional discussion (oral and written) that is grounded in the complex new roles and experiences. Within one's immediate experiences are opportunities for deeper exploration of ways of observing, consideration of multiple perspectives, and consideration of ethical issues. However, inquiry must also be evidence-based. Thus, careful self-assessment using validated protocols and discussion of evidence must be a part of the professional dialogue.

We found that one cannot assume a sophisticated capacity for reflection so Reiman (1999) developed a guided inquiry process that differentiates written responses according to one's current preferred ways of conceptualizing and reflecting on ill-structured problems and ethical dilemmas. Teacher educators working with candidates that were less reflective, for example, provided higher structure, more encouragement, more links to concrete experience, and more conceptual scaffolds in the written dialogue journals. Conversely, candidates demonstrating higher levels of conceptual and ethical complexity in ongoing written analyses of student artifacts and classroom practice were provided with less structure, more encouragement to critically examine learner needs, more consideration of complex teaching tasks, and more frequent consideration of theoretical and ethical issues related to practice.

Support and Challenge

Vygotsky's (1978) zone of proximal growth helps describe the support and challenge principle. Support (encouragement) and challenge (prompting the learner to accommodate to new learning) are necessary for learning and development. We refer to this challenge as the constructive mismatch.

This is the most complex pedagogical requirement of the ILF approach. Piaget uses seemingly circular language when he refers to cognitive as the affective and the affective as the cognitive, a parallel process during decentration (Piaget & Inhelder, 1969, p. 95). If, however, we think of a situation in our own experience when our method of problem solving and understanding no longer fits and then think of the feelings aroused, we have a clearer sense of the effects of disequlibrium during new learning and the connected roles of support and challenge. Learning how to manage support and challenge as an educator is the most difficult of the seven principles. Beyond the goal of balancing support and challenge, there is a second goal of realizing that each individual differs in their needs for support and challenge. Differentiation is required to meet individual needs.

Balance

Neither action nor reflection alone is enough to promote development. It is important that there is a balance between the new roletaking experience (action) and reflection. In our programs this means that the practice-based experiences are sequenced with guided inquiry each week. Too great a time lag between action and reflection appears to halt the growth process. For example, Pobywajlo's (2004) analysis suggests that the balance of experience and reflection could be improved in her ILF tutor training design by cutting down the amount of hours of tutoring in the first month, giving tutors more opportunities to observe experienced tutors, and by holding more frequent training seminars where tutors could reflect on their observations in relation to their own experiences.

Continuity

The complex goal of fostering changes in teachers' performance and moral reasoning and reflective judgment requires a continuous interplay between experience and inquiry. A 1- or 2-week workshop has not prompted changes in moral reasoning and reflective judgment. Typically, as least four to six months are needed for significant learning and development to occur.

Reflective Coaching

A reflective coaching process (e.g., Joyce & Weil, 1996) supports the learner as she/he attempts new skills and models of teaching. Support through coaching includes ascertaining prior knowledge, clarifying the supporting rationale and evidence for the performance, introducing demonstrations of the performance, providing opportunities for practice with self-assessment, and integrating observation and feedback by a more capable other for assessment of learning performance.

The integrated learning framework can guide the preparation of preservice teachers for their new role in teaching as well as guiding the staff development programs for teachers involved in complex new roles like mentor, school-based teacher educator, and collaborative action research.

The overall goal of a practice-based theory like the ILF is the development of more complex and more integrated understanding of oneself; the formation of greater conceptual judgment complexity and flexibility as one interprets and acts in one's practice; the growth of more complex ethical judgment reasoning; and the acquisition of new performances that enhance instruction and engagement with learners.

Evidence of Change

Can teacher professional development programs be created using the ILF conditions? What empirical evidence exists regarding the change process across the three judgment domains? Can teachers become more flexible, more empathic, and more principled in their practice? Such questions have been posed at an empirical and practical level. Our experience suggests that the framework for integrated learning can direct the nature and quality of teachers' new roles and leadership experiences such that it promotes new learning and development. Numerous studies have used the ILF to guide program design across the teacher professional career span and in other helping professions such as counseling and social work. The goal of these programs was to enlarge teachers' social perspective and sociomoral commitments, while simultaneously enhancing instructional performance and content knowledge. Empirical evidence takes many forms including longitudinal studies, meta-analysis of experimental and quasi-experimental studies, and case studies. This evidence is now reviewed.

Reiman and Johnson (2003) examined the effect sizes of 12 ILF studies that included developmental dispositions as dependent variables. Effect sizes were reported across the three dispositional domains described in this chapter—moral/ethical, ego, and conceptual judgment. Effect sizes were significant for the interventions and ranged from $+.75$ ($N = 10$, moral/ethical judgment), to $+.59$ average effect size ($N = 3$, ego judgment), and $+.50$ average effect size ($N = 10$, conceptual judgment). Effect sizes for the studies range from moderate ($+.50 - +.59$) for the ego and conceptual domains to large ($+.75$) for the moral/ethical domain. Nonsignificant findings were included as well per recommendations by Rosenthal (1995). The studies that were summarized reflected teacher professional development programming in the Southeastern,

Northeastern, and Midwestern sections of the United States and employed both urban and rural settings. The samples tended to have diverse makeup according to ethnicity, but lacked gender diversity (females were in the majority in all samples). A majority of the studies included dependent measures of performance as well. These outcomes are described in more detail when we describe specific programs.

Two longitudinal studies of teacher education candidates' moral reasoning were summarized by Reiman (2004). The average gain in postconventional moral reasoning across the two teacher education cohorts was 12.31 with an average effect size of +.62. This is a large gain score when compared with other national longitudinal samples. Only the Alverno studies (see Mentkowski & Associates, 2000) show similar effect sizes. The two teacher education samples participated in a unique program that was based on the ILF components. The evidence suggests that guided inquiry is important and should be integrated into teacher education programs in ways that permit future teachers to reason about and respond to the context of their progressively more "practice-based" experience.

But what do these programs look like? The following three summaries outline some of the programmatic features of a preservice program, mentoring program and a collaborative action research program that utilized the framework. Each program assesses teachers on their dispositions using a constructivist-developmental perspective (e.g., growth in moral judgment, reflective judgment, or ego maturity).

Application of the ILF to Preservice Programs

Senne and Rikard (2004) worked with undergraduate preservice teaching candidates. Their program included the *guided inquiry* method (self-assessment and guided reflection) using a teaching portfolio. As students participated in their practica field experiences, written discussion and guided analysis and reflection were prompted using Reiman's (1999) guided inquiry model. In the guided inquiry process the teacher educator differentiated responses and prompts in the portfolios to candidates who were less reflective and needed more structure versus candidates who were more reflective, needing less structure and more encouragement to critically assess their experiences. The teacher educator strived to acknowledge the ideas and contributions of the candidate. Written questioning by the teacher educator employed more theory, more discussion of the ethical/moral issues of teaching, and requests for candidate analysis of evidence related to instructional decision making.

The preservice program occurred over three academic semesters. The ILF component of *building trust and respecting contexts* is supported in the Senne and Rikard (2004) study through the portfolios which offered many opportunities for teacher candidates to individualize their learning based on their prior and present cultural and educational experiences. The significant *new role-taking experience* is fulfilled as teacher candidates assume the role of teacher during elementary and secondary teaching practica, and subsequently in an internship. The new experiences involve progressively more complex helping and teaching by the teacher candidate over 1 year. A *balance* between inquiry (reflection and self-assessment) and practice (teaching) was embedded within the field-based experiences of teacher candidates. Inquiry prompted teacher candidates to construct meaning derived from their teaching experiences.

Furthermore, concepts of matching and mismatching (*support & challenge*) were employed as the teacher educators read and responded to teacher candidates' portfolio patterns, in an effort to foster positive conceptual and ethical change. Acknowledging and reinforcing a candidate's current meaning making system is referred to as matching. When candidates demonstrated a readiness for more conceptual and ethical complexity, a mismatch or challenge was provided via the guided inquiry process. Differentiated responding by the teacher educator to the teacher candidate's written inquiry (reflection on experience and self-assessment of knowledge and skills) offers a more deliberate and research-based process for teacher educators as they guide the learning and development of candidates.

The *reflective coaching* component of the framework was embedded in the Senne and Rikard study through the use of professional growth plans that the teacher candidates worked on as a part of their portfolio. A key part of this process was effective demonstration by a more capable other on selected instructional skills with subsequent opportunities for teacher candidates to practice and self-assess using structured protocols. Finally, *continuity* was addressed by making sure that all conditions of the ILF were employed during the practicum and internship (total of 1 year). In this program the teacher candidate construction of a portfolio served as a developmentally responsive pedagogical tool for the teacher educator. The portfolio provides a touchstone for ongoing written guided inquiry between the teacher candidates and teacher educator where the aim of the program was positive changes in teacher candidates' knowledge, skills, and dispositions (e.g., conceptual and ethical change).

Application of the ILF to Induction and Mentor Programs

In the mid-1980s, North Carolina mandated that schools assign mentors to beginning teachers and that mentors receive professional development for their new roles. A collaborative program was developed between North Carolina State University and partner school systems. Subsequently, teachers collaborated with faculty in a professional development program to coach and educate teachers as teacher educators (and mentors) in their own districts.

School-based teacher educators complete a 12-credit hour sequence of professional coursework in the *new roles and experiences* of coaching and assistance. The curriculum includes a one-semester seminar, a one-semester practicum, and a two-semester internship. The curriculum is based on theory and research about teaching, integrated adult learning, and moral and conceptual development. Clinical teachers (mentors) are educated locally by teacher colleagues (school-based teacher educators) and complete a 6-credit-hour sequence resembling the seminar and the practicum taken by their school-based teacher educators. Clinical instructors are practicing school-based teacher educators who assume an additional new leadership role of teaching methods courses to prospective teachers and student teachers at a school site or at the university, often teamed with a university instructor. These clinical instructors have been extremely successful in their teaching and are uniquely suited to bridge the cultures of university and schools. Design of the curriculum for mentor teachers and school-based teacher educators is based on the ILF principles.

A recent federally-funded project supported a collaborative induction program for mentors and lateral-entry teachers. The new teacher-mentor dyads participated in the ILF curriculum for 1 year. All lateral-entry teachers who completed the program remained in the classroom. External evaluation indicated that lateral-entry teachers acquired relatively high levels of competence in cooperative learning strategies and varied instruction when contrasted with the comparison group. Disposition made a difference as well. Mentor teachers at more complex conceptual and moral stages were better able to differentiate their assistance according to the needs of the new teacher colleague (Reiman, 2005).

Application of the ILF to Collaborative Action Research Programs

A number of staff development projects used the ILF principles and *new roles and experiences* for teachers as action researchers. In action research groups, teachers collaborated to identify new skills and practices, compare to prior understandings, and investigate current theories and research related to their new roles. In collaborative action research teachers consistently reflect on their new behaviors and responsibilities in the classroom or school and use each other as advisors, consultants, and coinquirers when the new roles are creating periods of discomfort. Teachers are active in trying out their new, more complex roles in teaching or supervising. Teachers build interpersonal skills and relationships that create a supportive environment that is necessary for development when they are involved in the challenges of new experiences. Continuity is evident as the collaborative action research groups are ongoing, often meeting weekly over the course of the year or more. Balance is achieved as time is allowed for the necessary cycles of action and reflection in the action research process. We have found it helpful to identify the role of a developmental facilitator in school-university collaborative action research groups (Oja & Smulyan, 1989, pp. 166-167). The developmental facilitator is a member of the group and models and demonstrates the action research process and coaches group members as needed along the way.

In one project (Oja & Pine, 1987) two collaborative action research groups were formed from junior high school teachers who wanted to improve their schools and faculty from the local university who were skilled in the action research process. One action research group investigated teacher morale and the other group in a different school focused on block scheduling. We used a case study design to describe ten teachers as they participated in the action research, and thus we began to better understand different teachers' judgments and actions in the new role of teacher as researcher, the process of collaborative action research, and the relationships to the teachers' development in the conceptual, ego, and moral judgment domains (Oja & Smulyan, 1989).

In a different project three collaborative action research groups of elementary teachers were formed as they took on new supervisory roles as cooperating teachers with student teaching interns (Oja, 1990-1991). Teachers in the groups were involved for up to 2 years in cycles of action research to examine their own practical knowledge and evaluate the theoretical knowledge base in supervision strategies. The teachers attempted to vary their new supervisory practices to match the capabilities and flexibilities they observed in their student teaching interns. Measurements of the development of the teacher-researchers in the three action research groups showed high conceptual complexity scores, ego levels averaging E7, and high moral reasoning with an average of 60% principled judgments. The work of these school-university collaborative action research groups initiated the revisioning of the student teaching internship placement process, the establishment of a new course on mentoring free for all interested cooperating teachers, greater support for new university supervisors, and a joint decision-making body called the school-university collaborative that includes school principals and teachers and faculty from the university (see Oja, 2000, 2003).

IMPLICATIONS AND CONCLUSIONS

We are proposing that a constructivist-developmental perspective on dispositions presents a promising direction for teacher education and teacher professional development. Evidence has consistently linked teacher conceptual judgment to teacher decisions about curriculum, learners, and instruction; teacher moral judgment with professionalism and principled action; and teacher ego maturity with self-maturity and professional identity. In this section we ask: What are the implications for program design, curriculum, and assessment? And what are the implications for clinical experiences?

What are the Implications for Program Design, Curriculum, and Assessment?

The central message of this chapter is that disposition is best understood within the context of our understanding of thoughtful and responsible teacher professional judgment. In this regard, research on conceptual judgment, moral judgment, and ego can offer important insights and implications for program design and assessment.

- How can programs create a model of integrated course design that includes the elements of the ILF? Such integration implies that all faculty have a working applied knowledge of how to *guide inquiry* while students are engaged in *significant new learning experiences.* This is a tall order for most large teaching institutions that prize specialization and new knowledge production.
- How can curriculum and instruction be designed to emphasize the *continual* interplay between the significant new learning experiences and reflection? Curriculum can explicitly focus on developmental goals for candidates and teachers to reach their intellectual, interpersonal, and ethical potentials.
- How can teacher educators differentiate instruction for their protégés? Curriculum and instruction designed from a developmental perspective encourages educators to understand *candidate's cultural background and the contexts of candidates' prior learning and development.* These contexts include an understanding of the current preferred assumptions of moral reasoning, reflective judgment, and

ego maturity of candidates. Educators can attempt to predict how a preservice teacher, beginning teacher, or supervising teacher/mentor is going to act if they have information on the teacher's assumptions and judgments from assessments or from developmental trends that are observed. This knowledge provides a basis for providing *differentiated support and challenge* appropriate to individuals.

- How can assessment be integrated into program coursework? Although assessment has become the mantra of most teacher education programs, the fact remains that it is difficult to document program achievements on a sustained basis. Our ILF model gives primacy to candidate self-assessment. Thus, an implication may be that authentic and ongoing student self-assessment could be sustained and could be the fulcrum of program assessment. If teacher education programs coupled candidate self-assessment with selected pre and postassessments of teacher candidates using developmental measures, they could begin to develop a data base on how their program fosters positive changes in teacher dispositions and professional judgments.

What are the Implications for Clinical Experiences?

ILF research and practice over the past 25 years suggests that clinical educators working with student teachers or beginning teachers need to develop competence in a set of developmental pedagogies. Among these pedagogies are the following:

- Understanding how novice teachers' development across the conceptual, ego, and moral domains express themselves in judgments and actions (see Reiman & Thies-Sprinthall, 1998);
- Recognizing the signs of disequilibrium and knowing how to assist during periods of disequilibrium;
- Knowing and applying *differentiated inquiry* with student teachers and new teachers;
- Designing and utilizing a variety of meaningful and authentic assessment tools to assist novices as they self-assess the teaching/learning process;
- Recognizing and applying the *reflective coaching* process as a more deliberate approach toward skill formation;
- Applying challenges that are meaningful and timely for novice colleagues. During clinical experiences *balance* is needed so that candi-

dates' reflection on their experiences happens in a timely way, with no great lags, to keep the growth process going.

This partial list of competencies would imply that clinical education is not a casual process. Rather, such preparation requires deliberate preparation that models the very practices and pedagogies that will be employed once mentoring of a student teacher or beginning teacher commences.

The central message of this chapter is that disposition is best understood within the context of our understanding of thoughtful and responsible teacher professional judgment. We proposed that professional interpretation, judgment, and action should be a core characterization of teacher disposition. Professional judgment is a disposition toward interpreting and deciding based on one's developmental position, theoretical knowledge, and skills in meeting the needs of learners. However, because teacher professionalism involves social purposes and responsibilities, it must be morally grounded (Shulman, 1998). In this regard, research on conceptual judgment, moral judgment, and ego maturity can offer important insights and implications for program design and assessment because the research describes the nature and process of persons' interpretations, judgments and related actions in ill-structured professional contexts.

The ILF is a promising theoretical and conceptual model of intervention for teacher education and teacher professional development programs. As such, it addresses one of the long-standing problems in teacher education which has been the lack of directing constructs that are evidence based. Yet Murray's (1996) review illustrates just how far we have to go. It seems very far indeed from current debates about standard-based reform. These issues notwithstanding, linking the national call for assessment of dispositions to current and future scholarship on domains of teacher professional judgment and responsible action has potential.

NOTES

1. The validity for the DIT has been established along seven criteria as reported in Rest et al. (1999), and the reliability of the DIT has been demonstrated in over 200 studies. Both the Cronbach alpha and test-retest are reported to be in the upper .70s to lower .80s. The validity and reliability of the PCM (CL) test were described by Gardiner and Schroder (1972). Subsequently, a comprehensive review of content and predictive validity was reported in Miller's (1981) meta-analysis of over 200 studies. The LEP has a psychometric validity of between .63 to .84 and a test-retest reliability of .89 (Moore, 1989). Evidence for homogeneity, reliability, and validity (substantive validity, structural validity, exter-

nal validity, and clinical validity) of the WUSCT is summarized by Loevinger (1998) as being moderate to high.

REFERENCES

Ball, D. L., & Cohen, D.,K. (1999). Developing practice, developing practitioners: Toward a practice-based theory of professional development. In L. Darling-Hammond & G. Sykes (Eds.), *Teaching as a learning profession* (pp. 3-32). San Francisco: Jossey-Bass.

Brabeck, M. M., Rogers, L. A., Sirin, S., Henderson, J., Benvenuto, M., Ting, K., & et al. (2000). A measure to assess ethical sensitivity to instances of racial and gender intolerance in schools: The Racial Ethical Sensitivity Test. *Ethics and Behavior, 10*(2), 119-137.

Chang, F. -Y. (1994). School teachers' moral reasoning. In J. Rest & D. Narvaez (Eds), *Moral development in the professions* (pp. 71-84). Hillsdale, NJ: Erlbaum.

Diez, M. (1999). Critical components in the preparation of teachers. In R. Roth (Ed.), *The role of the university in the preparation of teachers* (pp. 226-240). Philadelphia: Falmer Press.

Fachin-Lucas, K. M. (1999). *Mentoring in adolescence: A sociocultural and cognitive developmental study of undergraduate women and sixth grade girls in a mentoring program.* Unpublished doctoral dissertation, University of New Hampshire, Durham.

Fischer, K., & Pruyne, E. (2002). Reflective thinking in adulthood: Emergence, development, and variation. In J. Deick & C. Andreoletti (Eds.), *Handbook of adult development* (pp. 169-198). New York: Plenum.

Harvey, L. J., Hunt, D., & Schroder, H. M. (1961). *Conceptual systems and personality organization.* New York: Wiley.

Hunt, D. (1975). The B-P-E paradigm for theory, research, and practice. *Canadian Psychological Review, 16*(3), 185-197.

Hunt, D. (1976). Teachers' adaptation: Reading and flexing to students. *Journal of Teacher Education, 27*, 268-275.

Hunt, D. E., Butler, L. F., Noy, J. E., & Rosser, M. E. (1978). *Assessing conceptual level by the paragraph completion method.* Ontario, Canada: Ontario Institute for Studies in Education.

Hy, L. X., & Bobbitt, K. H. (1991). *Ego development theory and methods: A review of developmental levels, tests, and scoring rules.* Manuscript submitted for publication.

Hy, L. X., & Loevinger, J. (1996). *Measuring ego development* (2nd ed.). Mahwah, NJ: Erlbaum.

Johnson, L. E., & Reiman, A. J. (2005, April). *Professional judgment and professional action in the moral/ethical domain: Key components of teacher disposition.* Paper presented at the meeting of the American Educational Research Association, Montreal, Canada.

Johnston, M., & Lubromudrov, C. (1987). Teachers' level of moral reasoning and their understanding of classroom rules and roles. *Elementary School Journal, 88*, 65-78.

Joyce, B., & Showers, B. (1995). *Student achievement through staff development*. White Plains, NY: Longman.

Joyce, B., & Weil, M. (1996). *Models of teaching*. Englewood Cliffs, NJ: Prentice-Hall.

Kegan, R. (1982). *The evolving self: Problem and process in human development*. Cambridge, MA: Harvard University Press.

Kegan, R. (1994). *In over our heads: The mental demands of modern life*. Cambridge, MA: Harvard University Press.

King, P. M., & Kitchener, K. S. (1994). *Developing reflective judgment: Understanding and promoting intellectual growth and critical thinking in adolescents and adults*. San Francisco: Jossey-Bass.

King, P. M., & Kitchener, K. S. (2004). Reflective judgment: Theory and research on the development of epistemic assumptions through adulthood. *Educational Psychologist*, 39(1), 5-18.

Kohlberg, L. (1969). Stage and sequence: The cognitive-developmental approach to socialization. In D. Goslin (Ed.), *Handbook of socialization theory and research* (pp. 347-450). Chicago: Rand McNally.

Lahey, L., Souvaine, E., Kegan, R., Goodman, R., & Felix, S. (1987). *A guide to the subject-object interview: Its administration and interpretation*. Unpublished manuscript, Harvard University Graduate School of Education.

Lapsley, D. K. (1996). *Moral psychology*. Boulder, CO: Westview Press.

Lapsley, D. K., & Narvaez, D. (2004). *Moral development, self, and identity*. Mahwah, NJ: Erlbaum.

Loevinger, J. (1976). *Ego development: Conception and theories*. San Francisco: Jossey-Bass.

Loevinger, J. (1998). *Technical foundations for measuring ego development*. Mahwah, NJ: Erlbaum.

Maher, M. (2005, April). *An investigation of teacher candidates' ethical identity*. Paper presented at the meeting of the American Educational Research Association, Montreal, Canada.

Mead, G. H. (1934). *Mind, self, and society*. Chicago: University of Chicago Press.

Mentkowski, M., & Associates (2000). *Learning that lasts*. San Francisco: Jossey-Bass.

Miller, A. (1981). Conceptual matching models and interactional research in education. *Review of Educational Research, 51*(1), 33-84.

Moore, W. S. (1989). The learning environment preferences: Exploring the construct validity of an objective measure of the Perry scheme of intellectual development. *Journal of College Student Personnel, 30*, 504-514.

Murray, F. (1996). Beyond natural teaching: The case for professional education. In F. Murray (Ed.), *The teacher educator's handbook: Building a knowledge base for the preparation of teachers* (pp. 3-13). San Francisco: Jossey-Bass.

Newmann, F. (1993). Beyond common sense in educational restructuring: The issues of content and linkage. *Educational Researcher, 22*(2), 4-13.

Oja, S. N. (1990-1991, Winter). The dynamics of collaboration: A collaborative approach to supervision in a five-year education program. *Action in Teacher Education, 12* (4), 11-20.

Oja, S. N. (2000). The unique place of roletaking and reflection in collaborative action research. In A. L. Communian & U. P. Gielen (Eds.), *International perspectives on human development* (pp. 531-549). Berlin, Germany: Pabst Science.

Oja, S. N. (2003). Collaborative action research and social roletaking. In W. Veugelers & F. K. Oser (Eds.), *Teaching in moral and democratic education* (pp. 127-149). Bern, Switzerland: Peter Lang.

Oja, S. N., & Ham, M. C. (1984). A cognitive-developmental approach to collaborative action research with teachers. *Teachers College Record, 86*(1), 171-192.

Oja. S. N., & Pine, G. (1987). Collaborative action research: Teachers' stages of development and school contexts. *Peabody Journal of Education, 64*(1), 96-115.

Oja, S. N., & Reiman, A.J. (1998). Supervision for teacher development across the career span. In G. Firth & E. F. Pajak (Eds.), *Handbook of research on school supervision* (pp. 463-487). New York: Macmillan

Oja, S. N., & Smulyan, L. (1989). *Collaborative Action research: A developmental process.* London: Falmer Press.

Oja, S. N., & Sprinthall, N. A. (1978). Psychological and moral development for teachers: Can you teach old dogs? *Character Potential: A Record of Research, 8*(4), 218-225.

Oser, F. K. (1992). Morality as professional action: A discourse approach for teaching. In F. K. Oser, A. Dick, & J. Patry (Eds.), *Effective and responsible teaching* (pp. 109-125). San Francisco: Jossey-Bass.

Perry, W. (1970). *Forms of intellectual and ethical development in the college years.* New York: Holt, Rinehart & Winston.

Peterson, P., Fennema, E., Carpenter, T., & Loef, M. (1989). Teachers' pedagogical content beliefs in mathematics. *Cognition & Instruction, 6*(1), 1-40.

Piaget, J. (1965). *The moral judgment of the child.* New York: Free Press.

Piaget, J., & Inhelder, B. (1969). *The psychology of the child.* New York: Basic Books.

Pobywajlo, M. C. (2004). *The role-taking experience of undergraduate peer tutors: A cognitive-developmental approach.* Unpublished doctoral dissertation, University of New Hampshire, Durham.

Raths, J. (2000). Teacher beliefs and teaching beliefs. *Early Childhood Research & Practice, 18*, 385-391.

Reiman, A. J. (1999). The evolution of the social role-taking and guided reflection framework in teacher education: Recent theory and quantitative synthesis of research. *Teaching and Teacher Education, 15*, 597-612.

Reiman, A.J. (2004). Longitudinal studies of teacher candidates' moral reasoning and related promising interventions. *Journal of Research in Character Education, 2*(2), 141-150.

Reiman, A. J. (2005). *Creating significant learning experiences in teacher induction.* (Technical Report 3-12133-01). Washington, DC: Department of Education.

Reiman, A. J., & Johnson, L. (2003). Promoting teacher professional judgment. *Journal of Research in Education, 13*(1), 1-11.

Reiman, A. J., & Thies-Sprinthall, L. (1998). *Mentoring and supervision for teacher development.* New York: Addison-Wesley Longman.

Rest, J. (1979). *Development in judging moral issues.* Minneapolis: University of Minnesota Press.

Rest, J. (1986). *Moral development: Advances in research and theory.* New York: Praeger.

Rest, J. (1994). Background: Theory and research. In J. R. Rest & D. Narvaez (Eds.), *Moral development in the professions: Psychology and applied ethics* (pp. 1-26). Hillsdale, NJ: Erlbaum.

Rest, J., Narvaez, D., Bebeau, M., & Thoma, S. (1999). *Postconventional moral thinking: A neo-Kohlbergian approach.* Mahwah, NJ: Erlbaum.

Rosenthal, R. (1995). *Meta-analytic procedures for social research.* Newbury Park, CA: Sage.

Schoenfeld, A. H. (1992). Learning to think mathematically: Problem solving, metacognition and sense making in mathematics. In D. A. Frouws (Ed.), *Handbook of research on mathematics teaching and learning* (pp. 334-370). New York: Macmillan.

Selman, R. (1980). *The growth of interpersonal understanding.* Orlando, FL: Academic Press.

Selman, R. (2003). *The promotion of social awareness.* New York: Russell Sage Foundation.

Senne, T. A., & Rikard, G. L. (2004). A developmental intervention via the teaching portfolio: Employing the teaching/learning framework. *Journal of Teacher Education, 23,* 1-17.

Shulman, L. (1998). Theory, practice, and the education of professionals. *The Elementary School Journal, 98*(5), 511-526.

Spillane, J. P., Reiser, B. J., & Reimer, T. (2002). Policy implementation and cognition: Reframing and refocusing implementation research. *Review of Educational Research, 72*(3), 387-432.

Sprinthall, N. A., & Thies-Sprinthall, L. (1983). The teacher as an adult learner. In G. A. Griffin (Ed.), *Staff development: Eighty-second yearbook of the National Society for the Study of Education* (pp. 24-31). Chicago: University of Chicago Press.

Vygotsky, L. (1978). *Mind in society.* Cambridge, MA: Harvard University Press.

Windschitl, M. (2002). Framing constructivism in practice as the negotiation of dilemmas: An analysis of the conceptual, pedagogical, cultural, and political challenges facing teachers. *Review of Educational Research, 72*(2), 131-175.

Wood, P. K. (1983). Inquiring systems and problem structure: Implications for cognitive development. *Human Development, 26,* 249-265.

CHAPTER 5

TEACHER DISPOSITIONS
IN CONTEXT

Larry Freeman

THE ARGUMENT

For at least the last century, teacher educators have strenuously attempted to develop and implement an approach to preparing teachers that claims to prepare teachers who can effectively teach in any school in a given state, if not any school in the United States.[1] This is the Boy Scouts approach—be prepared. This approach rests on a belief that there are laws that govern effective teaching and learning and, by implication, the laws that govern the preparation of teachers and other educational personnel. Thus, the National Council for the Accreditation of Teacher Education (NCATE) can set forth standards applicable to every teacher education institution in the United States, and its constituent organizations can evolve standards for programs preparing personnel ranging from early childhood to administration to school psychology. The beliefs underlying the desire to create these standards is that just as medicine assumes that there are laws governing the development, health, and illness of the human body, so there are laws that govern preparation of teachers. Since these laws have universal application, it makes no differ-

Dispositions in Teacher Education, pp. 117–138
Copyright © 2007 by Information Age Publishing
All rights of reproduction in any form reserved.

ence where one is going to teach, whether in a small rural school or a
large urban school. Moreover, there is a regularity and predictability with
which this preparation takes place—it requires completion of high school
followed by 4 years of study prorated between and among the liberal arts
and sciences and what is called professional education. In fact, each institution and each state or other agency that certificates teachers, develops a
set of arcane rules and regulations that simultaneously derive from beliefs
about how teachers are formed and that mystify the public at large, students seeking to become teachers, and often professionals themselves.

This set of beliefs lies behind much of the work that has been done on
one of the newest areas of teacher education—dispositions. Virtually
every teacher education institution has developed, often when anticipat-
ing a review by NCATE or state authorities, a list of dispositions. I participated in one such venture at Governors State University (GSU) located in
Northeastern Illinois. In its catalog, the University asserts that it assesses
the extent to which candidates display a long list of dispositions. Among
the dispositions identified for undergraduates is behavior indicating that
they "seek to excite and expand students' learning as well as their own,"
that they "understand and use a variety of teaching strategies," and that
they "believe that all children can learn and implement supportive structured behaviors." Graduate students are expected to display all the dispositions required of undergraduate candidates and in addition manifest
dispositions such as being "responsible risk-takers and agents of change"
and providing "leadership through collaboration to solve problems"
(GSU, 2004, p. 48).

The implication of this list of dispositions and the prose surrounding it
is that every candidate graduating from a program at GSU will manifest
each of these dispositions in their behavior. Further it is implied that each
and every graduate must display these dispositions in order to be an
effective educational professional. And yet, the problem for candidates
graduating from GSU is that they may be successful in some teaching situations and fail in others. There are major differences in public schools in
the region served by GSU. Within 35 miles of its campus, there are at
approximately 400 public schools, elementary through high school. The
differences between and among these schools are stark. Socioeconomic
characteristics vary widely since the area includes parts of Chicago and
the previously industrial cities of Joliet and Kankakee and since it
includes both very poor and very wealthy suburbs, and several rural areas,
including one rural township that is almost totally populated by African
Americans and is one of the poorest communities in the United States.

The fact is that graduates of GSU have to teach somewhere and most
will find jobs within a 35 mile radius of the University. They do not teach
in abstract or generalized settings. Depending on the district and the

school, they may find no established curriculum in a school, they may be required to follow a district wide plan where each grade is on the same page of the same textbook every day, and they may be in districts which encourage teachers to act entrepreneurially and develop curriculum. They may face students who are accustomed to national and international travel and students whose homes are not equipped with running water or telephones. They may work with parents who hover expectantly over their students as they watch each minute development and parents who keep themselves remote from the school because of their own schooling experiences and their sense of inadequacy in helping their children. Finally, I am not aware of any evidence showing a positive relationship between these required dispositions—or those that show up in the lists of other teacher education institutions—and student achievement. Yet even in the absence of such a showing, there is a compelling feeling that dispositions matter and matter greatly.

Another characteristic of the list appearing in the GSU catalog is that it is applicable to undergraduate students whether they are preparing to teach in the primary grades or chemistry in high school and to graduate students whether they will teach, administer or function as school psychologists. One would expect that the dispositions to be effective as an early childhood educator and those required to be an effective school business manager or a high school counselor are significantly different. There are more complexities that tend to be melted away under the desire to generate a generalized list of dispositions. For instance, educational roles that include direct contact with students such as classroom teaching also involve considerable interaction with other teachers, with superiors such as principals, with parents, and, in some cases, with teaching assistants. Successfully developing and elaborating relationships with adults in these various roles requires the acquisition and display of effective dispositions as well, but there is scant attention—usually one "disposition" under a heading of something like "collaboration."

Uhlenbeck, Verloop, and Beijaard (2002) summarize recent studies of teacher thinking and observe that the outcomes of these studies require attending to the specific situations in which teaching occurs:

Teachers act on what they think is best in a given situation, mostly on the basis of incomplete evidence, without much time for deliberation, and without clear criteria for judging the success of their actions (Airasian, Gullickson, Hahn, & Farland, 1995). While teachers may pursue the same goals, they may do so in different ways, using different strategies, depending on their personal theories about teaching and learning and their personal interpretations of the situation (Leinhardt, 1993; Tomlinson, 1995). The context, that is the school, the classroom, the particular students, the content, and the particular textbook, has considerable influence on teachers' decisions. Teaching shapes and is shaped by the context in which it takes place (Airasian et al., 1995; Leinhardt, 1993). In other words, teaching is defined as the interaction of teacher, students, content, and setting within the larger context of the school (Delandshere & Petrosky, 1994, 1998; Tomlinson, 1995). Consequently, what is judged as appropriate and effective teaching cannot be separated from the context in which it takes place and from the goals a teacher pursues. Teaching, in this view, is not at all like a technique in which teachers apply teaching methods that produce unequivocal learning results in students. Rather, teaching requires considerable judgment, a variety of pedagogical and instructional strategies, and a good understanding of the context in order to select those strategies that best fit. the situation. (p. 245)[2]

These findings concerning teaching in general would seem to be applicable to specific aspects of teaching, including dispositions. Moreover, these findings would seem to be applicable to the variety of responsibilities held by those occupying the wide range of positions typically referred to as "school personnel," that is, school psychologists, superintendents, principals, and so on.

The argument in this paper is that ignoring these complexities tends to render the notion of disposition eventually irrelevant and meaningless. Just as seeing effective teachers as those using generic teaching skills that allegedly promote student learning is now judged a limited view of what it takes to teach effectively, so it appears that requiring display of generic dispositions is likely to severely limit the work that needs to be done in the area of dispositions.

It is precisely in the details and complex web of expectations, aspirations, and limitations associated with a particular time and place that a teacher teaches and an administrator administers—these are the circumstances in which dispositions begin to make most sense. Attempting to overlook or ignore the differences between and among these educational settings can be done but the benefits of doing so are not clear except easing the demands on an assessment system. If we stick with the institution I described above, GSU, it is unlikely that all graduates of GSU displaying the desired dispositions would be equally effective in all of the different possible educational settings offered within the region served by GSU. The question is not whether graduates would be able to become effective in more than one setting, but whether merely displaying the required dispositions would insure their effectiveness. My focus here is delineating what else it takes for a specific individual to become an effective teacher at a specific time in a specific educational setting with a specific group of children, parents, and colleagues. I think of the "what else" as real dispositions.

I am arguing that the concept, disposition, most fully gains its power and usefulness, not in the development of lists of desirable patterns of behavior or lists of attitudes and beliefs, but in the fullness of the irregularity and unpredictably that occurs in the normal course of teaching and administering.

The Language of Dispositions

Before proceeding further it is necessary to distinguish between and among some of the several ways in which the term, dispositions, is used in relation to teachers and teacher education. There appear to be three major usages of the terms in this context. This list is not regarded as full and complete but as a initial step in cataloging uses of disposition.

Metadispositions

There is a usage of dispositions in which the term embraces what appear to be core personality characteristics or qualities or, perhaps, more accurately, general postures toward the self and the other. Metadispositions are basic ways of relating toward the outside world, the dispositional substrata that underlie more specific dispositions. For instance, a metadisposiition of "informed skepticism" might be said to underlie a tendency to ask questions about why something is done the way it is. GSU regards "reasoned eclecticism" as a metadisposition: "Reasoned eclecticism, then, might be well understood as an overarching habit of mind, or a *metadisposition* that encompasses all other knowledge, skills and dispositions" (GSU, 2001, p. 4) The University describes "reasoned eclecticism" in this way:

> Though dependent upon a developed and yet ever-developing grasp of a wide range of current and historical theory, reasoned eclecticism is an intensely pragmatic process by which a professional educator makes decisions at particular times and in particular situations. It continually discerns the key features of its environment with an eye toward productive adjustments which can be made in accord with learner needs. The reasoned eclectic professional understands that s/he is situated in a particular real context with particular dispositions, predilections toward thinking or behaving in a certain way in similar situations, and a repertoire of theory and strategy and other ways of responding that have been developed *a priori*. This approach, although intensely focused on practice, requires the professional educator to possess a growing variety of ready and relevant theoretical constructs with which to posit and critique alternative paths as well as predict likely outcomes.

From this point of view the "perceptual approach" described by Wasicsko and based on Combs work addresses metadispositons, what Wasicsko terms "perceptual orientations:" perception of self, perception of others, perception of purpose, frame of reference [Wasicsko, (n.d.)]. The concept of metadispositon allows seeing dispositions as not merely a pattern of behavior or a set of attitudes and beliefs but as the source and generator of subsequent action.

Dispositions related to ethical and moral standards belong in the category of metadispositions. These dispositions are expected of all individuals, whether or not they belong to the teaching professions: honesty, keeping agreements, respect for others, commitment to social justice. Finally, some commercial screening tests such as the teacher insight test (see http://education.gallup.com/) and the star teacher interview (Haberman, 1995) appear to focus on basic personal orientations or metadispositions.

A Priori Dispositions

A priori dispositions are declarations of how we hope we and/or others will be and behave most of the time. They appear sometimes to serve a creedal function—to provide a set of principles to guide behavior though the actual behavior is rarely specified. These statements appear often to remain at the level of "values." A typical and randomly selected disposition statement from the interstate New Teacher Assessment and Support Consortium (INTASC) core standards illustrates this point: "The teacher is committed to continuous learning and engages in professional discourse about subject matter knowledge and children's learning of the discipline." Without a full analysis of this statement, it is quite evident that this statement assumes a context—one in which teachers talk with each other about knowledge and how children learn particular kinds of discipline. This, however, is not a continuous activity, but one that takes place in specific kinds of contexts—professional development settings, the teacher's lounge, cocktails on Friday night, university classrooms. In addition, this preferred discourse might be manifest in innumerable ways.

Dispositions-in-Action[3]

At this level, dispositions are evidenced in behavior. and are shaped by the context in which the individual finds themselves. For this reason it is impossible to list the various ways in which individuals might display the INTASC disposition cited above; how it might play out in actual behavior depends not merely on "possessing" the disposition, but the context in which the person is working. Take Abraham, for example. He appears skeptical of new ways of thinking about knowledge and how children learn it. He is not an early adopter of the latest innovation. He engages in discussion but he is content to let others try it out first and will adopt a new way of doing something when he is dissatisfied with his current way of doing it. He has good reason for being cautious at his school. The culture of his school does not support innovators and risk-takers. Nancy, on the other hand, is constantly trying out new ways of thinking about the subject she teaches; she goes to conferences and subscribes to more journals than anyone could possibly read. Each of her professional years is littered with failed attempts as well as successes to find more effective ways to teach. And her principal holds her up as example of what a good professional should be doing. Who do we say exhibits the disposition in action?

As teacher educators we are most adept at producing lists of a priori dispositions. This is like producing a list of virtues without attending to how they are developed or displayed in someone's life. Too often we stop with this kind of an effort without analyzing the substrata on which they rest or how they are manifested in actual behavior. As a result much of the talk about dispositions takes on a catechismal aura. Seen in their proper context, a prior dispositions have a significant role to play in the development of candidates as do metadispositions. This paper however focuses on dispositions-in-action and undertakes to give an account of their character and use.

What is a Disposition-in-Action?

Mumford opens his study of dispositions by observing that

> Dispositions are considered ethereal: properties that somehow are not always manifest but which seem to lurk in a mysterious realm intermediate between potentiality and actuality. It is this feature that challenges us to bring dispositions down to earth and account for them in terms of what is actual. (Mumford, 1998, p. 4).

Because dispositions have this problematic quality, it is difficult to talk about them in an unproblematic way. Hopefully, this chapter will not fall victim to the difficulty.

Dispositions, as we intuitively understand them in the context of teacher education, differ from other kinds of dispositions. For instance, we might say that glass has the disposition of fragility. By this we mean that when hit with a certain amount of force, glass breaks. By and large, these kinds of dispositions can be expressed as cases of "if … then." Thus, if struck with a certain amount of force, glass breaks. But this is not the case with cases that are more complex and not susceptible to expression in a simple "if-then" statement. As Mumford (1998) points out, the disposition, bravery, is "an example of a disposition which is a complex of subdispositions" (p. 8) Describing someone as brave requires, first, that the person knows that the situation In which s/he will act is dangerous in some way and then acts appropriately in the face of that danger or fear. Further the disposition, bravery, raises a number of other questions, one of which is whether it is possible that a person is brave but has never had an opportunity to display bravery. Arnstine provides an extended discussion of the disposition, curiosity (pp. 267-291). For him, curiosity is usually ascribed to someone who engages in exploratory behavior for no known purpose. And he goes on to suggest that one can be in a state of curiosity even without overt behavior. I may be curious about how a mechanical device works and speculate about it while sitting in my sofa staring out the window.

Many of the dispositions that I have characterized as a prior dispositions that institutions and teacher education organizations have identified are in the complex category along with bravery and curiosity. Take, for instance, the so-called INTASC standards. I reproduce below the knowledge, disposition, and performance categories associated with Principle #4.

Knowledge

- The teacher understands the cognitive processes associated with various kinds of learning (e.g., critical and creative thinking, problem structuring and problem solving, invention, memorization, and recall) and how these processes can be stimulated.
- The teacher understands principles and techniques, along with advantages and limitations, associated with various instructional strategies (e.g. cooperative learning, direct instruction, discovery learning, whole group discussion, independent study, interdisciplinary instruction).
- The teacher knows how to enhance learning through the use of a wide variety of materials as well as human and technological resources (e.g. computers, audio-visual technologies, videotapes and discs, local experts, primary documents and artifacts, texts, reference books, literature, and other print resources).

Dispositions

- The teacher values the development of students' critical thinking, independent problem solving, and performance capabilities.

- The teacher values flexibility and reciprocity in the teaching process as necessary for adapting instruction to student responses, ideas, and needs.

Performances

- The teacher carefully evaluates how to achieve learning goals, choosing alternative teaching strategies and materials to achieve different instructional purposes and to meet student needs (e.g., developmental stages, prior knowledge, learning styles, and interests).
- The teacher uses multiple teaching and learning strategies to engage students in active learning opportunities that promote the development of critical thinking, problem solving, and performance capabilities and that help student assume responsibility for identifying and using learning resources.
- The teacher constantly monitors and adjusts strategies in response to learner feedback. The teacher varies his or her role in the instructional process (e.g., instructor, facilitator, coach, audience) in relation to the content and purposes of instruction and the needs of students.
- The teacher develops a variety of clear, accurate presentations and representations of concepts, using alternative explanations to assist students' understanding and presenting diverse perspectives to encourage critical thinking. (INTASC, pp. 20-21)

The dispositions listed here are of the complex, not the simple, variety. Moreover, there appears to be a logic at work in the distinction among knowledge, dispositions, and performances. The preface to the INTASC document provides some clues about this relationship. The task force says that it began with a "common core of knowledge and skills that should be acquired by all new teachers" (p. 6). The preface continues:

> Like the first tier of assessment for licensing in virtually all other professions, this "common core" is intended to outline the common principles and foundations of practice that cut across specialty areas—the knowledge of student learning and development, curriculum and teaching, contexts and purposes which creates a set of professional understandings, abilities, and commitments that all teachers share. (p. 6)

This declaration seems to suggest that a "set of professional understandings, abilities, and commitments" flow from this knowledge and understanding. It appears that these professional understandings, abilities, and commitments constitute dispositions. Later, the task force calls attention to an important aspect of these standards—they are "performance-based" which presumably accounts for the inclusion of the category, performances. The logic relating knowledge, dispositions, and performances can be represented, it would seem, in this way:

knowledge + disposition results in performance

This reading is supported by an analysis of the language used in the various categories. The knowledge statements use verbs such as "understands" and "knows;" dispositions statements use verbs such as "values," "appreciates," "believes," and "realizes"; and performances statements use verbs such "evaluates," "uses," "monitors," "develops," "creates," and so on.

The review of the categories used in the INTASC model standards suggests that dispositions function as intermediaries between knowing something—content matter, a process, a skill—and a performance, or an identifiable behavior or set of behaviors. The team that wrote these standards, however, does not provide an account of how dispositions carry out their role. As they appear in the INTASC standards, dispositions continue to appear, as Mumford suggests, "to lurk in a mysterious realm intermediate between potentiality and actuality." In the remainder of this section, I propose to develop an account of dispositions that brings their shape into sharper focus. I will suggest that a disposition might be conceptualized as a system comprised of three interrelated elements: *valuing, strategy,* and *intention.* [4]

Valuing

By *valuing* I refer to the desire for something to be realized, a want. It encompasses more than a favorable attitude or a mere belief that a certain state of affairs should be achieved. It has about the quality of envisioning, of seeing how the future can unfold. Examples of uses of the term, value, as I intend to use it, are provided by the sample from the INTASC standard quoted above and in instances I have selected from various other sources.

- NCATE's Standard 4 includes a this statement under the acceptable column: "Candidates learn to develop and teach lessons that incorporate diversity and develop a classroom and school climate that *values* diversity." (NCATE, 2002, p. 29)

- The College of Charleston includes the following statements in its list of dispositions expected of its candidates:

  o *Value* and respect for individual difference
  o *Value* positive human interactions
  o *Value* collaborative, and cooperative work (College of Charleston, 2004).

- Duke University describes its teacher education candidates as being "cooperative team members" who "*value* and seek out the experience and expertise of others" (Duke University, n.d., p. 8)

This list can be expanded almost indefinitely with examples from other teacher education colleges. These examples illustrate how the term "value" is used repeatedly in characterizing what candidates should be like and do. At the same time, there is considerable contamination in the air surrounding the concept of values and valuing. There are "value" stocks and portfolios for the investor. And a phrase such as the "value of human life" appears frequently in our talk. When pluralized to "values," the concept refers to those principles that we hold dear. It is in the last sense that the concept values functions as a component of a disposition.

Without the component of "values," whether implicit or explicit, there is no disposition. Values are the driving force, the aspect of a disposition that responds to the question, Why or why bother? Presumably these questions are addressed in the area of philosophical and social foundations and the area of curriculum that are conventionally included in teacher education programs. It would seem—though it is infrequently articulated—that these areas have explicit responsibility for assisting teacher education candidates in developing the values and vision that will drive their professional careers. Curriculum has a special responsibility in envisioning what students need to learn if they are to develop into competent adults in our society—though unfortunately curriculum has too often seen its purpose as developing endless lists of goals and objectives as though we can realize our visions if we atomize learning sufficiently.

Strategy

The second component of a disposition is *strategy*. Whereas values supply the response to the question why engage in a pattern of behavior, strategy responds to the question of how—How should behavior be organized in order to realize the sought after value? This is the domain of those areas that we refer to as "instruction," "methods," "techniques," and, yes, even "strategies." Although the terms I have just listed sometimes convey the notion I am after, the phrase, strategic planning, does a better job. I understand strategy as the means we use to relate some piece of thinking or action to a larger piece of thinking, action, or a vision. Strategy is inherently relational and is the means used to connect something to a bigger something, for example, a value. Strategies range from how to ask a question to lesson plans to curriculum, from ordering a student to sit down to a progressive discipline program, from processing a voucher to a budget. They represent the means by which something will (hopefully) be achieved.[5]

Intention

The third component of a disposition is *intention*. This is the most troublesome component of the notion of disposition and understandably so because delineating the concept, intention, is difficult.

Intention, as Searle has (1983) pointed out, is used in two different ways. One way manifests itself when a speaker declares what he/she will do. This is the kind of statement that often made in political campaigns, in interviews when candidates are asked what they would do if they were hired, in proposals submitted for funding. Searle describes this form of intention as "prior intention." Prior intention sets out the conditions that ensuing action will satisfy. The educational establishment, including teacher education, gives considerable attention to developing statements of "prior intention." "Prior intention" is called by many other names, including "vision," "goals," "objectives," "standards," "learner outcomes," "benchmarks"—the list seems very long, if not endless. In many cases, these statements of prior intention join values and strategy in the form of "I will do this in order that..." Moreover, often a great deal of attention is given to how some of these variants of prior intention are formulated. The aim is to insure that objective determination can be made about whether the conditions stated in the prior intention are satisfied by ensuing action.

Searle (1983) labels the other predominate usage of the term, intention, as "intention-in-action." Prior intention might be said to "represent" what someone will do. "Intention-in-action," on the other hand, "presents"—it is observable in the event which it produces. In the case of "intention-in-action" the correlate in teacher education consist of exercises which permit "authentic assessment" or of situations in which candidates carry out teaching, administrative and other relevant tasks in "real" situations usually in the context of practica or internships such as student teaching.

Intention, as Searle (1983) observes, represents our attempt to "fit" circumstances or events outside of us—the world—to representations or expectations in our mind. I accept Searle's notion that "prior intention" causes "intention-in-action" which causes some change in the external world so that it fulfills or moves the world closer to the representation implied in my prior intention. For instance, if I am an administrator, I might announce that I intend to develop and implement a specific program designed to increase parental participation in the school. In this case, I apparently have represented to myself a situation in which parents are more involved in the goings-on at school. Out of this emerges my declaration that I will make this representation reality by implementing a program—this declaration being my "prior intention." Presumably I develop and follow some sort of strategy as this program takes shape and becomes reality. My following out this strategy represents "intention-in-action and results in a series of identifiable events—meetings, memos, talks with individuals, and so forth.

Sometimes intention-in-action" occurs without a "prior intention." On any given morning, I might well walk to my garage, start my car, and drive to work. I may or may not declare to myself or someone else my prior intention to drive to work. Some things I just do and it is possible to infer my prior intention from what I do, but as the actor I do not always work from explicit statement of it. This provides a response to a troublesome aspect of Lilian Katz's (1993) tentative definition of a disposition: "A disposition is a pattern of behavior exhibited frequently and in the absence of coercion, and constituting a habit of mind under *some conscious and voluntary control*, and that is intentional and oriented to broad goals" [emphasis added] (p. 10). Katz goes on to explain why she uses the term "habit of mind":

> The term "habit of mind" is used to distinguish dispositions from mindless and unpremeditated habitual behavior like obeying traffic lights and fastening seat belts. Both such habits can be thought to have some motivational and intentional dimensions in an ultimate sense. However, they are such strong and frequent habits of action that they are typically enacted with little or no conscious engagement of motives or intentions. These habits, however, may relatively trivial and commonplace acts that are part of a general disposition to be obedient, law-abiding, or cautious. (p. 10)

Katz' view seems to create an almost impossible situation requiring that in teaching, at least good teaching, every action, every behavior, during the day derives from a "prior intention." That is, as I understand Katz, in order to demonstrate a disposition, I would be required to formulate a "prior intention" and then follow through with "intention-in-action." Searle, on the other hand, observes that some actions are spontaneous; as he says, "Like many things one does, I just do these actions: I just act." But that does not mean such actions are not intentional. If you were observing me teaching, you might ask, 'Why did you ask that question? Did you form an intention before you asked it?" I might well respond,

"No, I just asked it." Not having formed a prior intention or conscious intent does not render my action unintentional.

It appears that Katz (1993) is attempting to distinguish intentional from unintentional action when she uses words such as "mindless," "unpremeditated" and "no conscious engagement." There are unintended actions that occur frequently when teaching. The question that I asked in our previous example may have occurred during study of an historical event and the way I framed the question may have offended a student whose lineage includes participants in that event. I did not intend that offense, but it occurred as a result of my action.

Context

I have now outlined the three components of a "disposition:" values, strategies, and intention. But we are not finished with our analysis of what constitutes a disposition. So far what I have outlined is a way of looking at any intentional action or behavior. But disposition is, or results in, a particular kind of intentional action or behavior. It is behavior or action that is occurs in a given context at a given time; it is behavior or action that is related in an as yet unclear and complicated way to the context in which it occurs. The INTASC task force recognizes the importance of context when using the standards, if not only the dispositions, which it proposes:

> Recognizing that applications of these common understandings and commitments [as represented in the Standards] are manifested in specific contexts defined by students, subjects, and school levels, among others, we emphasize that "common core" standards are not analogous to 'generic' or context-free teaching behaviors. The assessment of specific teaching decisions and actions must occur in varied contexts that will require varied responses. In some cases, these are grounded in the discipline being taught: thus, subject-specific pedagogical decisions need to be evaluated in the context of subject-specific standards.... In other cases, contextual considerations must be made part of the assessment structure and response possibilities. (INTASC, 1992, p. 7)

It is tempting to employ any number of words to suggest the relationship between context and the manifestation of a disposition. One might say for instance that a context triggers, stimulates, provokes, evokes, or causes manifestation of a disposition. This might be the case if we are working with dispositions of the simpler "if ... then" variety. But still there is a discernible connection between disposition and context. Consider how parents sometimes instruct their children regarding dispositions: "When we are at Grandma's house, do not talk about that" (or "use that kind of language"); or, "You cannot wear that dress to church." When the young child goes to Grandma's house, it is not the context that causes the child to refrain from talking about certain topics and it is not necessarily the parent's admonition. The child simply does it and may or may not keep the parental admonition in mind.

There are a number of approaches that provide guidance in how we can appreciate how dispositions and context become entangled and how they may, in fact, successfully resist efforts to unentangle them. We might turn to Wittgenstein, for instance, to decipher why the child talks as s/he does at Grandma's house. In this case, the instruction from the parent might be instruction about what Wittgenstein (1958) labels "a language game" (*sprachspiel*) that, in turn is a part of a "form of life." Wittgenstein says it more formally when he writes: "Here the term 'language-game' is meant to bring into prominence the fact that the speaking of a language is part of an activity, or a form of life" (para. 23). And, it appears, from Wittgenstein, that "forms of life" are "what has to be accepted, the given" (p. 227). If we accept Wittgenstein's approach, we would say that the context, the school, the classroom—its culture, its customs, its way of doing things, is "a form of life" that is simply accepted and the teacher acts out "teaching games," behaves within the conventions of what is taken to be "teaching" in that situation. Dispositions then are manifested within a given way of doing things that is not questioned nor questionable by the participants. Further, the patterns of behavior manifesting dispositions are acted out by following conventions, agreed upon ways of doing things.

In addition to Wittgenstein (1958), we can appeal to Searle (1983; see also Searle, 1995, pp. 127-147) for help in understanding the relationship between dispositions and context. Searle introduces the notion of background in his book *Intentionality* as he attempts to explain how intentions are limited: to use Searle's (1983) example, we know what it means to say "I intend to run for the Presidency of the United States" but we have no idea how to understand someone who says, "I intend to become a coffee cup" (p. 142). Put more formally,

> The Background is a set of nonrepresentational mental capacities that enable all representing to take place. Intentional states only have the conditions of satisfaction that they do, and thus only are the states that they are, against a Background of abilities that are not themselves Intentional states. (p. 145)

With a tip of his hat to Ryle's distinction between "knowing that" and "knowing how," Searle argues that "in order that I can now have the Intentional states that I do I must have certain kinds of know-how I must know how things are and I must know how to do things" (p. 143).

Searle's (1983) explication of "background," like Wittgenstein's (1958) "forms of life," helps clarify that the relationship between "context" and behavior is not cause and effect; context does not trigger, does not cause, behavior. It permits and shapes intention and behavior. Bourdieu (1980) allows us to extend this analysis further, and I suggest we begin with a warning he provides:

> Those who have the monopoly on discourse about the social world think differently when they are thinking about themselves and about others (that is, other classes): they are readily spiritualist as regards themselves, materialists toward others, liberal for themselves and dirigiste for others, and with equal logic, ecological and intellectualist for themselves and mechanist for others. (p. 80)

Here Bourdieu warns against the tendency by "outsiders"—like this author and other writers and researchers—to regard others—teachers—as acting mechanically or as controlled by some outward force, "context," in this case.

To escape this dualism which wants to see individuals as mechanical agents following, say, "enlightened self-interest" or as controlled by social structures, Bourdieu (1990) proposes examining the practical actions of individuals. To do this, he develops two basic and interrelated concepts: habitus and field. This quotation outlines how Bourdieu thinks of habitus:

> The conditionings associated with a particular class of conditions of existence produce *habitus*, systems of durable, transposable dispositions, structured structures predisposed to function as structuring structures, that is, as principles which generate and organize practices and representations that can be objectively adapted to their outcomes without presupposing a conscious aiming at ends or an express mastery of the operations necessary in order to attain them. Objectively 'regulated' and "regular" without being in any way the product of obedience to rules, they can be collectively orchestrated without being the product of the organizing action of a conductor. (p. 53)

The other concept is *field*. Lingard and Christie (2003) provide a description of how Bordieu understands the concept, "field" and, they suggest in a general way, the relationship of habitus to field.

Bourdieu (1990) viewed fields as socially-constituted areas of activity. He wrote of the economic field, the political field, the fields of cultural production (the artistic field, literary field, scientific field, etc.), the educational field, and the field of the school. Fields have their own structures, interests and preferences; their own "rules of the game"; their own agents, differentially constituted; their own power struggles. It is in relation to particular fields that the habitus becomes active. Socially marked interests, agents and power relationships constitute fields, and an individual's habitus may be more or less well adapted to the demands of a particular field. There is a plurality of fields, thus a plurality of logics, a plurality of commonplace ideas, and a plurality of habitus (p. 324).

The Syntax of Dispositions

The foregoing discussion of the components of a disposition and their relationship to context suggests that the syntax of dispositions might be formulated as follows:

> Constraints and possibilities of context + an intention-in-action + values to be realized + pursuing selected strategies.

All of these elements must be present in order for a disposition to be activated and result in observable action. Thinking of the syntax in this way enables fairly quick and accurate analysis of observed behavior pursued by a teacher. If a pattern of teaching behavior is not producing the desired result, this syntax suggests that a systematic examination of context, levels of intention, strategies, and values will assist in identifying where change or adjustment is necessary.

It should be noted that dispositions do not appear in isolation from one another; they frequently appear to be tangled together and at times appear to defy untwisting and straightening out for the kind of analysis that is needed.

Some Examples of Analysis of Disposition

Elmer

When Elmer retired as a manager, he decided to pursue a teaching certificate by completing an alternative certification program. On the state basic skills exams and other tests of subject matter, he scored higher than most of his colleagues in the cohort finishing the program; on the state elementary education program he scored among the top 25%. Once of the university classroom and in charge of a classroom, disaster quickly loomed. As one of his supervisors put it, he wanted to be friends with his primary students rather than their teacher and while he appeared to have sufficient knowledge to teach reading. There was, to put it bluntly, little learning going on. Mentors were sent into his classroom and other forms of help were proferred and usually accepted.

At the time this case was developing, we did not have the framework I have outlined above. Now it is clear that the problems most likely stemmed from three areas: values, intention, and context. Elmer valued relating to the students as though he were a grandfather or an uncle, someone who would be emotionally supportive and allow a wide range of expression for the students. In short, his values were not appropriate for the context in which he was now operating. At the same time, though he professed the intention to implement different strategies in teaching reading and even wrote well developed lesson plans that reflected this intention, he failed on most days to carry through. In short he did not maintain his intention-in-action. He could conceptualize what was needed but did not carry it through at a detailed level.

Tanya

Tanya was a candidate in a graduate level early childhood education program. She was attracted to the program because she had served as a teacher's aide in early childhood education settings for a few years after her children began school.

Her grades in courses were mostly As; she was articulate both orally and in writing. She had completed more than 135 hours of prestudent teaching experiences in several different settings; there were no negative comments regarding her performance during these experiences.

When she began student teaching, problems began to surface. Tanya's performance was puzzling. Some days she would perform very well for part of the day; the rest of the day she appeared lethargic and without direction. Other days, she seemed to go through "the motions." As time went on, her daily lesson plans were less and less complete. Under the policies and procedures of the College of Education, her student teacher supervisor asked the Student Progress committee to review her student teaching performance. Her supervisor indicated that at her current level of performance, Tanya would not meet the criteria to be recommended for certification.

At a meeting with the student progress committee, Tanya complained about the demands of student teaching and explained that she was unprepared because sometimes by the time she finished caring for her children and her household, it was late evening before she had time to start planning for the next day. She told the committee that she went to bed at 11:00 pm because she needed her sleep and that getting her sleep was more important that finishing her planning for the next day. Besides, she said, she had never had to do all this planning when she worked as a teacher's aide.

A cursory review of Tanya's case suggests that her problems stem from the area of intention. Further discussion with her supervising teacher indicated that even when she had developed satisfactory lesson plans, her performance was less than satisfactory—she was disorganized and seemed "to run out of gas." Tanya was having trouble with both levels of intention—a priori and in action. Finally, the context in which she was now operating was not the same as when she was a teacher's aide. To help

Tanya develop the required levels of intention, an accountability system was set in place. One of her fellow students agreed to take a call from Tanya every morning so that Tanya could inform her fellow student of what she had done to prepare for the day; another fellow student took her call every evening during which Tanya described how she developed and maintained momentum throughout the day, including when her intention-in-action began to dissipate and how she managed to recover.

Pete

Pete was a student in an alternative certification program. He had successfully met the academic requirements for admission and had passed the star teacher interview. Shortly after he began the program, his behavior began to create minor problems. He frequently had excuses about why his work was late; these assignments were submitted a day or more late and without exception were at least acceptable. At other times, he seemed withdrawn and to be withholding judgments about his colleagues and with his teachers; a typical posture in class was arms folded across his chest. He was something of a grump, often being overheard complaining to his colleagues that the required assignments were "busy work." As he progressed through the program, several of his colleagues resisted when they were assigned to work with him on group projects. From time to time, Pete was simply absent without first notifying his instructor; he would return to class asking, "Did I miss anything?"

The assessment committee reviewed Pete's performance as it did the performance of all students. It decided that a representative of the committee should meet with Pete and explain to him that while his academic work was acceptable, his behavior seemed to signal potential problems. When confronted with this assessment, Pete became very defensive. He insisted on knowing precisely what he was doing wrong; he wanted to know where the rules and policies in the student handbook and other documents indicated that what he was doing was unacceptable.

As he proceeded into full-time teaching, these patterns became more pronounced, particularly as he now was responsible both to the school system in which he was teaching and to the academic program at the University. Pete seemed to have confused the context in which he was studying and working with an excessively bureaucratic entity, perhaps closer to the kind of organization he had worked at previously.

We have developed terminology to describe two of the intertwined dispositions in this example: linear thinking and uncoachability. Linear thinking often creates havoc for some students because it does not allow them to address effectively the messiness of teaching and even talk about teaching; students who predominately think in a linear fashion demand to know what the rules are and why there are not reliable rules. This is the strategy that Pete wants to make work in this situation, but it is the wrong for the context; it may have worked in his previous career but here matters are more ambiguous and "messy" which renders his strategy virtually useless and unworkable.

At the same time, this case presents an individual who is not open to coaching; he wants to control the context and shape it to his satisfaction—hence the demand for statements in the student handbook. Pete misreads the context. Not only is the strategy he pursues unworkable in this context, he will likely remain uncoachable until he "sees" that he is in a new context.

Pete's case is the most difficult of those described in this section. His ability to resist coaching rests on his belief in the thinking strategy he has adopted and in his apparent unwillingness to "read" the context. The approach most likely to successfully help Pete out of his situation is an approach that causes him to step outside of the context and his investment in it and to describe it empirically. This may be a long shot, but until he is able to develop the capacity to engage in reflexive activity, he will likely remain headed for disaster in the classroom.

Implications of Dispositions-in-Action

Focusing on dispositions-in-action allows one to escape the regulatory view of dispositions in which a pre-determined template is placed on individuals and problems result from deviance. The regulatory approach does not allow for response to context and often misses the most important undesirable and desirable dispositions.

NOTES

1. I am indebted, in part, to Elkind (1994 and 1997) for help in formulating the difference between modernist and postmodernist approaches to several aspects of education, including teacher education.
2. Bibliographic data for references in the quotation from Uhlenbeck's article appear in the references section.
3. I am aware that Ritchhart (2002) titles a section in one of his chapters as "Dispositions in Action." Ritchhart was not the source of my notion of "disposition in action." I am indebted to John Searle (for this suggestion—I simply worked by analogy from his notion of "intention-in-action" to arrive at "disposition in action."
4. I am well aware that the model of disposition presented below is similar in some ways to the model developed by David Perkins, Eileen Jay, and Shari Tishman (1993) and to the four-aspect model presented by Ritchhart (2002) in *Intellectual Character*. While I may have been unconsciously influ-

enced by the work of these authors, my recollection is that I arrived at a triad notion of dispositions in 2000 as my colleagues and I were developing the conceptual framework for teacher education at GSU.

5. I am aware that this version of what constitutes a strategy is incomplete. A fuller discussion of strategy would require at least taking up Bourdieu's (1990) notion of strategy which I understand as being analogous to "moves in a game" that may not be consciously chosen but derive from a feel for the game and as different from "following the rules." The definition I provide here is preliminary.

REFERENCES

Airasian, P., Gullickson, A., Hahn, L., & Farland, D. (1995). *Teacher self-evaluation: The literature in perspective.* Kalamazoo, MI: CREATE.

Bourdieu, P. (1990) *The logic of practice.* (R. Nice, Trans.). Palo Alto, CA: Stanford University Press.

College of Charleston. (2004) *School of education dispositions of effective teachers: Advanced study M. Ed.* Retrieved August 15, 2005, from http://www.cofc.edu/SchoolofEducation/Accreditation_2004/Evidence_List/concept_frame/0048_MEd_Dispos.doc

Delandshere, G., & Petrosky, A. K. (1998). Assessment of complex performances: Limitations of key measurement assumptions. *Educational Researcher, 27*(2), 14-24.

Delandshere, G., & Petrosky, A. R. (1994). Capturing teachers' knowledge: Performance assessment and post-structuralism. *Educational Researcher, 23*(5), 11-18.

Duke University (n.d.) *The conceptual framework for the Duke University teacher preparation programs.* Retrieved May 3, 2007, from http://www.duke.edu/web/teaching/documents/ncate/dutppcf.pdf

Elkind, D. (1994). *Ties that stress: The new family imbalance.* Cambridge, MA: Harvard University Press

Elkind, D. (1997) The death of child nature: Education in the postmodern world. *Phi Delta Kappan, 79*(3), 241-245.

Governors State University. (2001). *Conceptual framework.* Retrieved July 3, 2005, from at http://www.govst.edu/uploadedFiles/CF_112901.pdf

Governors State University. (2004). Evaluation of student knowledge, skills, and dispositions. *2004-2005 catalog.* Retrieved July 12, 2005, from at http://www.govst.edu/catalog/teach_ed_cert_cat.htm

Haberman, M. (1995). *Star teachers of children in poverty.* Indianopolis, IN: Kappa Delta Pi.

Interstate New Teacher Assessment Consortium. (1992). *Model standards for beginning teacher licensing, assessment and development: A resource for state dialogue.* Washington, DC: Council of Chief State School Officers.

Katz, L. (1993) *Dispositions: Definitions and implications for early childhood practice.* Retrieved December 15, 2004, from at http://ceep.crc.uiuc.edu/eecearchive/books/disposit.html

Leinhardt, G. (1993). On teaching. In R. Glaser (Ed.), *Advances in instructional psychology* (pp. 1-54). Hillsdale, NJ: Erlbaum.

Lingard, B., & Christie, P. (2003) Leading theory: Bourdieu and the field of educational leadership. *International Journal of Leadership in Education, 6*(4), 317-333.

Mumford, S. (1998). *Dispositions.* New York: Oxford University Press.

National Council for the Accreditation of Teacher Education. (2002). *Professional standards: Accreditation of schools, colleges, and departments of education.* Washington, DC: NCATE.

Perkins, D., Jay, E., & Tishman, S. (1993). Beyond abilities: A dispositional theory of thinking. *The Merrill-Palmer Quarterly, 39*(1), 1-21.

Ritchhart, R. (2002). *Intellectual character: What it is, why it matters, and how to get it.* San Francisco: Jossey-Bass.

Ryle, G. (1949). *The concept of mind.* Chicago: The University of Chicago Press.

Searle, J. R. (1983) *Intentionality, an essay in the philosophy of mind.* New York: Cambridge University Press.

Searle, J. R. (1995) *The construction of social reality.* New York: Free Press.

Tomlinson, P. (1995). Can competence profiling work for effective teacher preparation? Part II: Pitfalls and principles. *Oxford Review of Education, 21*(3), 299-314.

Uhlenbeck, A. M., Verloop, N., & Beijaard, D. (2002). Requriements for an assessment procedure for beginning teachers: Implications from recent theories on teaching and assessment. *Teachers College Record, 104*(2), 242-272.

Wasicsko, M. M. (n.d.) Assessing eductor dispositions: A perceptual psychological approach. Retrieved September 13, 2005, from http://www.educatordispositions.org/dispositions/Training%20Materials/Manual103.pdf

Wittgenstein, L. (1958) *Philosophical investigations* (G. E. M. Anscombe, Trans.). New York: MacMillan.

CHAPTER 6

WE TEACH WHO WE ARE

The Intersection of Teacher Formation and Educator Dispositions

Sally Z. Hare

We teach who we are.

Parker J. Palmer's words have resonated with me since I first heard him talk about teacher formation in 1994. A few years later, I enthusiastically accepted Parker's invitation to facilitate the *Courage to Teach*[1] in one of four pilot sites in the United States. I have now been involved in this work for the past decade, creating space for educational professionals to renew their vocational energy. My heart is heavy with the realization that we are losing teachers at the rate of nearly a thousand every school day ("Teacher Attrition," 2005, p. 1). After a lifetime in teaching and teacher education, I feel deeply the pain and turmoil in our educational world. I have great respect for teachers, and I am passionate in my desire to support them in their important work. We, in teacher education programs like the one in which I have taught for more than 30 years, seem to be inadequately providing educators with the inner

Dispositions in Teacher Education, pp. 139–149

resources to stay the course, to hold onto the passion that drew them to teaching.

With the NCATE (National Council of Accreditation for Teacher Education) standards incorporating dispositions and with the National Academy of Education's Committee on Teacher Education report also including a discussion of dispositions in *Preparing Teachers for a Changing World* (Darling-Hammon & Bransford, 2005), I have felt hopeful that this emphasis on dispositions might offer insights for teacher education. When Dr. Larry Freeman, retired Governor's State University dean of education, invited me to reflect on educator dispositions through the lens of teacher formation for a book he was editing, I was pleased to enter the discourse. Larry was already a leader in the growing work of educator dispositions when he was drawn to the *Courage to Teach* and completed the national facilitator preparation program. Then Larry's tragic death in 2006 interrupted his plans for this book on dispositions. I am grateful that Mary Diez and James Rath have picked up the mantle, determined to see Larry's vision to fruition. I especially appreciate this opportunity to honor Larry's memory by reflecting from this spot at which he stood, this intersection of teacher formation and teacher dispositions.

TEACHER FORMATION

Teacher formation is grounded in Parker Palmer's (1998) theory that "teaching, like any truly human activity, emerges from one's inwardness, for better or worse" (p. 2). In his book *The Courage to Teach*, Palmer not only explores the importance of the teacher's inner life, but also raises the question of how the teacher's selfhood might be a legitimate topic in education. "Good teaching," he writes, "requires self-knowledge; it is a secret hidden in plain sight" (p. 3).

In *Courage to Teach* retreats across the continent, skilled facilitators create the space for teachers to explore the question of who is the self that teaches. As I have become grounded in the principles and practices of teacher formation, I have come to understand that methodology and teaching techniques, although unquestionably important in teacher education, take a distant second to teachers' knowing who they are. My graduate and undergraduate students over the years have taught me the same holds true for educational philosophy and teaching styles. How can we possibly develop a teaching philosophy or create a teaching style until we are clear about our own personal identity, until we are able to define our own integrity? Palmer (1998) explains the role of technique as unfolding in this way: "as we learn more about who we are, we can learn techniques that reveal rather than conceal the personhood from which good teaching comes" (p. 24).

Holding Larry's questions of how dispositions look through a lens shaped by teacher formation, I reflect on where dispositions fit into my understanding of the critical role of self-knowledge in teacher development. Katz and Raths' (1985) framing of dispositions as "habits of the mind, not mindless habits" (p. 303) rings true for me, and I see Parker Palmer's (2004) illustration of life on the Mobius strip[2] (pp. 39-49) as offering insight into the development of these mindful habits. Palmer writes that we come into this world as whole human beings with birthright gifts, with the seed of true self. In that birthright wholeness, I recognize that our inner core also contains the seeds from which our dispositions develop, for better and worse.

Palmer (2004) illustrates this stage with a strip of paper, one side of which represents our outer life, the other side our inner life. Representing the earliest stage of life, he says the paper symbolizes our wholeness, with total integration between the outer and inner. The next years of our lives—through elementary and high school and young adulthood—are too often filled with such deforming experiences that we may forget who we are. Our lives become divided, and Palmer uses the strip of paper to represent the wall or barrier between the inner truth and outer world. At best, we may lose sight of our innate dispositions, the potential of our seeds of true self; at worst, we give them up when our culture and the significant adults in our lives convince us that our birthright gifts, including our dispositions, are not valued.

Instructing us to join the ends of the strip of paper, giving one a half-twist, Palmer (2004) guides us into creating a Mobius strip. The resulting figure seemingly has no outside or inside, but rather, two apparent sides which cocreate each other. The sides, of course, are an illusion, and we can trace our finger, without lifting it from the paper, across the entire strip. The Mobius strip, Palmer tells us, symbolizes our full-circle journey to the place we began, "for the Mobius strip is the adult version of the wholeness into which we were born" (p. 48). In this stage our dispositions and our actions, our inner and outer, are seamless. We truly teach who we are.

Teaching comes from the identity and integrity of the teacher, according to Palmer (1998, p. 10). He describes the concepts of identity and integrity in *The Courage to Teach: Exploring the Inner Landscape of a Teacher's Life* as **not** "only our noble features," but also as our "shadows and limits, our wounds and fears," as well as "our strengths and potentials" (p. 13). Our identity results from the complex forces that make us who we are, the intersection of inner and outer that converge into "the irreducible mystery of being human." Our integrity is the wholeness within that intersection, wholeness that we must reclaim throughout our lives as the forces of the outer world continuously form and reform and even deform us. Palmer writes that "(i)ntegrity requires that I discern what is integral to my selfhood, what fits and what does not" (p. 13). As I live into Larry's questions, I realize this discernment also includes our dispositions.

DEFINING DISPOSITIONS

Using the lens of teacher formation, I think about how I want to define the word *disposition*. In the current education literature, some writers use the words *attitudes* or *beliefs* or *values* synonymously with *dispositions*; others use those words in their definitions of *disposition*. For example, the NCATE definition refers to dispositions as

> the values, commitments, and professional ethics that influence behaviors toward students, families, colleagues, and communities and affect student learning, motivation, and development as well as the educator's own professional growth. Dispositions are guided by beliefs and attitudes related to values such as caring, fairness, honesty, responsibility, and social justice. (NCATE, 2002, p. 53)

Freeman's (2003) analysis of the literature suggests that dispositions replaced attitudes in teacher education discourse in the mid-1980s (p. 2).

In the language of formation, we often use metaphors, particularly those of nature and gardening, so I choose the metaphor of soil in a flower pot to help me to define *dispositions* (see Figure 6.1). Picture the uppermost layer of soil as dispositions. The second layer is thought, the thinking that informs the dispositions. Going a bit deeper, we find the third layer, feelings, which we know from current brain research are interdependent with thought, so the second and third layers are not cleanly separated, but each bleeds a bit into the other. Next we dig into the fourth layer, or values. Parker Palmer (1995) writes about the clear connection in his own life between thinking, feeling, and values:

> I tend to think most about that which I value, and my feelings are often related to my values—I feel joy when something I value is honored, I feel anger or sadness when something I value is trampled. In some significant way, what we value sets the agenda for both thinking and feeling. (p. 2)

The next layer, as we climb down into the flower pot, is composed of our beliefs, the perceptions in which our thoughts and feelings and values

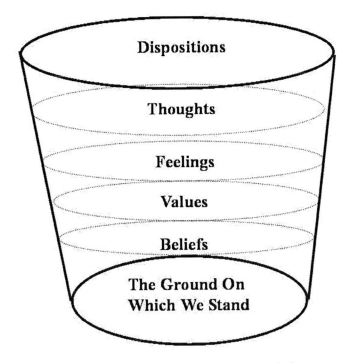

Figure 6.1.   Soil in a flower pot metaphor to help define
dispositions.

are grounded. At the bottom of the pot we find the most important layer,
a vital and yet nameless core. Palmer (1995) writes that this core is where

> we make the deeply inward response to the question, "Do I/we have
> ground on which to stand?" This is, of course, the ultimate question in
> everything we do, for without ground on which to stand life becomes dan-
> gerous and our responses to it become fearful and eventually violent.
> Despite the fact that this is a wordless realm, we must name it as the ulti-
> mate goal of formation—reminding ourselves that the formation process
> itself must be kept open to that which is beyond words, lest we miss the
> ultimate point. (p. 3)

We teach who we are. So **who** is the Self that teaches? From a perspective grounded in teacher formation, that Self is the **who** we are
"disposed" to be, not the **who** external forces maintain we are "supposed" to be. An important part of teacher preparation is adequate
time and safe space and skilled guidance to enable the individual to
discern which of those dispositions that are integral to selfhood also
serve the Self that teaches.

DISCERNING DISPOSITIONS

As I explore the literature on dispositions through a lens shaped by my work in teacher formation, I see the naming and claiming of one's dispositions as part of self-knowledge, especially vital to looking at the Self who teaches. I also see the function of discernment of dispositions as important in two different ways and at two different times in teacher education: (1) discernment on the part of the institution in deciding which applicants to admit into its teacher education programs, and (2) discernment on the part of individuals in naming and claiming those dispositions that are an integral part of who they are.

The first discernment seemingly would take place before a student is admitted to a teacher education program. The importance of dispositions, or personal qualities including feelings and beliefs and values, is not new in teacher education, nor is the idea that there must be some kind of discernment process in admitting students into teacher education programs. Mark Wasicsko, in his introduction on the Web page of the National Network for the Study of Teacher Dispositions (NNSED), reports that Arthur Combs and others investigated dispositions, or what Combs called **perceptions**, over a period of 40 years. Wasicsko describes the issues of dispositional mismatch with some students and a teaching career, and the importance of encouraging candidates to make self-assessments about their dispositional fit. "Ultimately, teacher educators have an ethical responsibility to encourage and admit candidates who have the dispositions that will foster growth and learning in students and not to admit those who cannot demonstrate that they posses the needed dispositions" (Wasicsko, 2005, ¶ 2). That is congruent with my formational lens through which I see dispositions as qualities to be discerned and developed, rather than to be taught or required.

CREATING THE SPACE FOR NURTURING DISPOSITIONS

The second discernment, requiring future teachers to identity those dispositions that are an integral part of who they are, would be an important part of the students' education within the program. Formation work during this time in preservice teachers' lives would allow them to claim and strengthen their own dispositions that are recognized as essential to good teaching, as well as those dispositions that will allow them to sustain themselves during their teaching careers.

"By formation," Palmer (2003) has explained to an audience of educators at Greensboro College,

I mean an educational process rooted in the assumption that each of us has that spot of grace or truth within ourselves—an ongoing source of truth-telling and well-being that needs only to be released from deforming pressures and allowed to reclaim its rightful role in the centering and grounding of our lives.

Formation work is in part the process of creating a quiet, focused, and disciplined space in which the noise within us—and the noise around us—can subside, allowing us to access that "spot of grace or truth."

The concept of space is important in teacher formation; in fact, we often talk about teaching as creating space. We are referring not only to the physical arrangement of the room, but also to the constructivist notion of learning with adequate time and resources and encouragement, resulting in an environment in which we trust the learner to construct understandings based on inner knowing and outer experiences. The space created in teacher formation settings[3] allows and encourages the nurturing and strengthening of dispositions, of thoughts, feelings, values, beliefs, of knowing the ground on which we stand. Gaining access to our inner truth, named in various wisdom traditions as soul, spirit, heart, or inner teacher, gives us an invaluable source that can guide our work, but is often neglected in teacher training and professional development. The recognition of teaching as vocation acknowledges in many of us a sense that we are "called to teach" that exists long before we begin any formal program of teacher education. By creating open and trustworthy spaces in which people can listen for and speak their own truths without fear and listen to the truths of others without rushing to judgment, we also create the conditions for vocational clarity.

STANDING AT THE INTERSECTION

Good teaching comes from the identity and integrity of the teacher, so it follows that an effective program of teacher education would develop teachers with a strong sense of identity and integrity. When I stand at the intersection of teacher formation and dispositions, I know that a vital aspect of the development of identity and integrity is identifying and encouraging those dispositions within individuals that enhance their teaching and sustain them as teachers. "The *Lehrergarten*: A Vision for Teacher Education" (Intrator, 2005, pp. 197-207) describes my concept for such a teacher education program. The *lehrergarten* (from German, *Lehrer*, teacher, and *Garten*, garden, a garden in which we nurture the seeds of future teachers) respects the need for special attention to the importance of creating the space for remembering who we are and knowing the ground on which we stand, so we can name and claim in ourselves the gifts, including our dispositions, that are integral to good teachers. The teacher education faculty in the *lehrergarten* recognizes that all gifts have their shadow sides, but that if we eliminate the shadows, we often also lose the gifts. To prepare teachers who are able to bring their inner lives into their outer work, these *lehrergartners* (teacher gardeners) understand the embracing of our shadows is necessary to claiming our dispositions, to learning to hold the world and ourselves as "both/and" rather than in the traditional "either/or" mode of our culture. A good program of teacher preparation must provide not only theory and foundation, methods and techniques, knowledge and skills; in addition to the *what*, the *how*, and the *why*, teacher educators must develop the *who* that teaches.

Who is the Self that teaches? Who are we disposed to be? The principles of the *lehrergarten* offer the opportunity for creating the space for identifying and strengthening those dispositions that contribute to good teaching, as well as the space for learning to live with the shadow side of our gifts and dispositions:

1.   We teach who we are. Craft, skills, techniques are important and necessary to our teaching, but who we are, our seed of true self, including our dispositions, is more important to how we teach than any method or procedure.

2.   Learning is a lifelong cyclical process, not a linear one. The pace of learning is organic—requiring not only enough time, but also attention to the cycles of work and rest, experiences and reflection, as nature attends to the cycles of light and dark, winter and summer.

3.   Every person has access to an inner source of truth, a source of strength and guidance that is the place of truth within us where we know the difference between reality and illusion. A vital relationship exists between inner clarity and sustaining our work in the world.

4.   The creation of a quiet, focused and disciplined space is essential for teacher education students to hear their own inner voices. The practices of reflection and journaling, silence and solitude, are important elements in creating that space. Darling-Hammond and Bransford (2005) include the disposition to reflect and to learn from practice in their category of teacher dispositions (p. 387).

5.   There is an interdependent, reciprocal relationship between teaching and learning. The roles of teacher and learner are dynamic, with the student often becoming the teacher. The importance of teachers' learning and development is also stressed in the litera-

ture on dispositions (Darling-Hammond & Bransford, 2005, p. 389).

6. Opportunities for embracing paradox, for seeing the world as both/and instead of either/or, abound in education. The teacher who can move with ease between the poles of seeming contradictions holds a key to sustainability in the profession. Cochran-Smith and Lytle (1999) describe this disposition as "inquiry as stance" (p. 250), crediting its importance in the ability of teachers to deal with the complexity of teaching and "the messiness of teaching and learning" (p. 279).

7. The relationship between education and community is the core of teaching and learning, the essence of being human. Learning is social; perceiving oneself as belonging to a learning community makes a difference for learners of all ages (Intrator, 2005, p. 199). Preservice teachers need the opportunity to experience this relationship, to develop the skill of dancing along the continuum of the individual and the community, to be able to stand with grace at the intersection of education and community.

The *lehrergarten* describes one program for teacher preparation grounded in formation, creating the space to name and claim and "grow" their dispositions in the future teachers. *Courage to Teach* and other programs, including the Center for Courage & Renewal's circle of trust retreats,[4] based on Parker Palmer's *A Hidden Wholeness: The Journey toward an Undivided Life* (2004), offer an opportunity for educators, as well as others, to remember who we are, including our dispositions.

When I stand at that intersection of teacher formation and educator dispositions, I get a glimpse of Larry Freeman's (2003) vision of what the teacher formation lens has to offer in the teacher education discourse. I know Larry's spirit is smiling at the idea of the importance of creating a space for naming and claiming, for discerning and nurturing, dispositions in teacher education.

NOTES

1. COURAGE TO TEACH® (CTT) is a program of the Center for Courage and Renewal (www.CourageRenewal.org), formerly the Center for Teacher Formation, consisting of quarterly retreats for the personal and professional renewal of teachers, administrators, and counselors. COURAGE TO TEACH® retreats focus neither on "technique" nor on school reform, but on renewing the inner lives of professionals in education. In large-group, small-group and solitary settings, educators explore concepts of teacher formation and "the heart of the teacher," using personal stories, reflec-

tions on classroom practice, and insights from poets, storytellers, and various wisdom traditions.

2. The Mobius strip, named for the German mathematician A. F. Mobius, is a one-sided surface, made by joining the ends of a rectangle, after twisting one end though 180 degrees (Oxford University Press, 1996).

3. Parker Palmer (1998) details his six paradoxes for creating teaching/learning space in *The Courage to Teach*: (1) bounded and open; (2) hospitable and "charged"; (3) inviting of both the individual voice and the group voice; (4) honors "little" stories of student and "big" stories of disciplines and tradition; (5) solitude and community; and (6) welcoming of silence and speech (p. 74).

4. Palmer describes the circle of trust as a rare form of community, one that is necessary for help in discerning the inner teacher's voice. For more details, see *A Hidden Wholeness*, pp. 22, 59-60. Information on opportunities to participate in circles of trust is available at www .couragerenewal.org

REFERENCES

Cochran-Smith, M., & Lytle, M. (1999). Relationships of knowledge and practice: Teacher learning in communities. *Review of Research in Education*, *24*, 249-306. Washington, DC: American Educational Research Association.

Darling-Hammond, L., & Bransford, D. (Eds.). (2005). *Preparing teachers for a changing world: What teachers should learn and be able to do*. San Francisco: Jossey-Bass.

Freeman. L. (2003, November). *Where did dispositions come from and what can we do with them?* Presentation at the Second Annual Symposium on Educator Dispositions, Eastern Kentucky University.

Intrator, S. M. (2005). *Living the questions: Essays inspired by the work and life of Parker J. Palmer*. San Francisco: Jossey-Bass.

Katz, L. G., & Raths, J. D. (1985). Dispositions as goals for teacher education. *Education and Teacher Education*, *1*, 301-307.

National Council for the Accreditation of Teacher Education (2002). Professional standards for the accreditation of schools, colleges, and departments of education. Washington, DC: Author.

Oxford University Press. (1996). *The Oxford Dictionary and Thesaurus*. USA: Author.

Palmer, P. J. (1995, September). Unpublished letter to Rob Lehman, President of the Fetzer Institute.

Palmer, P. J. (1998). *The courage to teach: Exploring the inner landscape of a teacher's life*. San Francisco: Jossey-Bass.

Palmer, P. J. (2003, September). *Lecture*. Greensboro, NC: Greensboro College.

Palmer, P. J. (2004). *A hidden wholeness: The journey toward an undivided life*. San Francisco: Jossey-Bass.

Teacher attrition: A costly loss to the nation and to the states. (2005). *Alliance for excellent education*. Retrieved August, 2005, from http://www.all4ed

Wasicsko, M. M. (2005). *The national network for the study of educator dispotions.* Retrieved February 22, 2005, from http://www.educatordispositions.org /moodle/moodle/mod/resource/view.php?id=4

PART II

EXPERIENTIAL PERSPECTIVES ON EDUCATOR DISPOSITIONS

CHAPTER 7

EXPERIENCES WITH DISPOSITIONS IN TEACHER EDUCATION

James Raths

INTRODUCTION

"Dispositions in teacher education" is surely a timely topic. At the 2006 AACTE (American Association of Colleges for Teacher Education) meeting in San Diego, there were 24 sessions devoted to dispositions. At the 2006 annual AERA (American Educational Research Association) conference, there were a similar number of such sessions. Furthermore, there have been numerous op-ed pieces hostile to the notion of dispositions in general and more specifically to the idea that teacher educators take dispositions into account in either admitting candidates into programs or assessing their progress in the program. For example, Will (2006) wrote disparagingly "Many education schools discourage, even disqualify, prospective teachers who lack the correct "disposition," meaning those who do not embrace today's progressive political catechism" (p. 98). Most of the critical commentaries focus on cases where teacher educators elected dispositions with political connotations as goals of their programs. The

Dispositions in Teacher Education, pp. 153–163
Copyright © 2007 by Information Age Publishing
All rights of reproduction in any form reserved.

controversies and trends in teacher education concerning dispositions prompt the questions: What is the history of dispositions in teacher education? What are the various definitions of dispositions in the teacher education literature? What are some enduring problems associated with teaching dispositions to our candidates and assessing their dispositions?

HISTORY OF DISPOSITIONS IN TEACHER EDUCATION

Early History of Dispositions in Teacher Education

While the term "dispositions" is a common one found in most dictionaries, Professor Larry Freeman of Governor's State University in Illinois searched extensively in the literature for the origins of the concept "disposition" as it applies to teaching and teacher education (see his chapter in this book). Freeman found what may be the first use of the term in this context in the seminal book, *Philosophy of Education: Learning and Schooling,* by Donald Arnstine of the University of Wisconsin published in 1967. Arnstine made the concept or construct of "dispositions" the centerpiece of his work, advocating that teaching dispositions is perhaps the most important contribution schools and teachers can make on behalf of their students. He defined dispositions as behaviors that were "thoughtful and discriminative of situations" (p. 28).

The notion of dispositions as program goals in teacher education was probably first brought to the consciousness of teacher educators by the work of Lilian Katz of the University of Illinois (Katz & Raths, 1985). Katz had the insight that some of our candidates have skills, but lack the dispositions to use them. For example, in most teacher education programs candidates are taught the skills to plan lessons, but as most teacher educators know, those particular skills are rarely practiced by experienced teachers. Katz hypothesized that often the ways that skills are taught in schools actually weaken the dispositions to use them. An example that comes to mind is reading. There is a danger that some of the reading programs that advance particular narrow subskills of reading actually weaken the disposition to be a reader. People learn how to read, but that does not guarantee that they will be readers. The thesis of the Katz-Raths essay was that teacher educators should adopt as goals not only pedagogical skills but also the dispositions to use them.

Recent History of Dispositions

A concentrated effort to reform teacher education was undertaken by Linda Darling-Hammond under the flag of INTASC (Interstate New

Teacher Assessment and Support Consortium, 1992). Working at state levels, Darling-Hammond enunciated principles that explicated best practices of teaching and lobbied to have the principles adopted by State standards boards. Her initiatives were quite successful in this regard. The INTASC principles included the notion, disposition—in an attempt to prevent teacher candidates from getting a license simply because of their high grade point averages when some of the A students treated pupils cruelly.

At the close of the decade (1999-2000), NCATE (National Council for Accreditation of Teacher Education), following INTASC's lead, decided that dispositions should be added to the list of "what teachers should know and know how to do." During the comment period, when proposed NCATE standards were reviewed by many teacher educators, a number of persons wrote to NCATE asking for some patience in adopting the expectation that teacher educators measure dispositions. If there were examples where dispositions were scaled, where the psychometrics of such scales had been studied, then they would support the proposed standards related to dispositions. But without such studies, NCATE was urged to omit dispositions from its litany of expectations.

DEFINITIONS OF THE TERM *DISPOSITION*

The field of teacher education, perhaps more than most, is known for widely differing definitions of key concepts. For example, the term "reflection" comes to mind. Many teacher education programs seem to be hoping to graduate teachers who are reflective practitioners; but it is difficult to recognize consensus in the literature about what counts as reflection and what constitutes better reflections as opposed to weaker reflections. It is no surprise that the same levels of disagreement are found concerning the concept, "dispositions."

In the original Katz and Raths (1985) article on dispositions as goals for teacher education, the notion of disposition was defined as an attributed characteristic of a teacher, one that summarizes the trend of a teacher's actions in particular contexts (p. 301). This definition builds on the work of Buss and Craik (1983) who defined dispositions as "summaries of act frequencies."

This definition does not equate "dispositions" as *causes* of behavior. A teacher, according to Katz, does not praise students because he has a disposition to be supportive. Rather, a teacher who is observed making use of praise in a number of contexts and on frequent occasions might be described as having a supportive disposition. In this sense, the concept, "disposition" is descriptive and may have a predictive element. Someone who is supportive over time is likely to be supportive "next time."

While INTASC did not formally define "disposition," one might infer a definition from the examples it advanced. INTASC (1992) links sets of dispositions with each of its ten basic principles. The "root words" associated with disposition include the following: the teacher realizes, appreciates, has enthusiasm for, believes, respects, is sensitive, values, and recognizes. As is clear, this version of the construct of "disposition" represents beliefs, values, and perceptions rather than a summary of behaviors.

Next, consider the NCATE (2002) definition of disposition, the one that is apparently causing so many problems for people engaged in the accreditation process.

> The values, commitments, and professional ethics that influence behaviors toward students, families, colleagues, and communities and affect student learning, motivation, and development as well as the educator's own professional growth. Dispositions are guided by beliefs and attitudes related to values such as caring, fairness, honesty, responsibility, and social justice. For example, they might include the belief that all students learn, a vision of high and challenging standards, or a commitment to a safe and supportive learning environment. (p. 53)

As in the case with INTASC, the NCATE definition posits that something "inside the brain," guides teachers' behaviors—including beliefs and attitudes, and so on. The collection of beliefs and attitudes constitutes a disposition.

In 2001, the National Research Council's Mathematics Learning Study Committee issued a report titled, "Adding It Up." The authors advocated that schools and teachers work to develop "mathematical proficiency" in their students. Mathematical proficiency was defined as having five strands—one of which was a "productive disposition." This goal was defined as "habitual inclination to see mathematics as sensible, useful, and worthwhile, coupled with the belief in diligence and one's own efficacy" (p. 5). Again, disposition according to the mathematicians, entails beliefs or other cognitive entities of the mind that can be fixed or manipulated.

In an important statement about dispositions published by AACTE, Hugh Sockett (2006) sees dispositions as "The professional virtues, qualities, and habits of mind and behavior held and developed by teachers on the basis of their knowledge, understanding, and commitments to students, families, their colleagues, and communities" (p. 23). He offers examples of desirable dispositions as "professional qualities of character" including courage, sincerity, and trustworthiness.

In the same publication, Mary Diez (2006) illustrates what she posits as three important dispositions—using the term "willingness" to define two of them. (The third is simply, "respect for others."). For example, the willingness "to do what it takes to help students learn."

What we see in this array of definitions is the concept, disposition, portrayed as a "cause" of behavior—akin to traits or character or will, that evidently must be shaped and changed if teachers are to act in effective ways in the classroom. Further, when dispositions are defined as values, beliefs, or character traits, it is easy to see how social advocates in our field would use mandated attention to dispositions as an opportunity to raise issues of social justice, racism, and peace as goals of teacher education. In this manner, the term "disposition" is taken apparently as a politically correct substitute for words such as values and beliefs. Teacher educators may sense that using the concept of "disposition" as a criterion for program admission or completion might be more acceptable than the alternate terms "values" and "beliefs." Here is where the problem identified by Will begins. It is not altogether clear what beliefs or actions count as indicators of the disposition to advance social justice. It seems likely that students and faculty might disagree about the meaning of the term. For example, it seems certain that those who voted for welfare reform act in the Clinton years thought they were doing so in the name of social justice, while others feared that a broken safety net in our society would lead to social injustices. How can candidates be evaluated for dispositions in the area of "social justice" without causing all sorts of problems with the First Amendment and with our sense of academic freedom for faculty as well as students?

APPROACHES TO DISPOSITIONS IN TEACHER EDUCATION

There seem to be two important steps to be taken in addressing the NCATE expectation that teacher education programs meet the following standard: Candidates for all professional education roles develop and model dispositions that are expected of educators." The first is to select the dispositions that a program wishes to strengthen and the second is to find ways to assess the strength of those dispositions. Both steps are exceedingly difficult. The following sections of the paper address these steps.

Selecting the Dispositions

Moving from Katz' original observation that teachers (and professors as well) may have skills that they don't use or apply, it would seem to follow that once a teacher education faculty has identified skills (competencies) to teach candidates, there is an implied, allied goal for teacher educators to aim toward—namely to strengthen candidates' dispositions to use the skills in the classroom. So, if a teacher education program elects to teach candidates to ask higher level questions, or to employ think-pair-share techniques in discussions, or to practice "wait time" in recitation lessons, the faculty has implicitly also chosen as goals to strengthen the dispositions to use those skills in practice. Thus, every teacher education program that lists competencies as targets within its program is also pronouncing associated dispositions as goals. However, this approach can be problematic if the conceptual size of the skills is small. During the competency based movement in teacher education, sponsored in part by the U.S. Office of Education and advocated by AACTE, teacher education programs would write out the competencies they were fostering in their candidates. The lists were formidable and long. One Midwestern university, for example, had as many as 1,500 competencies in its list of goals. The 1,500 competencies imply 1,500 dispositions as well. Teaching toward 3,000 goals and assessing 3,000 goals is a formidable task.

It would be important that the skills we teach our candidates be of a certain conceptual "size"—to merit our attention and theirs. An example of goals for teacher education that have an apparent hefty conceptual size was advanced by Bruce Joyce (1969) on behalf of Teachers College, Columbia University. In a proposal written to the U.S. Office of Education which was seeking to identify and fund competency based programs, Joyce advanced several important goals, written at the level of abstraction illustrated as follows: Candidates would be prepared (1) to be interactive teachers—sensitive to individual differences; (2) to be innovative teachers, rather than bureaucratic functionaries; and (3) to be scholars, permitting teachers to test and create knowledge about their own teaching. Joyce acknowledges that after defining these three areas as goals of his program, there was an opportunity to specify "the detailed sets of behavior that make up complete performance in the domain(s)" (p. 116). He chose not to do that and instead turned to define ways that these goals could be addressed within a teacher education program. For our purposes, taking the road Joyce left unchosen, we could spell out some skills associated with each of the broad goals, and accept that teaching the skills would also take into account ways of strengthening dispositions to use them. It is interesting that a 1969 Joyce comment about the application of the goals was as follows: "Hopefully, there will be reasonable transfer to their teaching situation" (p. 119). Evidently, Joyce was aware that teachers might acquire skills without applying them. The current emphasis on dispositions goes beyond Joyce's "hope," to a more systematic approach. To address the question of dispositions in teacher education, take the first domain in the Joyce list, "the interactive teacher." What are some dispositions associated with the goal of being an interactive teacher? A faculty might select the following:

- Teachers reward students' approximations of classroom goals
- Teachers listen carefully to their students
- Teachers let students know that they remember previous conversations
- Teachers seek causes of students' unproductive behaviors

It is important to recognize that teachers may have dispositions, either learned within the teacher education program or earlier in life, which may need to be weakened. So, in a sense, a teacher education faculty could espouse negative goals—to weaken dispositions such as:

- Teacher interrupts students as they are speaking
- Teacher makes trait attributions to students.
- Teacher raises her/his voice to students

It is also important to note that dispositions imply certain contexts in which the dispositions are to be observed. The "situational" aspect of disposition plays an important role. It implies judgment. As Arnstine (1967) suggested, a person with a truth-telling disposition has no difficulty responding untruthfully to a question from a friend, "Are you planning a surprise party for me?" Someone with a truth-telling, mindless habit might "spill the beans," but the situation calls for a thoughtful response, calls for judgment, surely an aspect of professional competence.

Another problem with the process of selecting dispositions is the inevitable one of "incompleteness." A faculty cannot choose to strengthen all the dispositions that might have a significant bearing on education within a classroom. Consider again how a Midwestern university selected 1,500 competencies to address in its program. Almost surely, that is too many. When a faculty chooses to narrow its focus, members must also resign themselves to incompleteness. The resignation to "incompleteness" is apparently an important attribute of selecting dispositions as goals.

In sum, a teacher education program could adopt the goal of strengthening candidates' dispositions to be interactive. This decision identifies a goal at a reasonable conceptual level. In clarifying the goal for candidates, specific instances that reflect the goal could be identified as well as instances that appear to be counterindicators of the goal.

It might be helpful to take another example. Gage (1966) claimed that "indirectness" was a practice associated with effective teaching. His notion might be operationalized by the work of Flanders (1970). Flanders listed the following behaviors as indicators of being indirect as a teacher:

1. Accepts and clarifies an attitude or a feeling tone of a pupil in a non-threatening manner (p. 34).
2. Uses praise and other encouraging statements which carry the value judgment of approval (p. 41).
3. Accepts or uses ideas of pupils (p. 34).

The teacher education program goal would be to strengthen candidates' dispositions to be indirect, in the Flanders sense. The behaviors associated with this goal would not be stated as goals themselves, but as indicators of the broader concept, "indirectness" which is the goal. Again, associated with this goal would be dispositions on the part of candidates the faculty would seek to weaken—sarcasm, excessive teacher talk, and so forth.

Assessing Dispositions

Buss and Craik (1983) suggested ways of assessing dispositions, after a target is selected. There are several steps in the process.

1. After identifying the target disposition, let us take "being indirect as a teacher," a panel of teaching experts—professors, supervisors, teachers, and principals, perhaps, is asked to generate examples of acts on the part of teacher candidates that would exemplify the disposition to be indirect in the Flanders' sense. In this exercise following Buss and Craik's specifications, perhaps 100 examples might be generated by a panel of a dozen people.
2. Next, a second panel would be asked to rate how typical each of the 100 examples would be of the "indirectness" disposition. The instruction to the second panel is of interest here. Panelists are asked to assume that while there are 100 various shades of red, for instance, as we can observe in an expensive box of crayons, some reds are more "red" than other "reds." In an analogous case, some acts are more representative of the disposition, "being indirect," than others. The results of the second panel winnow down the 100 examples to a few—say 10 examples.
3. Next, faculty are asked to observe teachers over a period of time, marking the instances in which one of the target acts was observed. The assumption is that a candidate who is seen as more frequently "acting" in line with the exemplars of "indirectness," has a stronger

disposition than another doctoral candidate with less frequent "acts."

We have tried a number of ways to assess dispositions that are perhaps less labor intensive and less time sensitive. For example, we have had supervisors rate student teachers on Likert scales where the "dispositions" themselves and not the acts are posed for ratings. In these cases, supervisors were asked to rate each candidate on his/her degrees of "indirectness."

At the University of Illinois, we tried ipsative measures—asking supervisors to rate for each candidate his/her two strongest and the two weakest dispositions from a list of dispositions. For example, if a program had taken on the following four dispositions as goal—being indirect, using technology, demonstrating subject matter knowledge, and planning aligned with curriculum standards—an ipsative task would ask the supervisor to say, for each candidate, what are his/her two strongest dispositions and what are his/her two weakest dispositions. In this approach, each candidate receives news about strengths and weaknesses. The "comparisons" implied by the ipsative technique are within an individual. The level of one teacher's performance in the area of "indirectness" might be a strength, compared to his other performances, but that same level of "indirectness" might be a weakness for another teacher who is extremely strong in the other areas. Both cooperating teachers and candidates themselves resisted the ipsative scales—finding the assumption built into this approach that every teacher must have a "weaker" disposition as unprofessional and even insulting. When it was used briefly, the program faculty found it useful to form a frequency distribution over all the candidates to locate potential program weaknesses. For example, in this instance "using technology" was advanced as a weakness far more frequently than any other disposition. The faculty was able to inquire into this aspect of its program to develop improvements. Of course, it is possible to over-interpret ipsative scales. Even though the disposition to use technology was cited as the greatest weakness within the set, it is possible (but surely not probable) that using technology was acceptably strong as a disposition, but weaker than the other dispositions the candidates demonstrated in their student teaching.

None of our approaches to assessing dispositions have been satisfactory—essentially because of low coefficients of agreement among raters. It seems that we have not been able to successfully teach raters what is meant by a specific disposition. Another factor associated with the weak psychometric characteristics of the scales we used was the reluctance on the part of supervisors and cooperating teachers to give marks away from the highest end of the scales. For example, in an effort involving 200 student teachers who were rated on 10 items each, yielding 2,000 ratings, over 90% of them were at the top of the scale. At the time, we were confident that our teacher education program was effective, and that our candidates were really well prepared to become teachers, but we did not think our program was as effective as the 90% mark suggested. Other factors are involved in rating student teachers—a process that calls for additional study.

ENDURING PROBLEMS WITH DISPOSITIONS

In a way of summary, let me cite what I see as the enduring problems associated with using dispositions in teacher education as one of several bases for assessing candidates.

1. We need to select a finite set of dispositions with which to work. Given the notion that we want to graduate "complete" teachers after four years of study, it is difficult to take on some dispositions and not others. For example, in any set of nominated dispositions, someone could advance a new one that almost everyone would agree is important. The point is that to have 1,500 goals in a teacher education program is not practical—and some interesting and apparently important goals need to be overlooked to give focus to a program's efforts.

2. We can, with some effort as described above, judge that some candidates have stronger dispositions than other candidates, but we cannot determine a cut score that asserts that if a disposition is as weak as level X, the candidate should not be licensed.

3. We need to consider how dispositions are learned and strengthened. Bandura's research on "observational learning" may be of help to us—but that is not at all clear. (See Breese &Nawrocki-Chabin, 2006 for a helpful explication of the application of Bandura's model to the teaching of dispositions.)

REFERENCES

Arnstine, D. (1967). *Philosophy of education: Learning and schooling*. New York: Harper & Row.

Breese, L., & Nawrocki-Chabin, R. (2006, April). *Social cognitive perspective in dispositional development*. Paper presented to the annual meeting of the American Educational Research Association, San Diego, CA.

Buss, D. M., & Craik, K. H. (1983). The act frequency approach to personality. *Psychological Review, 90*, 105-126.

Diez, M. E. (2006). Assessing dispositions: Five principles to guide practice. In H. Sockett (Ed.), *Teacher dispositions* (pp. 49-68). Washington, DC: AACTE.

Flanders, N. A. (1970). *Analyzing teaching behavior.* Reading, MA: Addison-Wesley.

Gage, N. A. (1966). Desirable behaviors of Teachers. In M. D. Usdan & F. Bertolaet (Eds.), *Teachers for the disadvantaged* (pp. 4-12). Chicago: Follett.

Interstate New Teacher Assessment and Support Consortium. (1992). *Model standards for beginning teacher licensure and development. A resource for state dialogue.* Washington, DC: Council of Chief State School Officers.

Joyce, B. R. (1969). A teacher-innovator: A program to prepare teachers. In J. L. Burdin & K. Lanzillotti (Eds.), *A reader's guide to the comprehensive models for preparing model elementary teachers* (pp. 105-157). Washington, DC: AACTE ERIC Clearinghouse on Teacher Education.

Katz, L. G., & Raths, J. D. (1985). Dispositions as goals for teacher education. *Teaching and Teacher Education, 1*, 301-307.

National Council for Accreditation of Teacher Education. (2002). *Professional standards for the accreditation of schools, colleges, and departments of education.* Washington, DC: Author.

National Research Council. (2001). *Adding it up: Helping children learn mathematics.* In J. Kilpatrick, J. Swafford, & B. Findell (Eds), *Adding it up: Helping children learn mathematics.* Washington, DC: National Academy Press.

Sockett, H. (2006). Character, rules, and relations. In H. Sockett (Ed.), *Teacher dispositions: Building a teacher education framework of moral standards* (pp. 9-25). Washington, DC: AACTE.

Will, G. F. (2006, January 12). Ed schools vs. Education. *Newsweek*, p. 98

CHAPTER 8

ALTERNATIVELY CERTIFIED
TEACHERS' PERCEPTIONS
OF DISPOSITIONS

Karen Peterson

This chapter is a discussion of an exploratory study of alternatively certified teachers' views on the dispositions needed to be a successful teacher, and the differences in expectations in previous careers which may indicate different dispositional behaviors necessary in education. The subjects are career changers who have been certified through the Governors State University (GSU) Alternative Certification Partnership, a collaborative program with 12 south suburban school districts in the Chicago metropolitan area. Their views provide insight into the dispositions they view as necessary for success in teaching, as well as the challenges of changing careers when dispositions linked to success in their former field may be different than what they view as contributing to success in education. The chapter discusses the origin of the study, a brief background on alternative certification to provide a backdrop for the research, the Governors State program and the Professional Education Unit's concept of dispositions, and the description of the study, results, and implications for further research.

Dispositions in Teacher Education, pp. 165–179
Copyright © 2007 by Information Age Publishing

165

This study grew out of the analysis of two types of program evaluation data: (1) The fact that in the program's performance based assessment model, the area in which candidates were most often ranked less than satisfactory was in the area of dispositions and (2) Building administrator evaluations' indication that many candidates were having difficulty making the transition to school culture from their previous careers. We decided to interview and survey teachers who had completed the program to determine their views both on teacher dispositions and the transition to school culture to provide data to assist the program in strengthening these areas of concern.

ALTERNATIVE CERTIFICATION

Although there are still strong opponents to alternate paths, in the last several years the dialogue regarding alternative certification programs has generally moved from discussion of whether or not states should approve certification through these routes, to discussions of the importance of quality teacher preparation in both alternative and traditional programs. Zeichner (2006) elaborates,

> We need to support teacher education programs of all kinds that have ... characteristics that are shown by research to enable the achievement of desired outcomes, whether they are traditional or alternative, and criticize and/or close down those that do not have them. (p. 332)

The reality is that approximately 50,000 teachers were certified through alternative routes in 2005 (Feistritzer, 2006), and while the research base is in its early stages, the one area of agreement is that the programs have been successful in bringing in a more diverse teacher pool of minorities and males (Jacobson, 2005). With the increasing number of new teachers coming into the field through alternate paths, there is an opportunity to view many aspects of teacher education and new teacher induction through different lenses which may provide opportunities for teacher preparation and development improvement on many levels. This study seeks to add insight from our teachers who come from diverse professional backgrounds.

Stoddart and Floden (1995) highlight this potential positive impact of alternative certification teachers on schooling. They note that "alternate route programs give school districts a choice between hiring teachers with two kinds of qualifications: those with academic and professional credentials and those with academic credentials alone" (p. 1). With this added institutional and organizational experience, alternative certification candidates also bring experience which can "challenge the status quo or conceive of different ways of organizing schools" (p. 1).

THE GOVERNORS STATE UNIVERSITY ALTERNATIVE CERTIFICATION PARTNERSHIP

There is a growing number of alternative certification programs, but there is a tremendous range in quantity and quality of preparation. When we began planning the Governors State University Alternative Certification Partnership 8 years ago to meet the needs of high need schools in our region, we were determined to go beyond what has been called "the six week summer wonder" model. Our candidates take 16 credit hours of professional education coursework before they begin their internship, when they become teachers of record after the initial 5 months of preparation. This is a standards-based, performance-based teacher preparation program, with a focus on working with children of promise (our alternative to the term "at-risk") incorporated throughout the coursework.

The program is a 16 month elementary certification program for individuals who hold a minimum of a BA or BS degree. The candidates are mid-life career changers, and they include candidates whose previous careers were attorneys, corporate trainers, accountants, social workers, and journalists. In line with the research noted previously, our program has prepared more than 150 elementary teachers, 60% minority and 25% male, significantly higher in these areas than our traditional program.

There is a four stage (application, testing, interviews, presentations) selection process to find quality candidates with 5 years of work experience following their degrees who are willing to make a 3 to 5 year commitment to work in high need schools. The Alternative Certification program addresses the same objectives as our traditional program in a more compact format, and includes mentor support of at least half a day per week, with special assistance contracts provided for candidates who need additional support.

The mission of the program is to provide quality teachers to high need schools in our region. The goals are:

- to recruit midlife career changers with a commitment to urban teacher education,
- to provide quality, standards-based teacher preparation in an abbreviated design, blending theory to practice and meeting all the objectives of our traditional elementary program,
- to improve teacher retention in high need schools in our region,

- to train candidates to develop as teacher leaders in their districts.

The Governors State Alternative Certification Partnership was recently named as one of six national finalists for the 2006 Christa McAuliffe Award for Excellence in Teacher Education by the American Association of State Colleges and Universities. In the first six cohorts, of the 182 candidates who began the program, 145 have been recommended for certification, 8 have been recommended pending completion of general education coursework requirements, 20 were not recommended to continue/complete based on their performance, and 6 left by choice, only 3 during the teaching internship. Of those recommended for certification, approximately 90% are still teaching or have gone on to administrative positions.

As a program in an NCATE (National Council for the Accreditation of Teacher Education) accredited institution, the Alternative Certification Partnership assesses all candidates in the areas of knowledge, skills, and dispositions in a performance based model at multiple gateways before recommending candidates for certification. Before Governor State's initial NCATE visit in 2001, there was a great amount of discussion regarding the concept of dispositions and how to address assessing them. It began with discussion of the NCATE glossary definition of dispositions:

> **Dispositions.** The values, commitments, and professional ethics that influence behaviors toward students, families, colleagues, and communities and affect student learning, motivation, and development as well as the educator's own professional growth. Dispositions are guided by beliefs and attitudes related to values such as caring, fairness, honesty, responsibility, and social justice. For example, they might include a belief that all students can learn, a vision of high and challenging standards, or a commitment to a safe and supportive learning environment. www.ncate.org/search/glossary.htm

Dr. Larry Freeman, the originator of the concept of this book on dispositions, led the way in the discussion on how to approach dispositions with the NCATE expectation of assessment. After much debate, our Unit determined that we found Katz and Raths' (1985) work in the area of dispositions to be most helpful, particularly moving from the concept of attitudes to dispositions. When attitudes is used in a conventional way "the focus is upon pre-dispositions to act" and that "we employ the term disposition as a summary of actions observed." The authors conclude that

> among the reasons underlying our belief in the usefulness of their (dispositions) inclusion (in teacher education), the most important is that they can orient our efforts toward designing and evaluating teacher education programs in terms of their enduring impact upon the candidates. (p. 307)

From this evolved our language of looking for patterns of behavior in assessing teacher candidates' dispositions.

The Professional Education Unit then delineated dispositions expected of all professional education candidates in the Unit System of Assessment, which are highlighted in each course syllabus as noted below: professional behavior

- appreciation of human diversity,
- commitment to collaboration with colleagues,
- commitment to ethical behavior,
- commitment to life-long learning, including professional development, and
- habits of mind that reveal reasoned eclecticism.

As indications of positive and professional dispositions, we expect students to:

- be actively involved during in-class activities,
- contribute to class discussions,
- be on time for class and when submitting assignments, and
- cooperate in and make significant contributions to group activities/ assignments.
- Interactions with faculty, other candidates, and pupils should be consistent with the dispositions listed above.

The Unit's description of the dispositions highlights categories of dispositions which are then discussed in each course. It provides opportunities to discuss applications of the expectations of the dispositions. For example, how does a professor approach expectations for candidates related to "appreciation of human diversity" in a foundations course discussing social foundations issues compared to "appreciation of human diversity" in a student teaching experience in a diverse school setting in a classroom with five students with individual education plans (IEP)? In our Unit's assessment of dispositions, each professor would observe patterns of behavior that would indicate an issue with appreciation of human diversity. In the foundations course, it might mean a candidate who consistently demonstrates intolerance as other candidates' voice views regarding their diverse life experiences. In a student teaching experience, a candidate might be regarded as having an issue with appreciation of human diversity if he/she is not actively seeking ways to differentiate for the IEP students.

Our experience in The Governors State University Alternative Certification Program demonstrates the importance of a focus on teacher dispositions in teacher education. The data in the table below indicate that of candidates in our first three cohorts who had lower than acceptable assessments, 37% were academic and 63% were dispositional in nature. Candidates were evaluated on multiple measures at four gateways throughout the program and ranked satisfactory, satisfactory with concern, marginal, or unsatisfactory. Nearly half of candidates were ranked at satisfactory with concern or lower on at least one of the four gateway evaluations, demonstrating the developmental process of evolving as a teacher. To be recommended for certification, candidates must be ranked satisfactory at the final gateway (see Table 8.1).

Of four candidates who completed all components of the program and were given a summative rating of unsatisfactory, three received the ratings solely because of dispositional problems and the other exhibited problems related to both skills and dispositions (Freeman, Peterson, & Erikson, 2004). Serious dispositional issues which precluded candidates from being recommended for certification have generally been related to commitment, work ethic, flexibility, and being open to suggestions, considered under the dispositional category "professional behavior" by the Professional Education Unit (PEU) at Governors State. Some candidates who have not been recommended for certification have had the knowledge and skills to be successful teachers, but have not demonstrated the dispositions of professional educator at the level required by program and PEU guidelines.

This is in line with the study by Katz and Raths (1985) when they surveyed preservice instructors of methods courses and the instructors believed that dispositions contributed more to teacher effectiveness than

Table 8.1.   Summary of Assessment Committee's Reasons for Ratings Below Satisfactory[1]

Cohort	Total Candidates	No. Rated Below Satisfactory	Percentage Rated Below Satisfactory	Percentage of Reasons for Ratings Below Satisfactory	
				Academic	Dispositional
1	25	10	40%	40%	60%
2	18	7	39%	29%	71%
3	21	14	66%	36%	64%
Total	64	31	48%	37%	63%

1. The number of ratings below satisfactory includes all candidates who were rated as less than satisfactory at any of the gateways.

skills or knowledge. Katz and Raths, in their analysis stated, "It is not a matter of emphasizing skills or dispositions; it is our view that the acquisition of skills and the dispositions to use them must be mutually inclusive goals" (p. 304). This chapter reinforces the need to explore the importance of dispositions in teacher education which was highlighted more than 20 years ago and is currently central to the performance based assessment work in NCATE accredited institutions. This study takes the approach of looking through the candidate/teacher lens to do so.

As mentioned previously, the other evaluation data that precipitated the exploration of these dispositional issues evolved partly as a result of a survey of building administrators of alternative certification candidates in the Governors State program. That survey's results emphasized the success of the partnership and the satisfaction with the program (3.84 on a 4 point scale) and the candidates (3.56 on a 4-point scale), but also highlighted suggestions for program improvement.

When asked to identify weaknesses, about one-fourth of the respondents identified unfamiliarity with schools or not understanding school culture as a weakness. This is understandable given that many of the candidates have no work experience in schools and it appears that acquiring an understanding of school culture requires such experience. One respondent suggested a workshop at which new candidates talk with experienced teachers and principals about how education and school culture as a work setting are very different from the work background they may have. This recommendation responds directly to observations that candidates do not have sufficient familiarity with schools and their culture. This finding led us to explore more deeply the connection between teacher dispositions necessary to assist candidates in making a successful transition from other careers to teaching.

THE STUDY AND RESULTS

The research questions of this study were: "What are the dispositions necessary to be a successful teacher?" and "What are the differences in the dispositions necessary to be a successful teacher compared to dispositions necessary for success in your previous career?" Teachers in the study were very familiar with the concept of dispositions as they had received feedback on their evaluations on knowledge, skills, and dispositions at each of four gateways. Each course syllabus outlines the Unit dispositions and each professor elaborates on dispositional expectations for each course. Many candidates had been required to attend conferences with assessment committee members to discuss concerns regarding dispositions and in the mentoring and coaching processes of the program dispositions were also addressed. They were familiar with the Unit's definition of dispositions as patterns of behavior.

One main purpose of the study was to provide insight into how to address the issue of better preparing alternative certification candidates for success in school settings and improvement of the dispositions helpful in acclimating them to school culture.

Nine teachers who have made a very successful transition from another field to the school setting were selected for interviews based on faculty recommendation and outcomes on their performance based evaluations. They were interviewed at length about dispositions necessary for success in their former fields and in teaching and comparing the two. Additional teachers certified through the program were sent surveys by e-mail. Thirty five of 110 surveys were returned (32%). The survey questions were: (1) What are the dispositions you feel are necessary to be an excellent teacher? (2) Please list dispositions necessary for success in previous work area(s). (3) What is the difference in the dispositions necessary in teaching compared to other fields? (4) Has becoming a teacher changed your work dispositions? If yes, please elaborate. (5) Please note any other comments in the area of teacher dispositions.

Interviews were transcribed and a content analysis was completed on the surveys and the transcriptions. Three individuals reviewed the data, coding by emerging themes. After reviewing the results, two individuals synthesized the variance in individual analyses. The results of the first research question are shown in the Table 8.2.

The most overwhelming response to the survey and interviews was the indicator that the human connection in the teaching profession is a disposition necessary for success. Candidates used multiple terms—caring, understanding, supportive, empathetic—in describing the need to make a personal connection with students and the importance of doing so. Flexibility was another disposition that had a strong response from both the surveyed and interviewed teachers. This finding was not a surprise as throughout the program we often speak about the importance of "flexibility in dealing with ambiguity" in working in high need schools. In fact, on our program faculty assessment of knowledge, skills, and dispositions, "flexibility in dealing with ambiguity" was added to the Unit's list of dispositions, as we judged it was so essential to candidates' success. At first, it appeared that this could have been a strong response based on a great deal of program input. However, when "reflective" received only one response, it was apparent that instruction and program focus alone did not determine how the teachers were responding since developing as a reflective practitioner is highlighted throughout the program. It may also be that teachers regard being reflective as more of a skill than a disposition, as the response on a recent program completer survey noted 94% of

Table 8.2. Alternative Certification Teachers' Views on Dispositions Necessary for Success as a Teacher *

Disposition Noted	Surveyed Candidates' Responses	% of 35 Total	Interviewed Candidates' Responses	% of 9 Total	Total Responses	% of 44 Total
Positive affect (kind, caring, supportive...)	23	66	8	89	31	71
Flexibility	17	49	8	89	25	57
Team player, cooperative	12	34	6	67	18	41
Patience	12	34	2	22	14	32
Persistence, determination	6	17	5	56	11	25
Open to suggestions	4	11	7	78	11	25
Dedication, commitment	6	17	4	44	10	23
Communication skills (speaking/listening)	6	17	2	22	8	18
Organization	5	14	3	33	8	18
Responsibility	6	17	2	22	8	18
Lifelong learner	6	17	1	11	7	16
Consistency (firm, strong)	6	17	1	11	7	16
Hard worker	3	9	3	33	6	14
Professional attitude	6	17	0	NA	6	14
Political savvy (related to school culture)	3	9	3	33	6	14
Child-centered	3	9	3	33	6	14
Innovation/creativity	4	11	1	11	5	11
Visionary/leadership	1	3	4	44	5	11

*Additional dispositions which had 2-4 responses were: sense of humor, communication skills, stamina, ability to multitask, motivating, forgiving, role model, culturally sensitive, open to change, ability to make learning meaningful, intrinsically motivated, thrive on challenge, ability to manage stress, honest, good planner, humble. Responses which were given only once were: realistic expectations, ability to manage self care, reflective, resilient, fortitude, commitment to quality, continual optimist.

teachers noted a 5 or 4 score beginning with "strongly agree" on a 5-point Likert scale on the question, "I developed as a reflective practitioner."

Comments regarding the importance of flexibility were, "You just can't be the kind of person who always expects things to go the same way every day, because it's never like that." Another noted, "You have to be able to make the right turn in a heart beat, right away, immediately. It happens really often. You cannot depend on anything being certain. Almost nothing is certain." Being cooperative and a team player were also highlighted by both groups. One teacher explained the importance of positive collaboration, "When talking about dispositions, we are saying that you must maintain a high level of professionalism when dealing with colleagues, because the students are witnessing every aspect of your actions which you are actually modeling."

The two areas where a stronger response was given by the candidates who were selected for the interviews based on their very successful transition to school cultures were persistence and determination and open to suggestions. Dedication and commitment were stronger, but to a lesser degree, although these concepts are very in line with persistence and determination. Open to suggestions was noted by 78% of teachers interviewed and only 11% of teachers surveyed. This difference would be interesting to follow up with further research with a larger sample to determine if these dispositions are in fact, found more often in teachers identified as successful by measures of teacher evaluation. In discussing dispositions necessary in former careers compared to teaching, it is interesting to note that many candidates stated that many of the dispositions are the same for various careers, particularly "if you work with others." One candidate noted, "People will be people regardless of their line of work." There were, understandably, more common themes with candidates who worked in the social service sector than with those from business.

What follows are comments regarding specific differences in certain fields and then two brief case studies of two teachers who felt there were stark contrasts in necessary dispositions in their former fields. Some teachers spoke of several fields in which they had worked. What is important to consider is that teachers are basing these views on the particular contexts of both their former jobs and their current teaching positions. The teachers are teaching in high need schools and these views could be different if they were in another school setting. Of course, there are contextual issues related to any job, for example, their administrators' styles (see Table 8.3).

These responses again focus on the more affective nature of teaching, particularly compared to various positions in the business world. They also reflect more intrinsic motivation and greater personal rewards in spite of challenges, particularly teaching in high need schools.

> For me, teaching is as much a calling as a vocation. Therefore you really have to forgive (students) because you come across students who will steal from you and will lie to you and will do all kinds of things and the next day you have to start anew.

The alternatively certified teachers also emphasized the rigor of the field of teaching. One former attorney commented, "I just don't know how you expect a kid that's just come out of college to handle this job without having gone through the rigor in some other field." Another

Table 8.3.   Alternative Certification Candidates' Views on the Differences in Expectations in Work Settings Which may Necessitate Different Dispositional Behaviors

Former Field	Difference in Teaching
Banking	• Unselfish focus on others in teaching, more task focus in banking
Instructional technology	• More likely to get "personal" in teaching
Executive assistant Health care worker	• Have more need to be "firm" as with students; required adaptation of natural style
Editor	• Multitasking essential; much narrower focus as editor
Retail sales	• Intrinsically rather than extrinsically motivated • More mental time commitment; teaching is 24/7
Self-employed	• Must teach all children; could self select clients
Military; corporate trainer	• More patient, concerned with feelings; less harsh dealing with others
Collection agent	• Share ideas more; more patient; less bossy and harsh
Business	• More creative; had to follow protocol at all times
Director of communications	• Transition from leadership to entry level was challenging • More ambiguity in teaching—constant change • More demanding than the public realizes
College english instructor	• Must work with and depend on others more in teaching
Executive director	• Must be even more prepared and organized
Public relations and sales	• Teaching more on task and structured • "I'm happier although more tired!"
Social work	• More time with students than clients; more chance of impact
College fine arts instructor	• More intense research needed to problem solve to meet needs of students
Business administrator	• Selflessness rather than selfishness in business world • Constant change in schools beyond your control
Non-profit management	• Teaching more pressure and hierarchical regimentation
Lawyer	• Must focus on bigger picture as there are many challenges in local politics and school culture • More opportunities for creativity
Law—Criminal prosecutor	• Opportunity to help students before it is too late
Music producer and singer	• Must be forgiving with kids—every day a new day • Must be "on-stage" for both • Structure of time commitment; used to more flexible schedule
Social worker	• Professional respect of adults in external world not a given with students; you must earn respect
TV producer	• Must be more open to change and suggestions as a teacher
Telecommunications analyst	• Teaching is more of a calling • Am doing my job 24 hours a day rather than 9-5 • Sensitivity to students' situations essential
Speech therapist	• More vested personal connections
Publishing manager	• Never leaving the job behind • Sense of personal responsibility

ex-attorney noted, "Some people can't imagine why I gave up law. Others don't think of teaching as a profession. They think it is easy to teach in the primary grades. I have become an advocate for teachers. It is fulfilling work, but it is not easy."

Several of the candidates discussed the fact that it is more than a career change, it is a lifestyle change.

> The biggest challenge that I had to make was spending my time doing my job literally 24 hours a day. When I left corporate America, at 4:30 or 5 o'clock, I was done. I did not bring work home at all. In teaching, there are times when I wake up in the middle of the night because I've come up with an idea and there are always papers you bring home.... It's a never ending job as far as I'm concerned.

Two teachers spoke very strongly about differences in their prior careers compared to their current teaching careers, one a TV producer and the other a newspaper reporter/editor. The former TV producer's comments reflect the missionary zeal of many candidates changing careers and committed to working in high need schools. The ex-editor's comments reflect the challenges of making the transition. They discuss the differences in the dispositional behaviors required in former fields which makes the transition to teaching challenging.

Former TV Producer

This teacher spent some time working on an infamous talk show and said, at that point, he was contributing to "the dumbing down of America." He went on to explain his view of the differences between his former career and his current as a teacher.

> The only similarity I think is the need to be able to work as a team.... Coming from the television and film industry, I was around people whose view of the world consisted of themselves and their own glorification.... Friends and family all took a back seat to the pursuit of that singular vision of success in the workplace.... That sort of attitude and self-centered world view must not enter the world of education.... To work in this profession, nay BELONG to this profession, you must realize that YOU, the educator, are not the central focus.... We must know that our behavior can lead a child to greatness, snatch him back from the brink of danger, or push him over the edge into desolation and nothingness.... A person in another profession, tv in my case, has a narrow world view focused on the self and self gratification... The teacher has to know that the world is bigger than him or her and that we must give everything we can to keep the wheels of society in motion.

Other teachers, as noted in the table, commented on the opportunity to have more impact through the career change. The criminal prosecutor said, "This is an opportunity to help students before it is too late." Several candidates spoke of intrinsic rather than extrinsic motivation and selfless-ness rather than selfishness as what may be found in the business world. Through the 7 years of the program's operation this has been a recurring theme. Career changers are choosing education, most taking very sub-stantial pay cuts, because they want to have an opportunity to make a dif-ference through a more fulfilling career.

Former Newspaper Reporter/Editor

The former newspaper reporter's placement is in a high need school setting with many school culture challenges. The school has a 97% low income rate and a 92% mobility rate. There had also been a change in administration in each of her first 2 years of teaching at the school. She had challenges adapting to school culture and her analysis on the survey regarding the differences in dispositions necessary in education com-pared to her previous career, demonstrate great insight into why her tran-sition may have been difficult. She discussed the affective skills necessary to teaching, "teachers need to be kind and patient and to come down to a child's level as needed." She spoke of the role of the reporter as one that required "boldness, fearlessness, and an ability to view people and events objectively" Teachers, she said, "need to be less skeptical and more inno-cent." Another challenge she noted which was mentioned by other career changers who had jobs as more independent contractors as well, was the issue of being "willing to stay in one room all day." As a reporter she had a "constant readiness for change of scene." As an editor, she also required the dispositions of perfectionism and high standards of accuracy. This reporter had challenges her first year of teaching as she exhibited disposi-tions in schools which had made her successful in her former career. Deal-ing with a difficult school culture, she said the insights gained which have both made her more successful as she remained at the school were,

> I had to learn to keep my bearings in the face of great disorganization; I've learned to loosen my standards of order and procedure, but maintain my fundamental ethics of good teaching and student care; and I've learned to accept that all concerned parties, will critique me—administrators, parents, students, coworkers, and even office staff.

Many candidates have had the challenge of accepting the fact that in some school cultures longevity can mean more than educational background or even competence, in some cases. The nuances of each school culture are something that must be explored and navigated carefully.

The reporter's comments highlight some of the challenges alternatively certified teachers face in adapting to school culture. Other issues noted in the interviews and surveys regarding school culture issues included the challenge of being a leader, a boss in their former career and now being the novice in the school setting. Some of our candidates have more managerial experience than their administrators and many find it challenging to find the balance between being helpful and being seen as a threat. Several candidates voiced frustration with teaching colleagues who were not open to change and who would be negative toward children. Exploring the challenges of having a positive impact in negative settings is an issue that would often arise in class discussions.

FUTURE RESEARCH POSSIBILITIES

The findings of this study have outlined alternatively certified teachers' views of the dispositions necessary to be a successful teacher. It has also provided insight to the challenges of changing careers and successfully making the transition to sometimes challenging school cultures. Some further exploration of these issues could include: comparing graduates' views of necessary dispositions in the field of education to the Professional Education Unit's given dispositions; comparison of dispositions necessary in high and low SES (socioeconomic status) schools; dispositions necessary in different types of school cultures or with schools with administrators with differing styles; continued discussion of necessary disposition for success in education to inform candidate selection and preparation; build on this work to provide additional resources for alternative certification candidates and their program administrators to see others' views of transitioning from previous careers to the field of education.

Our successful retention rate indicates that with a high level of support, candidates can successfully make the transition. The results of this study will help us better prepare candidates in a proactive manner. The voices of teachers who have previously made the transition will assist in preparing candidates as they begin their internship year and will be an excellent resource as candidates struggle with some of these challenges. The overall positive views and insights of the teachers who have completed the Governors State University Alternative Certification Partnership are illustrated by the comments below which articulate why many candidates feel that the transition to teaching is worth it.

Success is measured not by the amount of your paycheck, but by the teacher moments. When you get a bonus for closing a big deal, of course, it feels great, but to have a child look up at you with their eyes glowing because they get it, now, that's priceless!

REFERENCES

Feistritzer, E. (2006, February). *Overview of alternate routes to teacher certification*. Paper Presented at the third annual conference of the National Center for Alternative Certification, San Diego.

Freeman, L., Peterson, K., & Erikson, D. (2004). The performance of candidates in an alternative certification program. In J. Dangel & E. Guyton (Ed.), *Research on alternative and non-traditional education: Teacher education yearbook XIII* (pp. 105-121). Lanham, MD: Rowman & Littlefield.

Jacobson, L. (2005). Alternative routes attracting unlikely candidates. *Education Week, 24*(24), 3-16.

Katz, L., & Raths, J. (1985). Dispositions as goals for teacher education. *Teaching and Teacher Education, 1*(4), 301-307).

Stoddart, T., & Floden, R. E. (1995). *Traditional and alternative routes to teacher certification: Issues, assumption, and misconceptions*. East Lansing, MI: National Center for Research on Teacher Learning ED 383 697

Zeichner, K. (2006). Reflections of a university-based teacher educator on the future of college and university based teacher education. *Journal of Teacher Education, 57*(3), 326-340.

PART III

PERSISTING ISSUES RAISED BY DISPOSITIONS

CHAPTER 9

ASSESSING DISPOSITIONS

Context and Questions

Mary E. Diez

The assessment of dispositions needs to be set in the context of teacher assessment more generally. Over the past 30 years, challenges to well-established assumptions about measurement practice have emerged, and new forms of practice have been developed, spurred on in part by the work of the National Board for Professional Teaching Standards (NBPTS). Not only have scholars addressed the epistemology of approaches to evaluation (Shepard, 2000; Wolf, Bixby, Glenn, & Gardner, 1991), but they have also explored new frameworks for conceptualizing the task of assessing complex behavior such as teaching practice (Deland-shere,1996; Moss, 1996).

Overwhelmingly, measurement practice in teacher education has focused on separating bits of knowledge into items on standardized tests. Especially under the influence of the competency-based teacher educa-

A version of this chapter was originally published in *The New Educator,* Volume 2, No. 1, 2006, pp. 57-72. The current version is slightly modified and appears here with permission.

Dispositions in Teacher Education, pp. 183–201

tion movement of the 1970s, the same process was used to identify discrete bits of performance. Guided by what Wolf et al. (1991) call the "epistemology of intelligence," the identification of decontextualized items makes sense if the goal is to specify the specific items that will count in determining competence. They note that the "epistemology of intelligence" leads to a "culture of testing," in which "individual performances, rather than collaborative forms of cognition, are the most powerful indicators of educational progress" (p. 43) And in this view, tests are seen as scientific instruments, that themselves do not affect learning.

Wolf et al. (1991), Shepard (2000) and others describe the growing interest in alternatives to these measurement assumptions. Wolf et al. describe a competing view that they call an "epistemology of mind," which places the focus of competence in the action of the person and, in fact, in collaborative interactions as well. They see the "epistemology of mind" leading to a culture of assessment, whose goal is not to require performance on the same set of items by all persons, but rather to look at performance in context and to describe and interpret an individual's performance in its own terms, against a set of standards or expectations. Such assessment is seen as contributing to learning and is even termed "assessment-*as*-learning" (Alverno College Faculty, 2000). Clearly, standards like those developed by the NBPTS (1989) and the Interstate New Teacher Assessment and Support Consortium (INTASC) (1992) describe teaching as a set of highly complex tasks that are carried out in particular classrooms, with particular groups of students. Such standards can be more richly addressed in the "epistemology of mind" framework.

In principles aimed primarily at K-12 teaching and learning, but also applicable to teacher education, Stiggins (2002) outlines key differences between what he calls assessment *of* learning and assessment *for* learning. He is not just calling attention to the difference between summative and formative assessment. Rather, he is highlighting the purposes of assessment in each case. When assessment *of* learning is the focus, one looks at data in terms of what they tell about the progress of learners at a point in time; the purpose is often to make a decision, as at a "gate" for admission and advancement in a teacher education program. When assessment *for* learning is the focus, however, one looks at data to guide the teacher's planning and to provide feedback to the learner on strengths and weaknesses that can guide his or her next stages of growth. While not exactly the same distinction that Wolf et al. (1991) make about a culture of testing vs. a culture of assessment, the distinction between summative and formative assessment may be linked to particular kinds of data. Many K-12 districts and teacher education institutions make heavy use of standardized tests for summative decisions, and the individualized nature of formative assessment may link it more closely to the culture of assessment. However, it is possible to use standardized test data formatively, that is, to inform teaching practice. And it is also possible to use individualized, contextual assessment data, like portfolios, cumulatively, to make high stakes decisions at a point in time. Of concern to both K-12 and teacher education would be a narrow use of the epistemology of intelligence and a culture of testing, combined with more focus on assessment *of* learning than on assessment *for* learning.

The work of the NBPTS, in developing new formats for assessment that aim to capture the complexity of accomplished teaching practice in individual, contextualized classrooms, might be seen as an attempt change the link between an epistemology of intelligence and summative assessment practice. In doing so, it has raised many challenges to traditional measurement assumptions. Delandshere (1996), Delandshere and Petrovsky (1994, 1998), and Moss (1996) provide a rich source of discussion that addresses the role of interpretation in making judgments about complex performances.

Similar to the differences between an epistemology of intelligence and an epistemology of mind, these researchers critique what they call a "static and prescribed" system (Delandshere, 1996, p. 105) in the naturalist tradition of the social sciences (Moss, 1996) represented by traditional measurement practice. Delandshere and Petrovsky (1998) point to traditional practice as essentialist, devoid of meaningful context, and reliant on atomized items. Delandshere (1996) challenges the assumption that, with the exception of minimum skill, "there are essential and universal skills and knowledge that teachers need to have" (p. 115). She argues that defining "knowledge as fixed" (p. 115) has the impact of reducing teacher learning. Moss (1996) outlines the issues related to applying a priori categories to teaching practice rather than trying to understand it in the teacher's own terms.

Delandshere and Petrovsky (1998) point to the shift from the traditional measurement goal of sorting and ranking to a new interest in assessment supporting teaching and learning. To achieve that new goal, Delandshere (1996) argues for a "dynamic and principled" system "that is integrated with the continuous education and practice of teachers" (p. 106). With respect to the "dynamic" nature of the system, she advises that "a view of teaching as a continuous learning process will not become part of the culture of teaching unless the evaluation of teaching captures and values that process (p. 115). And she says that "a principled assessment of teaching outlines its constituent elements and the nature of the supporting evidence rather than a specific set of tasks to be performed" (p. 115). Moss (1996) argues that an interpretivist conception of social science has as a primary goal to understand meaning in its context. Delandshere and Petrosky (1994) cite "the trend toward new forms of performance assessment" as "an attempt to develop language, methods, and traditions around a different conception of knowledge within a different paradigm" (p. 18).

NATURALIST VERSUS INTERPRETIVIST APPROACHES

More recently, building upon much of the work cited above, Uhlenbeck, Verloop, and Beijaard (2002) propose a set of "implications from theories on teaching and assessment for developers of beginning teacher assessments" (pp. 262-264), which may be of particular use in looking at the assessment of dispositions. Arguing that a complete picture of performance requires assessment not only of a teacher's actions, but also of a teacher's cognitions, Uhlenbeck et al. call for teaching to "be assessed in context" (p. 46) and for assessors to recognize that the complexity of teaching can be addressed in different ways. Agreeing with the need to move from naturalist approaches in social science to interpretivist approaches, they argue that "criteria on which teachers are judged should not prescribe a particular way of teaching; but they should accommodate a range of acceptable ways to teach" (p. 46). For example, a criterion might be that the teacher uses data to inform decision making, but as Shirley and Hargreaves (2006) point out, the teacher has "to be intelligently informed by evidence, not blindly driven by it to teach a certain way (p. 32).

These two approaches, however, are actively competing for predominance in the literature on teacher assessment and teacher education. The naturalist approach argues for assessment to standardize expectations, with the resulting effect of screening out candidates who do not conform. It depends upon quantitative measures, often using the assumptions of psychometrics originally developed for multiple choice and other standardized tests, but now applied to teaching performance. The interpretivist approach argues that, while performance needs to meet a high standard, assessment must look at individual performance in context and can be used to develop candidates for teaching roles. The methodologies used in the interpretivist approach to assessment are more qualitative and interpretivist, drawing upon work from a number of research traditions as well as incorporating the communities of discourse within which teaching practice exists.

In some respects, the naturalist approach appears to be winning the day, perhaps showing the power of the psychometric tradition; but trends may also reflect the realistic costs involved in more contextualized assessment. Here it would be useful to acknowledge a distinction between what is possible and appropriate to assess within a teacher education program and what is affordable at the state level. As Stiggins's (2002) work suggests, assessment *for* learning, in the course of teacher education, might more appropriately follow the epistemology of mind and culture of assessment, that is, qualitative, individualized, contextualized, and interpretivist, even if state level summative measures follow the epistemology of intelligence and culture of testing, that is, quantitative, decontextualized, and standardized.

One must also acknowledge the impact of NCATE on teacher education assessment. NCATE's rubric for standard 2, the assessment system, uses terms that suggest a *quantitative approach* to assessment in requirements for the assessment system's work with data: "Data are regularly and systematically collected, compiled, summarized, analyzed, and reported publicly for the purpose of improving candidate performance, program quality, and unit operations" (p. 22). I use the term *suggest*, because of course it is possible to work with qualitative data from a range of assessment methods within an assessment system that meets NCATE standards. In fact the further demand to "establish fairness, accuracy, and consistency of its performance assessment procedures" (p. 21) may well require some *qualitative approaches*. But in many assessment plans in NCATE institutions, the language of the NCATE standards and rubrics may be promoting a sense that *only* quantitative data are acceptable, especially if these standards and rubrics are read in the context of the assumptions of traditional measurement approaches.

The interpretivist approach, however, is also evident in the literature and in teacher education practice, especially in work related to assessments developed for the NBPTS (see Delandshere, 1996; Delandshere & Petrosky, 1994, 1998, 1999) and INTASC (see Moss, 1996; Moss & Schutz, 2001) and in the nearly universal focus on portfolios in teacher education. Some states, like Wisconsin, require that teacher preparation institutions document portfolio assessment for any licensure program and that districts follow up with professional development portfolios for continuing licensure ("Beginning educator support," 2005). But Connecticut is still the only state to use the kind of portfolio envisioned by INTASC, building a careful case for the validity of the process (http://www.state.ct.us/sde/dtl/t-a/).

PROBLEMS IN TEACHER EDUCATION ASSESSMENT

Looking at the literature on teacher education assessment, as well as drawing upon my own experience as a teacher educator, an NCATE board of examiners member, a PETE (Partnership for Excellence in Teacher Education) consultant (working with institutions seeking NCATE accreditation for the first time through an American Association of Colleges for Teacher Education (AACTE) program, an INTASC standards writing group member, and the INTASC academy chair from 1999-2004, I suggest four problems that have dogged the credibility of assessment of teacher education candidates and beginning teachers. Reductionism, disconnectedness of aspects of the standards, superficiality in the design and implementation of assessments, and a culture of compliance stand out as problems that may also affect the assessment of dispositions.

Reductionism

When states and/or teacher education programs focus on standardization (as opposed to standards) in their assessment systems, reductionism is a real problem. Standardization means that the same elements must be present in the evaluation of each candidate. Given the expense of evaluation systems, only a limited number of elements are likely to be included. And, given the demands of the psychometric assumptions, those elements must lend themselves to straightforward judgment. Reductionism occurs when the evaluation system goes for what is easiest to measure, rather than seeking to measure what is most critical even though it may be hard or expensive to measure. Too often, this results in an examination that serves as a "proxy" for things that might really be important. States are using tests of basic skills and content knowledge, for example, as tests for readiness for teaching, recognizing that they are only part of what a teacher needs to know and be able to do to be successful in the classroom.

Most states require student teaching or an internship, so that there is some evidence of the candidate's ability to function at least minimally effectively in a classroom. But the American Board for Certification of Teacher Excellence (ABCTE, 2005) purports to have created a way to determine readiness for teaching with two multiple choice exams—one focused on content and the other on professional teaching knowledge, arguing that the latter exam can provide assurance that candidates can, among other things, manage a classroom (http://www.abcte.org/pdfs/ABCTEbrochure.pdf).

Problems of reductionism are also found in decisions by teacher educators. I recall the first summer of the INTASC academies, when teacher educator participants were introduced to samples of INTASC portfolios (more fully described in the next section). One participant said, "well, if that's what they're going to use for the teacher licensure decision, then that's all we'll do in our program." Clearly, that person did not understand the developmental processes required for a teacher to perform well two or three years into teaching. To look only at the portfolio for permanent licensure is another kind of reductionism that affects teacher education.

Disconnectedness

When the INTASC standards were developed, the writing group separated the knowledge, dispositions, and performance elements of each of the ten principles. We were attempting to address the problem of reductionism, where the only thing that was tested was knowledge or a limited set of skills performed out of context. Many of the standards writing group members argued that, while a potential teacher might have mastered a good bit of knowledge, we need to be concerned with what NCATE (2002) now defines as "the values, commitments, and professional ethics that influence behaviors toward students, families, colleagues, and communities and affect student learning, motivation, and development as well as the educator's own professional growth" (p. 53). And we also wanted to ensure that knowledge, skills, and dispositions came together in the performance of the teacher in the context of the classroom. In support of that view, INTASC worked to develop a prototype assessment for beginning teachers, whose focus was on the evidence found in 10 days of classroom practice, with accompanying lesson designs, videotapes, reflections, and analysis and feedback on student work leading to revision of planning over the course of the time period (see Connecticut's BEST system, http://www.state.ct.us/sde/dtl/t-a/).

The standards writing group saw the three sections under each standard as connected in practice, but pulled them apart to provide analytic frames for working with the development and assessment of teachers. What is occurring now in many places is the development of three separate forms of testing. Wilkerson (2005), for example, while acknowledging the relationships between knowledge, skills, and dispositions, argues that they are separate and must be assessed separately.

Superficiality

Delandshere and Arens (2003) conducted a study of the use of portfolios related to the INTASC standards in one state—Indiana, but their criticism of the process could probably be applied to many teacher education programs that have adopted portfolio assessment. The study focused on three teacher education programs, looking at the quality of evidence provided in candidate portfolios and the inferences drawn from them both by the candidates themselves and by the teacher educator instructors. What the researchers found troubling was "a pressing concern among teacher educators to rally evidence that the students are 'meeting the standards' without much opportunity for meaningful dialogue and debate about education, teaching, and learning" (p. 57). Most problematic were patterns on the part of teaching candidates of providing artifacts without clear explanation or rationale for how those pieces of performance linked to the requirements in the standards. Nor did such explanations or rationale seem to be required of them.

I have been concerned with similar superficiality in reviewing assessment systems for institutions preparing for NCATE or as a BOE (board of examiner) member. The focus on "collect, compile, summarize, analyze and report" too often means another kind of reductionism—that is, get the numbers! Numbers in themselves, of course, are not inappropriate; the issue is whether they stand for meaningful data. And there are too many examples of the numbers not doing so. For example, when teacher educators use electronic data systems that aggregate scores on rubrics, in some cases what gets points on the rubric is highly questionable. Consider a rubric for a presentation that includes five format criteria and one substantive one. A candidate's "score," computed by the system provides a number, and overall, the program could report high levels of performance in their aggregated data. Yet the meaning of the score had more to do with using titles appropriately, spelling accurately, and capitalizing titles using APA (American Psychological Association) style than it did with the use of evidence or critical thinking (neither of which was addressed).

Underlying the problem of superficiality is that teacher educators have not been well prepared to move into qualitative assessment; their assessment literacy is not strong. Delandshere and Arens's (2003) critique does cause one to wonder about the approaches to assessment employed before the move to performance assessment—perhaps these teacher educators focused in the past on discrete bits of information in objective testing formats. Serious attention needs to be focused on making distinctions between format (put two sample lesson plans in your portfolio) and substance (provide evidence of planning to meet learners where they are and move them to the next stage of growth) if portfolios are to be credible assessment tools for the complex performances of teaching practice.

A Culture of Compliance

Finally, I have been concerned for a long time that what is missing in teacher education, especially related to assessment systems, is the kind of rigorous thinking that most teacher educators should have learned in their doctoral programs. In a symposium at AACTE in 2005, Diez, Finch, Lasley, and Tom, recalling the 1979 movie about the wife turned labor organizer, suggested that teacher educators have fallen into "the *Norma Rae* Syndrome," reacting in a compliance mode that says "You want dispositions? I'll give you dispositions!" Pointing to the need to think through the implications of a program's conceptual framework (as suggested by Dottin, 2006), the panel decried the practice of putting together a list of dispositions to mollify NCATE and then, rather than seeing how meaningful dispositions might be integrated into and developed throughout a program, using a screening device as an admissions tool.

It is not simply dispositions, of course, that fall prey to the compliance mentality. At the beginning of the NCATE redesign, the requirement for a conceptual framework was treated similarly, and the development of assessment systems also gets short shrift when folks go into compliance mode. In a kind of perverse reductionism, the compliance mentality attempts to do the least possible to meet demands, while avoiding the careful, thoughtful work that makes the NCATE process so valuable to those who take it seriously.

QUESTIONS ABOUT THE ASSESSMENT OF DISPOSITIONS

Thus, a review of the literature on teacher education evaluation suggests a deep division between those who hold to the epistemology of intelligence and those who are engaging the epistemology of mind. The impact of the choice of one or the other is probably no where more clear and more important than in the assessment of dispositions. And the same problems—reductionism, disconnectedness, superficiality, and a culture of compliance—that affect the whole assessment system are also potential problems for the assessment of dispositions. In this section, I examine four questions and use the notions of epistemologies of "intelligence" and "mind" as well as the four problems to suggest competing answers:

Question 1: Are Dispositions Stable Traits or can Teachers Develop Appropriate Dispositions for Teaching?

Returning to the NCATE definition of dispositions as "the values, commitments, and professional ethics that influence behaviors toward students, families, colleagues, and communities and affect student learning, motivation, and development as well as the educator's own professional growth" (p. 53), how might the two epistemologies respond to the question?

The epistemology of intelligence would assume from the literature in psychology that uses "disposition" to mean the probability or likelihood that persons will engage in certain kinds of behavior (Bartussek, 1972) that "dispositions are dimensions of an individual's personality, which in turn is controlled by forces or drives which are hidden within" (Mullin, 2003, p. 8). Recent exploratory work by Educational Testing Service (ETS) described by Roberts (Martin, Milam, Diez, & Roberts, 2006; Roberts & Diez, 2006) has also been linked to psychology's "big five" factors or dimensions of personality traits. Roberts clearly argues that instruments based on personality traits are best used in the context of self-assessment and guidance; however, in a culture of testing, it is not far-fetched to picture the use of instruments testing personality resulting in a decision not to admit into teacher education persons who do not have the right "profile."

In contrast, the epistemology of mind would suggest a challenge to the "stable trait" theory in its assumption that teachers, as human beings, learn in many ways and on many levels. Combined with the connections assumed by the INTASC standards writers, one might argue, for example, that a teacher education candidate might come into a program not really believing that "all children can learn." Given his experience in the past, he may have drawn the conclusion that children vary greatly in their abilities and that some appear not to be able to learn very effectively at all. However, that judgment was formed in the absence of knowledge and skill; given a deeper knowledge of child development and teaching strategy, the candidate's disposition may be changed. Similarly, many urban teacher educators have worked with candidates whose lack of knowledge of cultures other than their own influenced their beginning disposition toward working in multicultural settings. Over time, building both knowledge and understanding and honing skills to interact effectively, these candidates can leave programs with a change in disposition, committed to respect for varied cultures and to social justice in meeting the needs of learners from all cultures.

Assessment can play a major role in the shifts described above. For example, in key assessments related to dispositions in the Alverno curriculum, candidates are asked to annotate lesson plans with an explanation of why the candidate chose to do what she chose to do, in terms of meeting the range of needs in the classroom. Through the assessment the candidate is directed to apply her knowledge and skills to be able to differentiate instruction—but overtime, she also shows evidence of a strengthening disposition to meet the needs of all learners as she consciously takes action to address those needs in her classroom.

Assessment instruments in this case are diagnostic, helping both the candidate and the teacher educator to see how dispositions are functioning. Some dispositions—brought to light in reflection—might lead the candidate to make a choice to move to another career (see Diez, 2006). But they also might solidify the candidate's choice to engage in the learning necessary to develop knowledge and skill required to change the disposition.

Are dispositions stable traits? I would argue no, if "stable" means that they cannot be changed in relationship to the knowledge and skills that a person develops. The impact of a teacher education program can, to use Bartussek's terms, adjust the *likelihood* of a person performing a particular behavior. Belief that dispositions are not affected by changes in knowledge and skill levels assumes the *disconnectedness* of the three INTASC standards categories, whereas the belief that dispositions can be affected by knowledge and skill development in context is possible only in a *connected* view.

Question 2: Are Dispositions Best Assessed in any Particular way?

The two epistemologies differ in the kind of evaluation that flows from their assumptions. Table 9.1 outlines four possible methods of assessing dispositions and also highlights benefits and problems related to each approach. It draws upon work by Wilkerson (2005) and Mullin (2003), as well as my experience in the Alverno teacher education program. The table suggests benefits and issues or problems related to each of the four methods.

Method 1: Response to a Common set of Statements
Psychodynamic personality tests, like the 16PF model, have been used for many years to screen applicants, and these tests are produced with highly sophisticated psychmetrics. Perhaps some of the new tests being developed for dispositions will meet the challenge and find an appropriate use (see Wilkerson & Lang, 2005). The teacher education community needs to be concerned, however, with scales being developed by individual teacher education programs that are not being tested with the same level of psychometric rigor. Most teacher educators have a passing familiarity with Likert scales; few are deeply trained in their development. Given a *culture of compliance* and NCATE's focus on aggregating data, it is tempting to gin up a quick Likert scale and have it filled out by faculty about candidates or filled out by candidates themselves. The data, however aggregatable, are questionable in those cases. Teacher educators need to ask this key question: What's the evidence for the judgment— whether it is made by teacher about candidate or a candidate self rating?

Table 9.1.   Possible Approaches to Assessment of Dispositions

Description of method	Benefits	Issues/Problems
Psychodynamic Give participants the same set of statements to respond to indicating their beliefs/dispositions; usually developed as a kind of Likert scale	Easy to do statistical research that compares everyone across a common set of statements; data can be aggregated easily (epistemology of intelligence)	• Assumes a set of right answers. • Possible to "scam" the system, saying what you expect is wanted • Possible to answer honestly about one's current sense of the possible and be ruled out as a teacher candidate. • Not contextualized, that is, not tied to evidence in practice.
Humanistic or existential: Give participants an open-ended response format question (in writing or interview) about what they believe/hold as dispositions	Allows participant to use own terms and thus may elicit responses not expected; respects the individual	• Possible to "scam" the researcher • Not necessarily contextualized • Requires interpretation and judgment • Difficult to aggregate data
Behavioral (perspective of the candidate) Ask participants to express reflection in relationship to specific actions related to beliefs/dispositions, for example, in developing a lesson/unit plan, how did they make decisions?	Expressions of beliefs/dispositions are tied to actual practice and thus are more likely to be "functioning" beliefs/dispositions; respects the individual (epistemology of mind)	• Difficult to "scam" the researcher • Because responses are contextualized and thus related to the practice of an individual, difficult to aggregate data • Requires interpretation and judgment
Behavioral (perspective of the candidate's students) In focus groups or interviews, ask the students of the candidate to describe how the candidate treats them	Kids' view of the behavior of the candidate and how they infer his/her dispositions; comes from experience in context; can be aggregated	• Difficult for the candidate to influence • Influenced by how the questions are asked • May require interpretation and judgment

Without a link from evidence to judgment, such an instrument is meaningless.

The other two assessment problems listed in Table 9.1 are also important to consider. Especially if a teacher education program is explicit about its values, commitments, and professional ethics, candidates could easily scam the system, giving the faculty what the see they want to hear.

Actually, an honest candidate not out to scam the system could be disadvantaged by answering honestly, if there is a high stakes decision tied to how he responds to an initial instrument assessing dispositions. But in either case—and in the case of faculty simply making judgments about candidate dispositions—the biggest problem is that the judgment about the candidate is not tied to any evidence that can be examined.

Lang (2005) acknowledges the possibility of responses that are intended to "self-report what was 'expected,' but not what they really believed or behaved," but he argues that instruments can be designed to minimize that problem. Again, I am not as concerned with the carefully designed instruments, as with those developed in house and then used in high stakes ways.

Method 2: Open-Ended Response (Interview or Written)

Drawing upon a humanistic or existential approach, several types of interviews that provide open-ended response opportunities are currently used in teacher education or in screening of beginning teachers. Some simply ask the candidate straightforward questions, like "why do you want to become a teacher?" While this format allows a candidate to express her own ideas and beliefs, in practice, the candidate may not know what is expected and so may not provide the depth of information that would fully express her readiness to enter a teacher education program. Lacking other contexts, a savvy candidate may scope out the program's language in public documents like the conceptual framework and give the program faculty what they want to hear, whether or not it matches his own beliefs. Mullin (2003) expresses concern that this approach may be "a dangerous entryway to "political correctness" (p. 8). And the recent, highly publicized cases challenging dispositions reinforce that concern, with Damon (2005) calling dispositions "an empty vessel that could be filled with any agenda you want" (p. 1).

The same two issues would apply to a written response to an open-ended question about one's beliefs as a teacher education candidate. Many programs ask for candidates to write letters as part of the application to the program. When these are assessed for dispositions (as opposed to quality of writing), candidates are disadvantaged unless they have a sense of what is expected in this context. And the tendency to appear "politically correct" may cloud the results if the expectations for kinds of dispositional statements are made clear.

Some interview protocols provide a series of brief scenarios and ask candidates "what *would* you do?" While candidates may respond honestly, they may not have faced a similar circumstance and so may respond differently that they would act, particularly because this type of question is particularly susceptible to the candidate "giving them what you think they want to hear." The Gallup Organization has moved from this type of interview (the Teacher Perceiver) to the "TeacherInsight" system, an online instrument that uses both Likert scale responses and some open-ended questions (http://education.gallup.com/content/default.asp?ci=868).

Some interview protocols ask the candidate to think about a past action, to tell the story about what they *did* do and why, and to respond to follow up questions that get at candidate thinking. This approach, originally developed by David McClelland (1978), comes the closest to linking responses to evidence. Candidates are asked to reflect on their own past action and the responses to the follow up questions are grounded in that action. This model is used in the Alverno College teacher education program (see Diez, 2006).

Method 3: Reflection Linking Actions and Dispositions

Elsewhere (Diez, 2006), I argue that dispositions can only be assessed indirectly, as they "leak out" in action or as they are described in reflection. In spite of Wilkerson's (2006) recent critique of the term "leak out" as implying the use of unsystematic approaches, my discussion of the phenomenon has always been within the context of carefully designed performance assessments. The combination of focusing on particular actions and reflecting on what those actions reveal about dispositions has particular promise for avoiding the *superficiality* problem in assessment of dispositions—precisely because, in the epistemology of mind, it attends systematically to the links between disposition, action, and reflection. Especially as candidates begin to develop knowledge and skill that allows them to engage in the beginning practice of the role they want to take on, they can complete assessments that ask them to describe what they did in a classroom interaction, for example, and debrief the event in terms of their decision-making: What did they do? Why did they do what they did? How does their choice of action link to particular value stances they hold? What impact did it have on the learners? How does it fit with the expectations of the profession?

And, faculty and candidate can use reflection to explore problematic behavior as well. Hugh Sockett (2006) gives, as an example, a teacher educator watching a student teacher, noticing that the student teacher "is particularly sarcastic with 6th-grader Susan, constantly puts the child down when she tries to answer, and generally bullies her intellectually" (p. 11). He provides three different scenarios for interaction about the problematic behavior, each based in a different philosophical/moral perspective (i.e., based in character, rules, and relationships). These perspectives suggest starting points for reflection on the candidate's action.

Method 4: Focus Groups of Students

Wilkerson (2005) proposes an approach that gets at the impact of candidate or teacher dispositions through asking students in the classroom about the way the candidate or teacher acts:

> What does the teacher do if you or your peers continue to have trouble understanding after he/she has explained it once? Does the teacher mind having to explain the same thing differently? Is he/she patient with you and your peers when someone does not understand? (slide 12)

Results from such focus groups would provide a good test of whether the self-reflection of the candidate or teacher about his/her behaviors is accurate in terms of the students' experience. One must be careful, however, not to underestimate the potential for mischief in student responses.

As in all good research, triangulation of data sources would be a good idea for having confidence that the data about candidate dispositions is accurate. None of the above methods is without problems if used by itself.

Question 3: Can the Assessment of Dispositions help to Develop Dispositions?

This question clearly resonates with the "epistemology of mind" approach; an "epistemology of intelligence" would tend to see dispositions as "stable" traits in the more narrow sense of that word. But given the assumption that candidates can develop dispositions appropriate for teaching, what kind of assessment *for* learning best promotes that development?

Literature on this question is just beginning to emerge, as teacher educators work with the notion of dispositions in the context of teacher practice, but it is worth looking at three examples of how teacher educators are using assessment to impact the development of dispositions. First, Cartwright and Blacklock (2003) asked intern teachers to develop interventions to assist struggling K-12 readers and to document their work over a 12-week period using a modified work sample assessment. Using a pre- and postquestionnaire, they documented significant positive change in dispositions toward teaching struggling readers.

Lamson, Aldrich, and Thomas (2003) developed a series of situational role plays that simulate experiences likely to take place in K-12 settings, such as parent-teacher interactions, discipline situations (dealing with biting, hitting, bullying), and adaptation of lessons for children with special needs. Participants have to justify their simulated actions and connect them to theoretical frameworks (e.g., related to parent involvement, classroom management, differentiation). While this report is primarily descriptive, the authors provide multiple examples of candidate testimony to the impact of such experiences on their self-understanding and dispositions for teaching.

Finally, McCombs (2003) describes the use of the ALCP (the Assessment of Learner-Centered Practices). This guided reflection survey tool assists teachers "to reflect on (1) their own beliefs and practices, (2) how these practices are perceived by their students, and (3) the impact of both teacher and student learner-centered variables on student motivation and achievement" (p. 2). The ALCP has been validated (McCombs, 1999) with more than 5000 teachers. McCombs (2003) argues that the use of the tool encourages "the development of learner-centered teacher dispositions" (p. 20).

Question 4: What Should Teacher Education Programs Consider as They Develop a Plan to Assess Candidate Dispositions?

The emerging literature on the assessment of dispositions suggests a number of key ideas to keep in mind as teacher preparation programs work to address NCATE and state requirements. The first is to make sure that the program has expressed in its conceptual framework a clear sense of "the values, commitments, and professional ethics" that guide courses, experiences, and assessments. Dottin (2006) lays out the danger of treating dispositions as "add-on features" and not naturally inherent in all aspects of the curriculum. An add-on approach is likely to fall prey to the problem of *superficiality*. The second is to recognize the links between and among knowledge, dispositions and skills, recognizing that dispositions will deepen as candidates develop the understanding and skill that support, for example, a disposition to work to meet the needs of all learners in a class. The third is to incorporate assessment of dispositions across the program, over time, using multiple methods, both structured instruments and ongoing observation of the candidate in action (Diez, 2006).

Finally, given the developmental nature of candidate growth in dispositions and given the complex nature of teaching, the assessment of dispositions should be guided by what Wolf et al. (1991) call an epistemology of mind and a culture of assessment, using qualitative, interpretivist approaches to look at each individual candidate's responses to the challenges of becoming a teacher. These qualitative approaches can lead to a cumulative picture of the candidate's readiness for teaching, at the point at which a summative decision must be made.

REFERENCES

Alverno College Faculty (1994). *Student assessment-as-learning at Alverno College*. Milwaukee, Wisconsin: Alverno Institute.

American Board for Certification of Teacher Excellence. (2005). *Passport to teaching certification brochure*. Retreived July 18, 2005, from http://www.abcte.org/pdfs/ABCTEbrochure.pdf

Bartussek, D. (1972). Disposition. In H. J. Eysenck, W. Arnold, & R. Meili (Eds.), *Encyclopedia of psychology* (p. 282). New York: Herder and Herder.

Cartwright, D. D., & Blacklock, K. K. (2003, January). *Teacher work samples and struggling readers: Impacting student performance and candidate dispositions*. Paper presented at the annual meeting of the American Association of Colleges for Teacher Education, New Orleans.

Damon, W. (2005). Arresting insights in education. *Fwd, 2*(3), 1-6.

Delandshere, G. (1996). From static and prescribed to dynamic and principled assessment of teaching. *Elementary School Journal, 97*(2), 105-120.

Delandshere, G., & Arens, S. A. (2003). Examining the quality of the evidence in preservice teacher portfolios. *Journal of Teacher Education, 54*(1), 57-73.

Delandshere, G., & Petrosky, A. R. (1994) Capturing teacher's knowledge: Performance assessment. a and post-structuralist epistemology, b) from a post-structuralist perspective, c) and post-structuralism, d) none of the above. *Educational Researcher, 23*(5), 11-18.

Delandshere, G., & Petrosky, A. R. (1998). Assessment of complex performance: Limitations of key measurement assumptions. *Educational Researcher, 27*(2), 14-24.

Delandshere, G., & Petrosky, A. R. (1999). It is also possible to quantify colors but that is not the point: A rejoinder to Brookhart. *Educational Researcher, 28*(3), 28-30.

Diez, M. E. (2006). Assessing dispositions: Five principles to guide practice. In H. Sockett (Ed.), *Teacher dispositions: Building a teacher education framework of moral standards*. Washington, DC: AACTE

Diez, M. E., Finch, M. E., Lasley, T., & Tom, A. (2005, February). *You want dispositions? I'll give you dispositions! The Norma Rae syndrome in teacher education*. Major symposium at the annual meeting of the American Association of Colleges for Teacher Education. Washington, DC.

Dottin, E. (2006). A Deweyan approach to the development of moral dispositions in professional teacher education communities. In H. Sockett (Ed.), *Teacher dispositions: Building a teacher education framework of moral standards* (pp. 27-47). Washington, DC: AACTE

Gallup Organization. (n.d.). *TeacherInsight Program*. Retrieved July 29, 2005, from http://education.gallup.com/content/default.asp?ci=868

Interstate New Teacher Assessment and Support Consortium. (1992). *Model standards for beginning teacher licensure and development: A resource for state dialogue*. Washington, DC: Council of Chief State School Officers.

Lamson, S. L., Aldrich, J. E., & Thomas, K. R. (2003, February). *Using social inquiry strategies to enhance candidate dispositions*. Paper presented at the annual meeting of the Association of Teacher Educators, Jacksonville, FL.

Lang, W. S. (2005, February). *Analysis of disposition measures of consistency with INTASC principles: Results of an initial study.* Paper presented at the annual meeting of the American Association of Colleges for Teacher Education. Washington, DC.

Martin, C., Milam, S., Diez, M. E., & Roberts, R. D. (2006, January). *Critical issues in identifying and assessing teacher candidates' professional dispositions.* Major Symposium at the annual meeting of the American Association of Colleges for Teacher Education, San Diego.

McClelland, D. C. (1978). *Guide to behavioral event interviewing.* Boston: McBer and Company.

McCombs, B. L. (1999). *The assessment of learner-centered practices: Tools for teacher reflection, learning and change.* Denver, CO: University of Denver Reseach Institute.

McCombs, B. L. (2003, April). *Defining tools for teacher reflection: The assessment of learner-centered practices.* Paper presented at the annual meeting of the American Educational Research Association, Chicago.

Moss, P. A. (1996). Enlarging the dialogue in educational measurement: Voice from interpretive research traditions. *Educational Researcher, 25*(1), 20-28.

Moss, P. A., & Schutz, A. (2001). Educational standards, assessment, and the search for consensus. *American Educational Research Journal, 38*(1), 37-70.

Mullin, D. (2003). *Developing a framework for the assessment of teacher candidate dispositions.* East Lansing, MI: National Center for Research on Teacher Learning. (ERIC Document Reproduction Service No. ED479255)

National Board for Professional Teaching Standards. (1989). *What teachers should know and be able to do.* Detroit, MI: Author.

National Council for the Accreditation of Teacher Education. (2002). *Professional standards for the accreditation of schools, colleges, and departments of education.* Washington, DC: Author.

Roberts, R. D., & Diez, M. E. (2006). *Assessing teacher dispositions.* Paper presented at the annual meeting of the American Association of Colleges for Teacher Education, San Diego, CA.

Shepard, L. A. (2000). The role of assessment in a learning culture. *Educational Researcher, 29*(7), 4-14.

Shirley, D., & Hargreaves, A. (2006). Data-driven to distraction: Why American educations need a reform alternative—and where they might look to find it. *Education Week, 26*(6) 32-33.

Sockett, H. (2006). Character, rules, and relations. In H. Sockett (Ed.), *Teacher dispositions: Building a teacher education framework of moral standards* (pp. 9-25). Washington, DC: AACTE

Beginning educator support and training (BEST) program. (2005). *State of Connecticut, Department of Education.* Retrieved from http://www.state.ct.us/sde/dtl/t-a/ on July 29, 2005.

Stiggins, R. J. (2002). Assessment crisis: The absence of assessment for learning. *Phi Delta Kappan, 83*(10), 758-765.

Uhlenbeck, A. M., Verloop, N., & Beijaard, D. (2002). Requirements for an assessment procedure for beginning teachers: Implications from recent theories on teaching and assessment. *Teachers College Record, 104*(2), 242-272.

Wilkerson, J. R. (2005, February). *Measuring dispositions with credibility: A multi-insti-tutional perspective.* Paper presented at the annual meeting of the American Association of Colleges for Teacher Education, Washington, DC.

Wilkerson, J. R. (2006). Measuring teacher dispositions: Standards-based or morality-based? *Teachers College Record.* Retreived April 20, 2006, from http://www.tcrecrod.org

Wilkerson, J. R., & Lang, W. S. (2005, February). *Measuring dispositions with practi-cality, utility, validity and reliability in mind.* Paper presented at the annual meet-ing of the American Association of Colleges for Teacher Education. Washington, DC.

Wolf, D., Bixby, J., Glenn, J., & Gardner, H. (1991). To use their minds well: Inves-tigating new forms of student assessment. In G. Grant (Ed.), *Review of research in education* (Vol. 17, pp. 31-74)). Washington, DC: American Educational Research Association.

CHAPTER 10

THE ROLE OF COACHING IN WORKING WITH DISPOSITIONS[1]

Mary E. Diez

The practice of coaching has been extended in recent years, encompassing not only sports and athletics coaching, but business and executive coaching, creativity coaching, performance coaching, life coaching, and even birth coaching (Bloom, Castagna, Moir, & Warren, 2005; Flaherty, 2005; Hargrove, 1995). In the realm of education, cognitive coaching and peer coaching are common terms (Costa & Garmston, 1994), and districts are following a business model in hiring coaches for principals and superintendents (see, for example, Milwaukee Public Schools, 2004).

Across these categories of coaching, some clarification about coaching in an educational setting is emerging. Bloom et al. (2005), contrast coaching with therapy, mentoring, consulting, and supervision. They explain that, while *therapy* focuses on an individual's psychological functioning, coaching is concerned with helping the individual accomplish professional goals. While *mentoring* usually involves a relationship with an expert in the field or an organizational insider, coaching is more like a partnership. While *consulting* offers information in an area of the consultant's

Dispositions in Teacher Education, pp. 203–218
Copyright © 2007 by Information Age Publishing
All rights of reproduction in any form reserved.

expertise, coaching is based on a more holistic set of knowledge and skill as the coach works with the coachee to create a plan of action.

While both *supervision* and coaching share the role of nurturing growth, the key difference is that a supervisor has power over one's employment, where a coach does not. Bloom et al. (2005) note that good supervisors will, of course, use coaching techniques, but coaches do not have access to the power differential available to supervisors. Coaching is defined as showing "people how to transform or stretch their visions, values, and abilities" (Hargrove, 1995); "helping an individual or team produce a desired result through increasing awareness and ability to solve problems" (Milwaukee Public Schools, 2004, p. 10); and "providing deliberate support to clarify and achieve goals" (Bloom et al., 2005, p. 7).

In a discussion of differentiated coaching, Bloom et al. (1995) identify instructional, collaborative, and facilitative coaching. In *instructional* coaching, the coach provides information, models a way or ways to approach a problem, and may even offer concrete suggestions about what to do. In *collaborative* coaching, the coach engages the coachee in working on problems together, reflecting together on what is learned. In *facilitative* coaching, the coach stands back, allowing the coachee to produce most of the information and make the decisions, asking questions to spark the coachee's thinking (see also, Milwaukee Public Schools, 2004).

What is a chapter on coaching doing in a book on educator dispositions? Whether one defines dispositions as unchangeable aspects of the person or as aspects that can be developed, the notion of coaching has some relevance and applicability. In the following sections of this chapter, I review varied ways in which dispositions might be addressed through a coaching model. Where terms like "guidance," "counseling," "self-assessment,"or "feedback" might also be used, the coaching model fits surprisingly well across this set of approaches. How coaching would be carried out differs, of course, based on the assumptions within those definitions.

DISPOSITIONS AS STABLE TRAITS

Kyllonen, Walters, and Kaufman (2005), in exploring noncognitive constructs and their assessment in graduate education, make the argument that many quasi-cognitive and attitudinal variables can be related to personality variables, which are stable. In a review of variables from research studies, they organize sets of variables, many of which would be typical dispositions as described in teacher education programs' conceptual frameworks (e.g., persistence/tenacity or collegiality/making professional connections), in relationship to the "big five" personality factors—extroversion, neuroticism (emotional stability), agreeableness, conscientiousness, and openness. Roberts (2006) describes work being undertaken by ETS that draws upon Kyllonen et al.'s work. Roberts and colleagues worked with the dispositions statements in the INTASC (Interstate New Teacher Assessment and Support Consortium) standards, finding that all could be linked to one or more of the "big five."

Roberts (2006) and colleagues suggest that, rather than creating a test of dispositions to determine eligibility or readiness for teaching, the role of a testing company might be to develop an instrument providing information for candidate self-assessment and/or guidance. Thus, for example, a candidate might use such an instrument to recognize that because she has a relatively high score on the introversion side of the introversion-extroversion continuum, she needs considerable solitude for quiet time to process and reflect. Should that person eschew a teaching career? Not necessarily, but the role of guidance or coaching might be to help the person learn how she can balance the demands of the classroom with her need for reflection and processing time. Alternatively, a person high on the extroversion side of the continuum might need guidance to learn how to engage in reflective practice, in order to get maximum learning from the activities of the professional day.

A second approach to identifying dispositions as stable traits was developed by Donald O. Clifton and a team of researchers at The Gallup Organization. The Clifton StrengthsFinder® is based on a simple question, "What would happen if we studied what is right with people?" (Lopez, Hodges, & Harter, 2005). The Clifton StrengthsFinder® is an online tool, used exclusively for development, which identifies an individual's signature (top five) talents from 34 themes of talent. Gallup defines talents as the "naturally recurring patterns of thought, feeling, or behavior that can be productively applied" (Hodges & Clifton, 2004, p. 257). Thus, talents are seen as the unique expressions of individual behavior. Strengths emerge "as the ability to provide consistent, near-perfect performance in a specific task," (Lopez, Hodger, & Harter, 2005, p. 4) and are most evident when talents combine with knowledge and skill for the task.

The 34 themes of talent range from "Achiever"—describing a person with an "internal fire" that pushes her "to do more, to achieve more" (Liesveld & Miller, 2005, p. 67), to "Woo"—describing a person who enjoys "the challenge of meeting new people and getting them to like you" (p. 167). In *Teach With Your Strengths*, Liesveld and Miller provide action items that elaborate on the themes and provide suggestions for a teacher.

For example a teacher who has the talent of "Deliberative" tends to be "careful," "vigilant," and may be a "private person." One of the action items suggested by Liesveld and Miller's (2005) to guide a teacher with this talent indicates the kind of *instructional* coaching that might be appropriate in working with this person:

Because teaching is, by its nature, quite public, you might need to deliberately carve out some time in the day to be by yourself. Better yet: if you can,
co-opt a private place for yourself so you can have time alone when you
need it. You might need to give your students and colleagues some simple
clues that indicate your need for privacy. (p. 106)

Gallup's strengths-based development concept uses the top five "signature" themes of talent as a beginning point for self discovery. With feedback from the assessment, a respondent customizes a group of
developmental suggestions to create a personalized view of self (Lopez,
Hodges, & Harter, 2005) Behavioral change is encouraged by using the
approach of moving from talent and managing areas of lesser talent, conventionally referred to as weaknesses. Gallup's strengths-based approach
suggests that while gains can be made in areas of talent or lesser talent,
the potential for excellence stems from developing talents.

In a teacher education program, where interaction with a coach over
time is possible, *collaborative* or *facilitative* coaching might also be applied.
For example, in facilitative coaching, a teacher educator might work with
a candidate with a high "Activator" talent, someone for whom action is a
form of learning. The coach might notice that the candidate is impatient
with group work, including the simulated school planning committees
that are part of his teacher education experiences. Because working collaboratively is critically important in today's schools, the teacher functions
as a coach for all the candidates, providing criteria for effective interaction, raising questions, and videotaping the group interaction for their
self-assessment and for her feedback. Key for the "Activator" candidate
would be understanding his behaviors, helping him realize the importance of his participation in groups, and underscoring his contribution in
taking the lead during the action phase that follows group deliberation.

The proposed ETS instrument and the Clifton StrengthsFinder® are
similar in that they are based on the assumption that persons have personality traits or talents that fit within the umbrella of the current discussion of dispositions. But the coaching roles may be very different. With
the proposed ETS instrument, the role is to help guide whether teaching
is a choice that fits a candidate; StrengthsFinder® focuses on the adjustments candidates can make to be more effective in the varied roles a
teacher takes on.

DISPOSITIONS AS DEVELOPED

As evident throughout the chapters in this book, not everyone sees dispositions as stable traits; some clearly argue that dispositions are learned

and developed (see, for example, Oja & Reiman and Nawrocki-Chabin & Breese, in this volume). Clearly, if one sees dispositions as integrated with knowledge and skill, then it is likely that one would expect these aspects of the person to grow and change as the person as a whole grows and changes. Derek Bok's (2006) critique of undergraduate education suggests a way to think about dispositions—and coaching—in this integrative way. Arguing that building character is an important role for higher education, Bok notes that university faculties have increased the number of courses on moral issues over the last 50 years. His discussion clearly links the teaching of moral reasoning with the noncognitive—one's empathy, sense of integrity, and moral will. While Bok notes that universities can set a positive example in their own ethical practice as well as reinforce moral values through enforcement of rules, he also suggests that "universities can try to foster ethical behavior by helping students develop greater concern for the needs of others. Empathy supplies the most powerful motive for acting ethically" (p. 166). Bok goes on to argue that "moral reasoning and the will to act ethically ... are closely interconnected" (p. 168), noting that education plays a key role in guiding the development of both.

Moral Dispositions

Sockett (2006) makes the same connection between moral reasoning and moral action, citing Norton's (1991) notion that the core of moral life is cognitive. In his thoughtful discussion about the ways in which moral perspectives grounded in philosophical positions view moral development, he makes clear that moral dispositions are *formed*. While Sockett does not use the term "coaching," I think that the questions he asks using each philosophical position to address a scenario about a sarcastic student teacher could be seen as instructional, collaborative, or facilitative coaching. "Are you deliberately choosing to become the sort of person and teacher who hurts other people?" (p. 11) engages the coach and student teacher in a dialogue about character. Depending upon what follows the first question, the approach could be instructional or facilitative. In the first case, the coach would be directly teaching the appropriate character for the student teacher to take on; in the second case, the coach would use the question to spark a response of ownership by the student teacher.

In asking "Why have you not yet learned the rule that you must not single out students and bully them in this way?" (Sockett, 2006, p. 12) the coach draws the student teacher into a consideration of "the social context of rules" (p. 12). Again, the coach might be using instructional coaching to suggest a particular desired response; the form of the question implies a single right response. But using facilitative coaching would also be possible here if the coach moved on to questions that helped the student teacher stand back and examine his behavior in relationship to expected professional behavior in the classroom.

"Let us talk together about how we all try to create caring relationships with children" (Sockett, 2006, p. 12) is an attempt to focus on relationships. The tone and structure of the opening sentence seems collaborative, at least on the surface, but the coach is taking the lead in suggesting a goal and plan of action.

Sockett (2006) goes on to discuss a set of primary dispositions implicit in each of these stances toward moral development. The point here is not to debate the value of these perspectives, but to point out that whatever perspective one takes on, coaching is a mechanism that can promote moral development within that perspective.

Professional Dispositions

NCATE (National Council for the Accreditation of Teacher Education) has recently revised its definitions, at least partially in response to some highly publicized incidents (e.g., at Brooklyn College, LeMoyne College, and Washington State University) where the assessment of dispositions was challenged by preservice teacher candidates. The highly politicized reports and editorials in the popular press (see Gersham, 2005; Leo, 2005; Will, 2006), were responded to in each instance by Art Wise, President of NCATE (Wise, 2006). In addition, NCATE attempted to clarify expectations by changing the term from "dispositions" to "professional dispositions" and eliminating references to terms like "social justice," which could spark ideological controversy. The new definition also makes explicit the expectation that candidates will "demonstrate classroom behaviors that are consistent with the ideas of fairness and the belief that all students can learn" and the expectation that institutions will "assess professional dispositions based on observable behavior in educational settings" (NCATE, 2006)

Using the term "professional dispositions" also implies the connection between the knowledge required for a professional, the skills developed by a professional, and the dispositions that guide the application of both knowledge and skill. To take an explicit statement in the new definition— "the belief that all students can learn"—is a good example of these connections. Many teacher education candidates enter the profession having experienced classrooms where they might reasonably come to believe that not all children can learn. These candidates' beliefs will be impacted by a teacher education program in at least two ways. First, they will study developmental and cognitive psychology, gaining a broader view of both "learning" and "ability." Second, they will learn techniques and strategies for working with students, gradually gaining skill in designing developmentally appropriate instruction and working with differentiation. Building knowledge and skill is intimately tied to changing the belief that all children can learn; the observable behavior linked to that belief would be their ongoing effort to work with children, recognizing their developmental starting point and being willing to make the effort to differentiate instruction to meet the needs of all the learners in a given class. Specific evidence, for example, might be found in work samples or portfolios that incorporate lesson plans, videotapes of teaching, samples of student work with feedback, and reflection that shows how the candidate made decisions based on review of student work.

Teacher educators could characterize as coaching their work with candidates as they develop the knowledge and skills that are necessary and build the professional dispositions to use that knowledge and skill to make a difference. The early stages are likely to be more heavily instructional coaching, with the teacher educator making explicit the implications for action in the knowledge being developed and carefully scaffolding the use of reflection to probe connections between theory and practice. As candidates move into field experiences, more collaborative coaching might be appropriate. For example, a teacher educator might provide samples of middle school student work in science and engage with candidates in examining it to determine how to approach the misconceptions they find there. During student teaching, facilitative coaching would be appropriate, with teacher educators asking questions to help candidates reflect on their particular classroom needs.

BUILDING STRATEGIES FOR COACHING IN TEACHER EDUCATION

While many districts are moving coaching into daily practice in schools, not all teachers and administrators come into practice ready to be coached or even recognizing its value. In this final section of the chapter, I want to explore how two teacher education programs are applying forms of coaching candidates with regard to aspects of practice that fall under the umbrella of "dispositions," however defined.

To begin, it may be helpful to look briefly at the history of interest in dispositions. Both Katz and Raths (1985) and the INTASC standards writing group in the early 1990's came at the issue because they recognized that it was possible to have the knowledge and skills required to be an effective teacher and yet not use them for good in the classroom. Katz and Raths describe the teacher who refuses to re-explain a concept for a student as punishment for not paying attention. The AFT (American Federation of

Teachers) representative in the INTASC work asked those of us teacher educators, "When are you going to stop recommending candidates for licensure who are mean to kids?"

Like Sockett's (2006) example, the concerns expressed in these examples have a deeper set of philosophical implications; hence, the effort on the part of NCATE to tie the notion of dispositions to the conceptual framework of a teacher education program. Milam (2006) supports that effort, citing court cases that recognize the responsibility of professional programs to clarify expected professional outcomes—including noncognitive outcomes like appropriate social interaction behavior—and to assess them.

A teacher education program, then, needs to identify the expectations for candidate behavior, just as it defines the knowledge and skills appropriate for professional practice. But just as candidates need to learn knowledge and skills needed for the profession, they likely need to learn to behave as professionals. Coaching may be a key factor currently missing from the "dispositions debate."

APPLICATIONS OF COACHING IN
THE TEACHER EDUCATION CONTEXT

Coaching as Intervention at Governors State University (IL)

At Governors State University (GSU), the alternative certification program offers coaching as a way to improve a candidate's performance. Faculty at Governors State see coaching as a strategy that allows candidates to identify, assess, and develop their dispositions; the program employs primarily facilitative and collaborative coaching methods. Key to the Governors State approach is the maintenance of the candidate's own value base and philosophy; thus the *Coaching Agreement with Assessment Committee of the Governors State University Alternative Certification Partnership* (GSU, n.d.) describe the purpose of coaching as

- Assist[ing] the candidate to clarify what he/she wants to achieve
- Encourag[ing] the candidate to identify the obstacles to achievement and resources to support achievement
- Elicit[ing] client-generated solutions and strategies
- Hold[ing] the client responsible and accountable

GSU's assessment committee may recommend or require that candidates participate in a minimum of three coaching sessions; if they elect to participate, they complete the coaching agreement document. As outlined in the document, the candidate maintains control, choosing the topics to be explored at each session. The coach's role is to listen and to contribute observations and questions that can help the candidate to "achieve clarity and develop a pathway of action and commitment to pursue action suggested by the pathway" (GSU, n.d.). It should be noted that participating in coaching does not guarantee success in the program. A letter sent to candidates recommended for coaching notes that

> the Assessment Committee of the GSU Alternative Certification Partnership will recommend candidates for certification based on their performance. Completion of all courses and the internship does not guarantee recommendation for certification. The program is providing this opportunity [coaching] to candidates to assist you in improving your performance to better meet program requirements and the needs of your students. [GSU, 2006, p. 1]

Two key principles guide the work at Governors State: Coaching to the candidate's vision and assisting the candidate in planning. In order to coach to the candidate's vision, faculty who serve as coaches are trained in questioning techniques that assist the candidate to articulate their vision, what they hunger for. One of the GSU coaches is a certified Paideia trainer and believes that Socratic dialogue plays an important part in helping candidates arrive at the core behaviors that contribute to their success in education through helping them realize what has led to their lack of success (K. Peterson, personal communication, 2006).

The second principle relates to moving toward the vision or planning for change. Here the key skills of the coach are questioning to help the candidate develop the outlines of a plan and then working to address details that will help him or her to achieve it. A GSU coach explains:

> Candidates are sitting down with another professional who is not in a position to hire, fire, or grade them, but rather to explore challenges, and get excited about solutions. It is possible to lose outstanding teachers without the advantage of the coaching process. I have worked with candidates who have excellent teaching skills and have had successful results, but who probably would not be rehired because they are not aware of how others perceive them.

From the perspective of a candidate, coaching at GSU is experienced as a help to move toward the change that they have come to understand is necessary for them to be successful. A student who was successful reflected about the experience, saying that

> [My coach] helped me to understand that the way I view things [isn't] always the way that my superiors or colleagues may view them. She helped me to see

that how you deal with situations may change depending upon the environment that you are in. In education, people expect you to be more personable rather than stand-offish and that was something I had to learn. Because of my coaching experience, I better understand how to deal with my principal and it has definitely helped me to understand what types of dispositions are expected of me. At first, I wasn't too thrilled about attending coaching sessions, to say the least, but it proved to be very beneficial to me.

As Peterson (personal communication, 2006) notes, the experience of the GSU program with coaching has led the faculty to integrate more conscious attention to mentoring all candidates in this alternative teacher education program. Thus, instructors focus on goal setting, brainstorming strategies for problem solving, and deepening candidate understanding of the challenges of a teacher's role. The more intensive coaching is recommended or required for students whose professional behavior has been assessed as needing the additional intervention to either move the candidate toward success or to assist him/her to determine that teaching is not a good fit for his/her personal vision.

Coaching as Feedback and Self-Assessment at Alverno College

At Alverno, faculty see themselves as coaches in their work with candidates, particularly through the use of two tools: feedback and self-assessment. Though not used frequently in the coaching literature, these tools implicitly match the goals and practice of coaching as laid out in much of the literature (Hargrove, 1995; Flaherty, 2005).

Elsewhere, I discuss five principles to guide practice in the assessment of dispositions (Diez, 2006), including that "dispositions should be assessed over time as part of an ongoing reflection process" (p. 49). The notion of assessment is itself compatible with coaching, because the etymological meaning of the word "assess," is "to sit down beside." Another principle is that "criteria used in the assessment of dispositions should be public and explicit" (p. 49). I want to use these two principles to explore how coaching within the context of teacher education can use feedback and self-assessment. Again, whether one looks at dispositions themselves as stable traits or more malleable aspects of character, coaching can focus on the behavior of the candidate.

Feedback

One of the most powerful interventions for learning goals documented in the literature is descriptive, formative feedback (Black & Wiliam, 1998; Davies, 2003; Stiggins, 2002). While the focus of most recent research related to feedback has been on cognitive learning, I would propose that feedback has a similar powerful role in building professional dispositions and professional behavior.

NCATE makes explicit the expectation that professional dispositions flow from the conceptual framework. Milam (2006) suggests identifying the expectations for professional behavior as a key legal requirement. For learning and development, the next step is to identify public and explicit criteria. So, for example, an explicit expectation in Alverno's conceptual framework is that teachers show respect for diversity in the classroom. Faculty at Alverno draw upon Purkey and Novak's (1996) invitational learning theory in providing a theoretical base that students study, but we also provide explicit criteria for their work in classrooms, from early field work to student teaching. For example, three criteria spell out the expectations that student will

- Show respect for varied learner perspectives
- Use positive terms in referring to specific students
- Thoughtfully link concrete examples of their practice to principles of invitational learning

Feedback is for us a form of coaching, because we use it to document what we see in the candidate's performance as evidence related to each criterion. In contrast to "grading a paper," where the emphasis might be on finding the errors and giving a summative judgment, "giving feedback" is focused on helping the candidate see what she does well—so that she can do it again—and on providing guidance on what might be her next step to come closer to the full set of expectations for professional behavior. Feedback can be characterized as formative assessment, focused on promoting growth in relationship to a clear set of criteria.

Taking the expectation above, it might be useful to look at a concrete example. Andrew, a teacher educator in the Alverno program, was observing Penny, a candidate who was assigned for field work related to his course in an inner city public school; the class of fourth graders was predominantly Hispanic. Penny had prepared a geography lesson, using a series of questions that she intended to tap into the students' prior learning. Andrew recorded the following exchange

Penny: Boys and girls, can you think of the name of a state that's also an island?

Children: Puerto Rico!

Penny: I believe I said a *state*.

Andrew noted that Penny, like many beginning field work students, was surprised to get a different answer than she had expected; she was looking, of course, for Hawaii. Her nonverbal communication clearly signaled to the students that they had missed her expected answer. Andrew used the experience to help Penny examine the exchange, coaching her with questions like these:

- Why might the children have immediately thought of Puerto Rico?
- And, more generally, why might it be important to maintain an awareness of the background knowledge and experiences of a group of learners so that you are able to interpret a response on the spot?
- (After reviewing a videotape of the lesson) How might your nonverbal response (including facial expression and tone) affect the likelihood of these children responding to future questions?
- How might you slow down your response to students' answers in order to give yourself time to see the connection that *they* are seeing or to ask a follow up question so that you can begin to interpret the connection?

Grounded in the statements of expectations, faculty coaching of this sort is critical feedback that makes the individual candidate aware of her behavior and also supports her in working to change that behavior. In the absence of such statements, candidates might take offense or argue about the right of the instructor to raise questions. In effect, the outcome statements put the issue on the table, and raise consciousness about professional behavior.

So much of what teacher educators work with in observing candidates in field settings involves the candidate as a whole person—not just what they know and can do, but the way in which they use their knowledge and skills in interaction with PK-12 students and with other candidates. Derek Bok (2006) suggests that many professors do not see this kind of coaching as their role; indeed, he points out that many professors are uncomfortable outside of the cognitive arena of their specialized knowledge. However, Milam (2006) reinforces the responsibility of professional education to address not only knowledge and skill, but also professional behavior.

Self-Assessment

If feedback is the work of the faculty, self-assessment is the parallel work of the candidate—learned through the modeling of the faculty coach. As defined by the Alverno College Faculty (1994), self-assessment is the ability of a student to observe, analyze, and judge her performance accurately on the basis of criteria and determine how she can improve it. The focus in self-assessment is on a particular performance, with the candidate examining her performance using the explicit, public criteria provided. Candidates need to be taught to self assess; it does not come naturally. What they are building is the capacity for judgment (Loacker, 2000).

At the beginning of their program, students are self-observers, learning to thoughtfully report their actions, thoughts, and emotions—describing both the performance itself and the process of producing a performance. Typically, they are challenged, initially, in learning to distinguish actions from emotions. After several semesters of practice, students become more sophisticated, applying disciplinary and/or interdisciplinary frameworks to the observation of performance. For example, if Andrew had not been observing Penny on the day when she asked the question about the island state, she might have recognized the problem in this exchange with students herself as she wrote the required reflection on how the lesson went. Reviewing specific actions and the responses of the students, she could use the process of self-assessment to examine this classroom performance.

Interpreting and analyzing performance also takes practice, as students look at samples of performance to identify patterns of strengths and weaknesses in their behavior. Students gradually begin to see and explain the significance of patterns in performance, making sense out of performances in relationship to disciplinary or interdisciplinary frameworks. Reflecting on invitational learning, Penny might become aware of how her words and the students' crestfallen expression were connected.

Criteria are central to the judging component. In self-assessment students look at the criteria for a particular performance to see if their work measures up. For example, the criteria guiding Andrew's work with Penny included these three:

- Show respect for varied learner perspectives
- Use positive terms in referring to specific students
- Thoughtfully link concrete examples of their practice to principles of Invitational Learning

Penny could have used them independently to look critically at her own performance. Indeed, while students initially go for the bottom line—whether the performance is satisfactory, criteria help them gradually learn to become more reflective. Judgment then becomes a tool to guide self-monitoring and to suggest adjustments in ongoing actions or plans. Reviewing the criteria, Penny might then address whether she did, in fact, show respect for varying student perspectives in dismissing the response of the student.

The final component of the self-assessment process is to plan for improvement. While students initially may simply focus on "doing better," without specifying how, they gradually learn to use feedback and to explore options for approaching tasks more effectively. Over time, they see the connection between planning and changes in performance, which helps them to refine their goals with a focus on continuous improvement. Based on her observation, analysis, interpretation, and judgment, Penny would then think about how she might better self-monitor and adjust her response when surprised by how students answer a question.

In considering growth in managing dispositions, self-assessment is particularly key because when candidates become more conscious about what they do and how they make decisions, they are able to take more responsibility for their actions and their ongoing growth. Lake (2000) provides this quotation from an early childhood education candidate at Alverno College:

> When I looked over my lessons and self-assessments, I saw that for each one I had talked about wanting to do a better job of getting and holding all the children's attention at the beginning of the lesson. But I also noticed that I wasn't really doing anything different to make this happen. For my next lesson I am going to ask my cooperating teacher for ideas about this. (p. 75)

The candidate shows not only the ability to find patterns in her work, but also to critique herself and to set a goal to take action. She is, in effect, showing that she is learning to coach herself. She is also building another benefit of self-assessment, recognizing that one can always improve. As a result, she is less likely to be defensive when faced with awareness that she could do better.

CONCLUSION

Whether coaching is seen as a special intervention, as in the case of Governors State, or is integrated as a practice in the exchanges between candidates and teacher educators across a candidate's experiences, as in the case of Alverno, it seems particularly appropriate for working with "dispositions," as acted out in professional behavior. Teacher educators would do well to consider the principles of coaching that show respect for the individual and work with his or her personal characteristics in the context of the role demands of the professional educator. Coaching, especially in its facilitative and collaborative modes, can be a powerful tool for both clarifying the vision of the teacher education candidate and assisting that candidate to produce the desired result in his/her professional practice.

NOTE

1. The original chapter on coaching was envisioned and outlined by Larry Freeman. I took on the task of completing the chapter and have perhaps taken it in a different direction, but I dedicate it with sincere respect to Larry Freeman.

REFERENCES

Alverno College Faculty. (1994). *Student assessment-as-learning at Alverno College.* Milwaukee, WI: Alverno College Institute.

Black, P., & Wiliam, D. (1998). Inside the black box: Raising standards through classroom assessment, *Phi Delta Kappan, 80*(2), 139-148.

Bloom, G., Castagna, C., Moir, E., & Warren, B. (2005). *Blended coaching: Skills and strategies to support professional development.* Thousand Oaks, CA: Corwin Press.

Bok, D. (2006) *Our underachieving colleges: A candid look at how much students learn and why they should be learning more.* Princeton, NJ: Princeton University Press.

Costa, A., & Garmston, R. (1994). *Cognitive coaching: A foundation for Renaissance Schools.* Norwood, MA: Christopher-Gordon.

Davies A. (2003) Feed back ... feed forward: Using assessment to boost literacy learning. *Primary Leadership, 2*(30), 53-55.

Diez, M. E. (2006). Assessing dispositions: Five principles to guide practice. In H. Sockett (Ed.), Teacher dispositions: *Building a teacher education framework of moral standards* (pp. 49-66). Washington, DC: AACTE.

Flaherty, J. (2005). *Coaching: Evoking excellent in others* (2nd ed.). Amsterdam: Elsevier.

Gersham, J. (2005). *"Disposition" emerges as issue at Brooklyn College.* Retrieved September 5, 2006, from http://www.nysun.com/article/14604

Governors State University. (n.d.). *Coaching agreement with assessment committee of the governors state university alternative certification partnership.* University Park, IL: Governors State University College of Education.

Governors State University. (2006). *Template for letter to recommend a candidate for coaching.* University Park, IL: Governors State University College of Education.

Hargrove, R. (1995). *Masterful coaching: Extraordinary results by impacting people and the way they think and work together.* San Francisco: Jossey-Bass/Pfeiffer.

Hodges, T. D., & Clifton, D. O. (2004). Strengths-based development in practice. In A. Linley & S. Joseph (Eds.), *Handbook of positive psychology in practice* (pp. 256-268). Hoboken, NJ: Wiley.

Katz, L. G., & Raths, J. D. (1985). Dispositions as goals for teacher education. *Teaching and Teacher Education 1,* 301-307.

Kyllonen, P. C., Walters, A. M., & Kaufman, J. C. (2005). Non-cognitive constructs and their assessment in graduate education: A review. In J. Abedi & H. O'Neil (Eds.), *Assessment of noncognitive influences on learning: A special issue of Educational Assessment, 10*(3), 147-152.

Lake, K. (2000). Self assessment in a fourth-semester course in teacher education. In G. Loacker (Ed.), *Self assessment at Alverno College* (pp. 69-81). Milwaukee, WI: Alverno College Institute.

Leo, J. (2005, October 24). Class(room) warriors. *U.S. News and World Report.* Retrieved on September 5, 2006, from http://www.usnews.com/usnews /opinion/articles/051024/24john.htm

Liesveld, R., & Miller, J. (2005). *Teach with your strengths: How great teachers inspire their students.* New York: Gallup Press.

Loacker, G. (Ed.). (2000). *Self assessment at Alverno College.* Milwaukee, WI: Alverno College Institute.

Lopez, S., Hodges, T., & Hafter, J. (2005). *Clifton StrengthsFinder technical report: Development and validation.* Princeton, NJ: The Gallup Organization.

Milam (2006, January). *Understanding the institutional context: Legal implications of decisions about individual candidates.* Paper presentation at the annual meeting of the American Association of Colleges for Teacher Education, San Diego.

Milwaukee Public Schools. (2004). *The Coaching Intensive. Handouts from a workshop on September 17-18, 2004.* Milwaukee, WI: Author.

National Council for the Accreditation of Teacher Education. (2006). *Revised definitions/glossary for unit standards.* Retrieved September 5, 2006, from http:// www.ncate.org/documents/Standards/May06_revision /GlossaryAdditionsEdits.doc

Norton, D. (1991). *Democracy and moral development.* Berkeley: University of California Press.

Purkey, W., & Novak, J. (1996). *Inviting school success: A self-concept approach to teaching and learning* (3rd ed.) Belmont CA: Wadsworth.

Roberts, R. (2006, January). *Technical considerations: Assessing dispositions in the continuum of professional preparation and practice.* Paper presented at the annual meeting of the American Association of Colleges for Teacher Education, San Diego, CA.

Sockett, H. (2006). Character, rules, and relations. In H. Sockett (Ed.), *Teacher dispositions: Building a teacher education framework of moral standards* (pp. 8-25). Washington, DC: AACTE.

Stiggins, R. J. (2002). Assessment crisis: The absence of assessment for learning. *Phi Delta Kappan, 83*(10), 258-765.

Will, G. (2006, January 16). Ed schools vs. education *Newsweek.* Retrieved September 5, 2006, from http://www.msnbc.msn.com/id/10753446/site/newsweek/

Wise, A. E. (2006, February 28). *NCATE news: Wise to Hess, Will, and Leo.* Retrieved September 5, 2006, from http://www.ncate.org/public/ 0228_postWise.asp?ch=150

CHAPTER 11

DISPOSITIONS AS A DIALOGUE IN TEACHER PREPARATION

Lisa M. Stooksberry

What do teacher educators mean when they define, develop, and assess dispositions in the preparation of teachers? In this volume Freeman (see chapter 1) suggests that dispositions arrived abruptly in the teacher education conversation with the introduction of the standards of the Interstate New Teacher Assessment and Support Consortium (INTASC, 1992). The discussion and debate heightened with the inclusion of dispositions in the revised standards of the National Council for the Accreditation of Teacher Education (NCATE, 2002). With the catalysts from these standards-based bodies, teacher education is engaging now in the discussion that was missing when the INTASC standards were introduced 15 years ago. It is a welcomed opportunity for dialogue that will contribute to the use of dispositions in teacher preparation.

In addition to the extensive foundation provided by Freeman (see chapter 1) in this text, a basis for the use of dispositions in teacher education was established historically in the field through examination of teachers' beliefs and attitudes (see Lasley, 1980; Nespor, 1987; Pajares, 1992).

Dispositions in Teacher Education, pp. 219–232
Copyright © 2007 by Information Age Publishing
All rights of reproduction in any form reserved.

However, identifying dispositions as part of the core expectation (along with knowledge and skills) for teachers has changed the nature of the discussion in teacher education.

In closing this volume, I argue for dispositions as a dialogue in teacher preparation. Because the dialogue was missing in early years after the introduction of dispositions as a core requirement, teacher education faculty find themselves now, in many cases for example, assessing dispositions of candidates without having a clear understanding of a program's definition and development of dispositions. The dialogue offers an opportunity to examine the role and contribution of dispositions in the development of teachers.

Dispositions are a messy construct (Schussler, 2006). While work in teacher knowledge and skills is far from simple, the field has progressed in identifying ways to facilitate candidates' development in those areas. Identifying and facilitating candidates' dispositions, however, is in its infancy in many ways in terms of how the field grapples with dispositional goals as a core expectation for teachers. Teacher educators are now called to the task of engaging in the dialogue to shape the next steps in using dispositions in the preparation of teachers. In this book, the authors represent the current issues in the field by offering different ways to conceptualize and to operationalize dispositions in teacher preparation.

I see three elements of dispositions as critical in framing the dialogue. These elements are: (a) defining dispositions; (b) systemic development of dispositions in teacher education programs; and (c) assessment of dispositions. These factors build upon one another, informing the use of dispositions in teacher preparation. Emerging from the three elements of the dialogue are core questions to consider; how the field responds to the questions will shape the next stage of work in dispositions in teacher preparation.

In this chapter, I will discuss the three elements that frame the call for dispositions as a dialogue in teacher preparation. I will consider the questions that emerge from the three elements and then close with the resulting implications. The challenge of engaging in the dispositions dialogue about how to define and to use dispositions creates the space for growth in programs and, if done well, in teacher candidates who will serve P-12 students.

DEFINING DISPOSITIONS

What is a disposition? This is not a simple question. In the opening chapter, Freeman takes us through a useful history on the evolution of dispositions in the fields of philosophy, psychology, and teacher education.

There are a range of definitions used in teacher education, raising a key question: Does the field need a common definition for dispositions?

Definitions for dispositions include notions about teachers' beliefs, attitudes, judgments, investments, and habits of mind and actions (for example see chapters by Breese & Nawrocki-Chabin; Hare; Oja & Reiman; and Wasicsko). Other definitions include the moral agency inherent in teachers' ethical, character-laden decisions (Sockett, 2006). Also influencing some definitions are the contextual factors of teaching. For example, Schussler's (2006) definition includes teachers' awareness of and reflection upon the external influences to think and to act in particular ways.

The different definitions used by the authors in this book represent the myriad ways teacher educators conceptualize dispositions. In some instances definitions may use different words but share a similar foundation. For example, Breese and Nawrocki-Chabin (see chapter 2) focus on dispositions as "intellectual and emotional investments in events, situations, and people" (p. 37) while Oja and Reiman (see chapter 4) define dispositions in their work as "dominant and preferred trends in teachers' interpretations, judgments, and actions" (p. 98); however, the authors share a foundation in suggesting dispositions develop over time and offer interventions to support teachers' development of their dispositions. A core difference in definition appears to be whether one believes dispositions are inherent, thus largely unchangeable, versus believing that dispositions can change and develop over time. There is a spectrum to this core, of course, allowing space for degrees to which dispositions are malleable under particular conditions and over time.

My argument is that as a field teacher education needs to understand the different definitions of dispositions being used in programs and how those differences inform the dialogue. Moreover, if the field can come to some level of agreement on the baseline of what a disposition is, then it might result in a shift from an apples versus oranges debate to a more productive, forward-thinking discussion. Defining dispositions is the starting place for the dialogue on dispositions in teacher education. I do not think teacher education can progress successfully without asking hard questions about dispositions, and faculty have to start at the beginning. Teacher educators need to understand what one another are saying, and be informed by what those in related fields are saying, about the meaning of dispositions. To grapple with the concept of dispositions will result in clarification in the field around a useful, clear definition. Through clarity of definition, teacher education faculty can then begin to consider how programs are designed to facilitate candidates' development of and demonstration of expected dispositions.

DEVELOPMENT OF DISPOSITIONS IN
TEACHER EDUCATION PROGRAMS

In most if not all teacher education programs, the expected knowledge, skills, and dispositions of graduates are identified. To develop knowledge, skills, and dispositions in teacher preparation programs, faculty must implement a systemic design. It is the responsibility of the program to provide up-front what is expected of a candidate to enter and to complete the program. This requirement leads to a key question of engaging in a dialogue on dispositions in teacher preparation: How are dispositions part of a systemic, developmental program in which candidates are aware of and have multiple opportunities to demonstrate the dispositions expected upon program completion?

The first stage in a systemic approach to dispositions is for faculty to engage in the first question essential to the dialogue, how is disposition defined in the program? Once faculty find common grounding in a programmatic definition, the next stages are to consider what dispositions are expected, how those expectations will be measured, and what types of program-based decisions will result from those measures.

Program expectations vary with regard to dispositions. At one end of the spectrum, many programs identify a list of observable behaviors that are either completed or not completed, thus checked off the list. Other programs develop something akin to professional guiding principles that are demonstrated across multiple measures and time. For example, program faculty might use a candidate's letter of application, interview for admission into the preparation program, clinical experience evaluations, and P-12 students' work samples to make decisions about a candidate's disposition toward the guiding principle that all students can learn. There are many programs that fall somewhere in the middle of checklists and multiple measures over time.

There is no common agreement around how to structure expectations of candidates' dispositions. For example, in this book Raths (see chapter 7) suggests it can be an unwieldy task to limit the dispositions expected of candidates while Wasicsko (see chapter 3) argues it is possible and useful to identify a reasonable number of dispositions that should be considered, for example, for admission into teacher education and for curriculum development in programs. I am not convinced there is a single, "right" way to structure dispositions in teacher preparation programs. Instead, I argue this is a pivotal point in the dispositions dialogue providing an opportunity for program faculty, first, to examine candidates' opportunities to demonstrate dispositions within the context of the program's definition and, then, to assess what is and is not learned about candidates' dispositions from those experiences.

Dottin (2006) describes faculty commitment to and collaboration in developing a unit's conceptual framework. While the phrase "conceptual framework" is invariably tied to NCATE accreditation, I contend that whether or not a unit and its programs are NCATE accredited, they must be driven by a common conceptual framework, that is, an established mission. If teacher educators build their programs around individual courses and expectations in syllabi, are candidates provided the foundation they need to develop, along a continuum, as a teacher? In this volume, Diez (see chapter 10) provides a description and two program examples of how a model of coaching can be used to work purposefully with candidates in developing dispositions throughout the course of their preparation.

Faculty must consider the dispositions they expect candidates to possess and consider how to assess those dispositions, but these and other questions around expectations of graduates must be considered within the framework of the program. Systemic development of dispositions is necessary whether a program subscribes, for example, to a developmental perspective of dispositions, use of dispositions criteria for admission, or something else altogether. How do expectations of dispositions (and knowledge and skills) pervade the program so that candidates know not only what is expected and are assessed accordingly, but experience those expectations across time and throughout the program? Reflecting the field, authors in this volume argue for the essentiality of systemic development in which to define, use, and assess dispositions in teacher preparation (see for example Breese & Nawrocki-Chabin; Freeman; Oja & Reiman; and Wasicsko).

ASSESSMENT OF DISPOSITIONS

Assessment may very well drive the current dialogue on dispositions in teacher education. Attesting to the wide range of dispositional assessments in teacher education, an internet search using the phrase "assessing teacher dispositions" yields over 700,000 hits for books, articles, and examples of institutions' measures. Assessment of dispositions, like that of knowledge and skills, should provide faculty and candidates with evidence of strengths, weaknesses, and growth. In this volume and elsewhere, Diez (see chapter 9; see also Diez, 2006) has provided guidance on developing and using effective assessments of dispositions. My purpose is not to restate her argument, but instead to consider the issue of assessment within a framework of faculty decisions in defining, developing, and assessing systematically dispositions in their teacher education programs. This leads to a third essential question in the call for dispositions as a dialogue: How does the assessment of candidates' dispositions provide evidence of strengths, weaknesses, and growth over time?

Just as there are a variety of ways to assess knowledge and skills, there are a variety of ways to assess dispositions. In this volume, Wasicsko (see chapter 3) describes how one program uses measures of dispositions, for example, as criteria for admission into teacher education. Faculty are well-trained in using the program's assessment measures to collect evidence of candidates' dispositions. Oja and Reiman (see chapter 4) depict a program's use of an integrated learning framework that can be used to guide the definition, development, and assessment of candidates' dispositions.

In teacher preparation, has assessment of dispositions taken on a life of its own for the purpose of complying with NCATE standards? The starting point for assessment of dispositions in programs is careful examination of the goals and use; thus, as Behling (2006) contends, faculty must determine first what the program will measure. If a program leaps to assessing dispositions before examining carefully what is to be measured, then faculty are limited from the start about what will be learned concerning candidates' dispositions. However, faculty have the opportunity to take a proactive position instead of operating compliantly. Programs that are designed, developed, and supported around what faculty have identified as best practices in preparing candidates to teach contribute to a proactive stance; then, from the systematically developed assessments of knowledge, skills, and dispositions throughout the program, data are available for the purposes required by accreditation.

Faculty have difficult yet productive decisions to make around the assessment of dispositions. If the goal of assessment is compliance for accreditation, then I imagine a checklist suffices. If the goal is to use assessment as a tool for supporting candidates' growth and development in knowledge, skills, and dispositions, then it is irresponsible to use assessments that do not provide useful information about candidates.

Of course, program assessment of dispositions must attend to issues of evidence. Diez (see chapter 9) warns that programs often assess in ways that provide limited information, forcing faculty to rely heavily on inference. When the stakes are high such as program admission, dismissal, or completion, sole reliance on inference is a dangerous endeavor. There are inferences, of course, from which one can chart a clear path from the evidence; conversely, there are inferences, such as those drawn from Likert scales, that do not have a clear tie back to evidence.

Legal defensibility in the assessment of dispositions is an area in need of attention, particularly in programs, for example, where candidates can be dismissed if they do not demonstrate dispositions identified by a program. To illustrate, incidents involving the threat of dismissal from teacher education programs have played out recently in the public forum, providing a foothold for those who argue that teacher education attempts to strong arm candidates based on their political views, under the guise of dispositions (Leo, 2005; Wilson, 2005). These events and others like them support the degree to which faculty must make careful decisions in how dispositions are defined and used in programs.

Finally, the assessment of dispositions should not take place outside consideration of candidates' awareness of the dispositions they bring to teacher preparation experiences (Sockett, 2006; Stooksberry, Schussler, & Bercaw, 2006). In this volume Hare (see chapter 6) argues identity and integrity are central to the construct of developing dispositions, thus understanding one's self and what one brings to the process is central to the development of candidates' dispositions during teacher preparation (Hamachek, 1999; McLean, 1999).

INFLUENCE OF CONTEXT ON DISPOSITIONS AS A DIALOGUE

In this chapter I argue that engaging in dispositions as a dialogue in teacher preparation can be guided by three key questions, focused on definition, development, and assessment. As is evident in this volume through explicit or implicit reference by authors, the key questions can not be addressed without considering the influence of context on the definition, development, and assessment of dispositions. Freeman (see chapter 5) contends that dispositions make sense within "the details and complex web of expectations, aspirations, and limitations associated with a particular time and place" (p. 126). Context influences how the field and how programs arrive at a definition of dispositions and how programs develop and assess dispositions. Ignoring context suggests that dispositions can be generalized across people and situations, but as is evident in this volume, the field does not share a common definition and programs define, develop, and assess dispositions in different ways. By considering context, teacher education faculty bring yet another challenging aspect into the dispositions dialogue. In this volume, context is more present in some authors' views than in others. For example, context is central to the Oja and Reiman (see chapter 4) argument that development occurs through interaction with the environment. On the other hand, Wasiscko (see chapter 3) describes use of an instrument to measure dispositions that appears largely context free.

If a definition put forth by the teacher education community is based on dispositions as inherent, stable characteristics that change little over time, then that is the context within which programs may consider how to define, develop, and assess dispositions. Conversely, if the field defines dispositions as malleable and, as Diez (2006) argues, changing as knowledge and skills increase, then this context informs programmatic defini-tions in a different way. Defining dispositions can not be considered without also addressing the influence of the conditions under which it is conceived.

Candidates bring to teacher preparation dispositions gleaned from a lifetime of experiences that inform their work with children and in teach-ing and learning. Faculty are challenged, then, to consider the context of individuals' dispositions while designing broad, program-based opportu-nities for candidates to develop their dispositions. As is the case with any consideration of teaching, one size does not fit all, and the needs of can-didates will drive how faculty respond within the context of opportunities to develop dispositions within the program.

What are the conditions under which dispositions are defined, devel-oped, and assessed in programs? Faculty will consider the definition they have established as it aligns with the mission of the institution (part of the context) and the program (a different aspect of context) to then design course and field-based opportunities (both contextual) for candidates (who bring context) to become aware of and to develop their dispositions. This suggests, over time, that a program continues to evolve in how it defines, develops, and assesses dispositions because a program is informed by and shaped by contextual factors. Programs should not be static but instead reflect the changing dynamic, the changing context if you will, of being informed by experiences, lessons learned, and the con-tribution of self study around what is and is not working in preparing can-didates with dispositions to work successfully with children.

Teaching is filled with complexities, and context adds a dimension to the dispositions dialogue that can not be ignored. Faculty must build into program design the consideration of context and its influence on defin-ing, developing, and assessing dispositions in teacher preparation.

IMPLICATIONS OF ENGAGING IN DISPOSITIONS AS A DIALOGUE

I have argued that a dialogue on dispositions in teacher preparation is necessary for the field to move forward in creating programs that clearly define, develop, and assess dispositions in ways that benefit candidates' growth as teachers. Three key questions can be used to shape the dia-logue; the questions support systematically designing teacher preparation programs by considering the following: (1) defining dispositions to frame the program; (2) providing opportunities in programs for candidates to develop and to demonstrate dispositions in multiple ways and over time; and (3) assessing dispositions in ways that yield useful evidence for faculty and for candidates. I turn now to the implications that emerge from these key questions.

There are two aspects to the issue of defining dispositions, the first is in the field and the second is in programs. The central question is: Does the field need a common definition for dispositions? The secondary question, then, becomes how does a program define dispositions as the initial stage in systemic development?

First, as a field, does teacher education have to agree on a definition of dispositions or, instead, is it acceptable to expect faculty will define and institute dispositions in ways that fit with program mission and goals? The authors of this volume did not attempt to reach a common definition, or consensus, around defining dispositions but instead identify significant questions about the nature of dispositions and how they are used in programs. In fact, Larry Freeman invited authors in this volume based on their differing perspectives. My intent is not to suggest that teacher educators must come to a form of unconditional agreement on a definition of dispositions, as different theories coexist, for example, on the nature of knowledge. Moreover, faculty will begin their examination of the use of dispositions in their programs at different starting points. However, is there a need to reach a degree of agreement in the field for the purpose of unifying the profession? If yes, what is the process for achieving this agreement and what will be the result? One implication of engaging in a dispositions dialogue in teacher preparation is considering, as a field, what might result from working toward and reaching consensus on the definition and use of dispositions in teacher education.

I shift now to the public forum, where a somewhat recent entry into the dispositions debate fuels the potential need for consensus on dispositions in teacher education. NCATE has been attacked for the use of "social justice" as an example of dispositions in the glossary of its standards (Wasley, 2006; Will, 2006). This attack had led to debate about whether or not social justice should be removed from the glossary. I argue this is not the issue for debate; NCATE standards may guide the work of many institutions, but it is up to the institution, the unit, and the program to make decisions about how social justice does or does not fit with its mission and goals of preparing teachers. Because education serves the public, it answers to a host of supporters and critics around how teachers are prepared to serve children successfully. The public conversation elicits a larger problem in teacher education; if a level of consensus around dispositions can not be achieved in the field, then teacher education is prey for those with strong opinions and large audiences. The most recent argument stems from one event, but it could be precursor to others if common ground is not reached in the field to define, develop, and assess dispositions. This debate is not solely going on in public, as Raths contends in this volume (see chapter 7) there is no viable means by which to measure social justice as a disposition of teacher candidates. How does the public debate contribute to or detract from the work in teacher education to identify appropriate use of dispositions alongside the knowledge and skills of candidates?

In light of debates within the field and in the general public, should teacher education consider consensus as a next step in the use of dispositions? Reaching consensus, if it is determined to be a useful endeavor is not without consequence, just as there is consequence in not making the attempt. Decisions have to be made, resulting in achieving some goals and adapting or mitigating others. The result of such a process of consensus might be a code of professional ethics. In the preface to *Teacher Dispositions: Building a Teacher Education Framework of Moral Standards*, Art Wise (2006), President and Chief Executive Officer of NCATE, calls for the creation of a code of ethics as a requisite step in the effort to professionalize teaching. How would the field engage in a consensus process with the goal of developing a code of professional ethics and who would lead the way? A task force, Teacher Education as a Moral Community (TEAMC), of the American Association of Colleges for Teacher Education (AACTE) has been charged to pursue a professional consensus on dispositions in teacher preparation. The work of TEAMC will contribute to the dialogue on dispositions and will provide guidance on developing a professional code of ethics if this is the direction taken by the field.

A variety of professions have a code of ethics, for example, social workers, journalists, and engineers, to name a few. Inevitably, developing and using codes of ethics in professions raises its own set of challenges worthy of debate. If teacher education forges into this territory, it will inform the dispositions dialogue in the preparation of teachers and will prove useful in terms of considering the advantages and disadvantages of a code of professional ethics in teaching.

A code of professional ethics would perhaps influence how programs define and use dispositions. Faculty could turn to the profession's statement about what is expected of candidates to inform how dispositions are defined, developed, and assessed in programs.

A second implication of engaging in a dispositions dialogue, and related to the implication of consensus, could result in the collection of evidence across diverse programs about how candidates' dispositions are successfully defined, developed, and assessed. As has been established in recent publications, most notably the volume published for the American Educational Research Association (Cochran-Smith & Zeichner, 2005), there is much work to be done in collecting evidence in teacher education, for example, around what constitutes best practices. Behling (2006) argues that best practices are typically identified through scholarly research in the field, yet she contends a valuable contribution to the current conversation might be a practice-based collection from programs that have evidence they are doing well in preparing candidates for teaching. Behling suggests "selecting a range of best practices from a diversity of schools might not spark creativity in program enhancement, but it might begin to coalesce program practices and key markers and requirements" (p. 5). If teacher education programs engage in systemic development of dispositions in their programs, then sharing those practices contributes to the dialogue. The sharing of practices, then, contributes to an informed dialogue around the work on consensus.

Program faculty should exercise caution when adopting or adapting the practices of other programs around the definition, development, and assessment of dispositions. Because dispositions (along with knowledge and skills) of candidates are systemic, faculty must take care in making decisions about how to use examples from other programs. There is no silver bullet; there is challenging yet rewarding work in considering how dispositions inform the practices of teacher candidates. Examples from this volume demonstrate a variety of ways dispositions can be systematically anchored and developed in teacher preparation programs.

Finally, a third implication of the work in dispositions as a dialogue in teacher preparation is engaging in research to inform current practices. A search of electronic education databases confirms that research on dispositions is occurring and is regularly presented at conferences. As well, journal articles on dispositions are increasing, with themed issues of teacher education journals being devoted to dispositions (i.e., *Journal of Teacher Education*, forthcoming, September/October 2007; *The Teacher Educator*, v41, n4).

Research needs will emerge from and contribute to the dispositions dialogue focused on the key questions of definition, development, and assessment. Teacher education must think both broadly and in depth to consider the questions to be examined by research. In this volume one example of research includes Peterson's work with dispositions of alternatively-certified career switchers (see chapter 8). Peterson's practice-based study examines how teachers view the influence and use of their dispositions in teaching.

By thinking creatively and by drawing from the work taking place in programs, faculty have opportunities to engage in a variety of types of research to inform the dispositions discourse. Different types of research will yield complementary pieces to the dispositions puzzle, all of which can be used by faculty to continue to improve their work with candidates. Opportunities for descriptive research will emerge naturally from the dispositions dialogue as teacher educators attempt to understand the nature of what is and is not known about the role of dispositions in teacher preparation and in teaching. The dispositions dialogue will foster other forms of research seeking to make sense, for example, of how candidates' dispositions contribute to the learning of P-12 students.

CONCLUSION

In closing this volume, I contend dispositions as a dialogue is an essential process for teacher education to move forward in the work of conceptualizing and using dispositions in working with candidates. I provide three key questions to provoke and frame the dialogue: (1) Does the field need a common definition for dispositions? (2) How are dispositions part of a systemic, developmental program in which candidates are aware of and have multiple opportunities to demonstrate the dispositions expected upon program completion? and (3) How does the assessment of candidates' dispositions provide evidence of strengths, weaknesses, and growth over time? I urge teacher educators to consider these central questions and the contextual factors that influence teacher preparation in defining, developing, and assessing candidates' dispositions.

The authors in this volume provide theoretical perspectives that generate useful ways of working with the conceptualization of dispositions and promising practical applications around the use of dispositions in teacher preparation. A reader will leave this volume with a richer understanding of how dispositions are used in preparing teachers.

In introducing this volume Freeman indicated the goal of the book was to enrich the discourse. My attempt in closing this volume is to identify central questions to frame a dispositions dialogue in teacher preparation. The questions emerge from how authors in this volume and others in the field apply dispositions in teacher preparation programs and examine dispositions in research. Some may misconstrue the questions to suggest I argue for standardization of dispositions; to the contrary, however, I see an array of ways in which dispositions will work in programs as long as faculty tend well to the processes of defining, developing, and assessing dispositions within the range of conditions that influence people, time, and place. The goal of the dialogue is to improve teacher education programs' use of dispositions and to provide candidates with opportunities to grow in their knowledge, skills, and dispositions of teaching.

REFERENCES

Behling, L. L. (2006). *Accreditation, accountability, and assessment across professions.* Unpublished manuscript.

Cochran-Smith, M., & Zeichner, K. M. (2005). *Studying teacher education: The report of the AERA panel on research and teacher education*. Washington, DC: American Educational Research Association.

Diez, M. E. (2006). Assessing dispositions: Five principles to guide practice. In H. Sockett (Ed.), *Teacher dispositions: Building a teacher education framework of moral standards* (pp. 49-68). Washington, DC: American Association of Colleges for Teacher Education.

Dottin, E. S. (2006). A Deweyan approach to the development of moral dispositions in professional teacher education communities: Using a conceptual framework. In H. Sockett (Ed.), *Teacher dispositions: Building a teacher education framework of moral standards* (pp. 27-47). Washington, DC: American Association of Colleges for Teacher Education.

Hamachek, D. (1999). Effective teachers: What they do, how they do it, and the importance of self-knowledge. In R. P. Lipka, & T. M. Brinthaupt (Eds.), *The role of self in teacher development* (pp. 189-224). Albany, NY: State University of New York Press.

Interstate New Teacher Assessment and Support Consortium. (1992). *Model standards for beginning teacher licensure and development: A resource for state dialogue*. Washington, DC: Council of Chief State School Officers.

Lasley, T. (1980). Preservice teacher beliefs about teaching. *Journal of Teacher Education, 31*(4), 38-41.

Leo, J. (2005, October 24). Class(room) warriors. *U.S. News & World Report*. Retrieved October 28, 2006, from http://www.usnews.com/usnews/opinion/articles/051024/24john.htm

McLean, S. V. (1999). Becoming a teacher: The person in the process. In R. P. Lipka & T. M. Brinthaupt (Eds.), *The role of self in teacher development* (pp. 55-91). Albany, NY: State University of New York Press.

National Council for Accreditation of Teacher Education. (2002). *Professional standards for the accreditation of schools, colleges, and departments of education*. Washington, DC: Author.

Nespor, J. (1987). The role of beliefs in the practice of teaching. *Journal of Curriculum Studies, 19*(4), 317-328.

Pajares, M. F. (1992). Teachers' beliefs and educational research: Cleaning up a messy construct. *Review of Educational Research, 62*(3), 307-332.

Schussler, D. L. (2006). Defining dispositions: Wading through murky waters. *The Teacher Educator, 41*(4), 251-268.

Sockett, H. (2006). Character, rules, and relations. In H. Sockett (Ed.), *Teacher dispositions: Building a teacher education framework of moral standards* (pp. 9-25). Washington, DC: American Association of Colleges for Teacher Education.

Stooksberry, L. M., Schussler, D. L., & Bercaw, L. A. (2006). *Conceptualizing a dispositions framework: Intellectual, cultural and moral domains of teaching*. Manuscript submitted for publication.

Wasley, P. (2006, June 16). Accreditor of education schools drops controversial "social justice" language. *The Chronicle of Higher Education, 52*, A13.

Will, G. (2006, January 16). Ed schools vs. education. *Newsweek* (U.S. Edition), *CXLVII*, 98.

Wilson, R. (2005, December 16). We don't need that kind of attitude: Education schools want to make sure prospective teachers have the right "disposition," *The Chronicle of Higher Education, 52*, A8.

Wise, A. E. (2006). Preface. In H. Sockett (Ed.), *Teacher dispositions: Building a teacher education framework of moral standards* (p. 5). Washington, DC: American Association of Colleges for Teacher Education.

ABOUT THE AUTHORS

Lee Breese retired as an assistant professor of education at Alverno College in 2006, where she had taught courses to preservice teachers in the areas of instructional design, methods of teaching, and diversity. She was an elementary teacher and principal for many years in urban schools in the Milwaukee area.

Mary Diez, a 1995 winner of the Harold W. McGraw, Jr. Prize in education, is former president of the American Association of Colleges for Teacher Education and currently professor of education and dean of graduate studies at Alverno College. She has served on the National Board for Professional Teaching Standards and is currently a member of the board of examiners of the National Council for the Accreditation of Teacher Education. She chairs AACTE's task force on Teacher Education as a Moral Community. Dr. Diez's writing focuses on standards and assessment in both teacher education and K-12 school reform.

Larry Freeman, as an administrator in state government and higher education, led the creation and significant reshaping of several organizations, programs, and initiatives, including the creation of both a college of education at a state university and a high quality alternative teacher certification program. Since the early 1980s, he served in various administrative positions at Governors State University, including dean, associate vice president for academic affairs and directors of information services. His publications reveal interests and expertise in the study of literature, cultural pluralism, technology integration, and legal and management issues related to the preparation of educational personnel, most recently in the area of dispositions.

Sally Z. Hare, distinguished professor emerita at Coastal Carolina University, is president of still learning, inc. She has worked nationally for the past decade with Parker Palmer and the Center for Courage and Renewal. Dr., Hare lives in Surfside Beach, South Carolina, with her husband Jim and their dog, Eleanor Roosevelt. She is the author of a children's book, *Lucas and the Terribly-Trying Trying-Terribly Test* and a number of other essays and articles, including "The Lehrergarten: A Vision for Teacher Education" in *Living the Question: Essays Inspired by the Work and Life of Parker J. Palmer.*

Rita Nawrocki-Chabin, associate professor and director of the Licensure to Master's Program (LTM) in the school of education at Alverno College. She teaches courses in mentoring, Dewey, assessment, and pedagogy. She has consulted nationally and locally on ability-based learning, curriculum alignment, assessment, and mentoring. Her research interests include character education, democratic education, and teacher dispositions.

Sharon Nodie Oja is a professor at the University of New Hampshire, where she has been awarded with the Kimball Fellowship and the Carpenter Professorship. She teaches and has coordinated the internship program in the 5-year integrated undergraduate-graduate master's program in teacher education. She has directed three research grants funded by the National Science Foundation and U.S. Department of Education. In her coauthored book, *Collaborative Action Research: A Developmental Process,* she looked at how the different roles that teachers take on in action research seem to be related to the cognitive-developmental stage of the individual. Additional publications include the textbook *Educational Psychology: A Developmental Approach* and numerous chapters and articles resulting from her research interests in the areas of school-university collaboration, action research, and continuing development for the experienced teacher and preservice teacher.

Karen Peterson is currently the director of both the Alternative Certification Program and the Beginning Teacher Program at Governors State University. She was an elementary teacher for more than 20 years and has also served as the coordinator of elementary education at GSU. Dr. Peterson's research interests are induction/mentoring, alternative certification, urban teacher education, and teacher dispositions. She has chaired several State of Illinois induction advisory panels and is currently serving on the panel of the National Association of Alternative Certification to develop national standards for alternative certification programs.

James Raths is professor of education at the University of Delaware. His areas of interest include the evaluation of teaching and teacher education. He has been active in developing materials for the training of members of the board of examiners for the National Council for the Accreditation of Teacher Education and for planning the accreditation procedures used by the Teacher Education Accreditation Council. Dr. Raths was also a member of a team of psychologists and evaluators who revised the classic Bloom's taxonomy.

Alan J. Reiman is an associate professor in the Department of Curriculum and Instruction at North Carolina State University and executive director of SUCCEED which advances a comprehensive approach to new teacher professional learning and development across the moral, epistemological, emotional, and performance domains. He has published two books addressing teacher development and new teacher induction and mentoring, and he has authored or coauthored over 50 journal articles and book chapters. He has received five university and national awards for his teaching, research, and partnerships with public schools.

Lisa M. Stooksberry is the director for professional issues and partnerships at the American Association of Colleges for Teacher Education (AACTE). Lisa supports projects focused on the preparation of teachers such as the Standards-Based Teacher Education Project and the Center for Improving Teacher Quality. Dr. Stooksberry works with the task force, Teacher Education as a Moral Community (TEAMC), which leads AACTE's efforts in work on dispositions. With two colleagues, she conducts research on dispositions in teacher preparation. Prior to joining AACTE, she was an assistant professor at Mississippi State University.

Mark Wasicsko presently holds the Bank of Kentucky Endowed Chair in educational leadership at Northern Kentucky University. His prior experience includes serving as faculty, department chair, dean of education, and provost. His major professional interest, growing from his close association with the late Arthur Combs, is investigating the human elements or dispositions that permit some educators to foster greater than average positive changes in students, colleagues, and institutions. For over 30 years he has applied his interest to the areas of educator selection and preparation.

Printed in the United States
87594LV00001B/40/A